AUTOBIOGRAPHY

OF THE

REV. JOSEPH TOWNEND:

WITH REMINISCENCES OF HIS

MISSIONARY LABOURS IN AUSTRALIA.

Yours Affectionately
Joseph Townend

AUTOBIOGRAPHY

OF THE

REV. JOSEPH TOWNEND:

WITH

REMINISCENCES

OF HIS

MISSIONARY LABOURS IN AUSTRALIA.

The Profits of this Publication will be given to the Australian Missions.

SECOND EDITION.

LONDON:
W. REED, UNITED METHODIST FREE CHURCHES' BOOK-ROOM,
15, CREED LANE, LUDGATE STREET.

1869.

INTRODUCTION.

Autobiographies are not very frequently published. This we do not regret, because we are of opinion that there are few persons whose history presents a sufficient number of interesting, remarkable, or instructive incidents, to justify them in writing and publishing their own antecedents. Yet, in some cases, this has very properly been done; and some of the most useful and pleasing biographies have been of this class.

Having very carefully read what the Rev. Joseph Townend has written concerning himself, we are of opinion that he has acted judiciously in preparing a sketch of his own most eventful life for publication. We are sure that the work will be read with great interest and profit; and especially so by those to whom he is personally known.

When we consider the afflictions which he endured in his youth—the slight educational advantages which he has enjoyed—the services which he has rendered to the Church and the world—in England, Scotland, and Australia—and the general esteem which he has obtained, wherever he has laboured, as a minister of the Gospel of Jesus Christ, we see the wonderful workings of Divine wisdom and goodness, in training and qualifying him for the work to which he has been called, and in which he is engaged.

If we had discovered, in what he has written, any attempt at self-laudation, it would have excited our disapprobation. We believe that his object has not been to magnify himself, but to record the riches of the Divine goodness; and to encourage others to be hopeful and cheerful when struggling with affliction and difficulties; and to devote themselves to the service and love of God.

INTRODUCTION.

There may be some circumstances contained in the following Narrative, which some persons of very refined taste would have had omitted. But they probably are those which will to other readers prove most acceptable and profitable. The value of the work is in our judgment greatly enhanced by the frank, open, and unvarnished honest simplicity, with which every event related is presented to view.

At the earnest request of the author, we consented to superintend the passing of this work through the press; and we earnestly pray and hope that it may be the means of benefitting many souls; that the life of its author may be long spared; that he may ever richly enjoy the Divine benediction, be honoured with extensive usefulness in that distant land where his labours have already been eminently successful, and that, if it be consistent with the will of God, it may be long before his Obituary can be added to his Autobiography.

ROBERT ECKETT,

LONDON, 1854.

PREFACE TO SECOND EDITION.

SINCE my return to England, and especially since being stationed in the Rochdale Circuit, I have been frequently importuned by many persons to republish my Autobiography, with the addition of Australian experiences, and some account of our Mission in that country. The first edition has been out of print some years, and I felt reluctant to undertake the task, having very little leisure for the labour required. Several reasons, however, have led me to comply with the wishes of my personal friends. I make no pretensions to literary ability, but I have tried in the following pages to give a plain and simple narrative of events and incidents, which may perhaps help to dispel some very vague and erroneous notions which I have found to prevail in the minds of many persons relative to matters connected with our Australian Mission.

In justice to myself and others, I have felt compelled to mention some circumstances which perhaps a few individuals would like to have had omitted.

J. TOWNEND.

ROCHDALE, *March 10th*, 1869.

CONTENTS.

PART I.

CHAPTER I.

Parents members of the Wesleyan Society—Birth—Death of a Sister—Removal of Family to Grassington, to Linton Mill, and to Burnley—Alarmingly burnt—Attended Sunday-school—Went to work in a Factory—Benefit of Religious Instruction—Removal to Rawtenstall—Happy Death of a Brother—Subject of serious impressions—Visit to a Roman Catholic Chapel—A patient in the Manchester Infirmary—Acts as Assistant Nurse—Undergoes an operation—Awful Scenes in the Infirmary—Visits of Friends—Beneficial effects of sympathy—Fatal effects of fruit and wine—Departs from the Infirmary . . 1

CHAPTER II.

Returns home—Maternal welcome—Visits the Manchester Infirmary, Blackpool, and Lytham—Itinerates to sell Confectionery—Obtains a situation of trust—Conversion—Begins to preach—First discourse—Becomes a Class-leader—Recommended to the Conference—Examined at the District Meeting—Opinions on the Divine Sonship—Distressing affliction and delirium of a female Friend—Joins the Temperance movement 20

CHAPTER III.

Leaves the Conference Connexion—Becomes a salaried Local Preacher at Burnley—Examined at the Leeds Annual Meeting—Appointed to the Keighley Circuit—Removes to the Hull Circuit—Visits an afflicted Family, and the Hull Infirmary—Father's and Mother's Death—Leaves Hull, and goes to the New Mills Circuit—Evils of Drunkenness—Temperance Meeting—Victims of Intemperance—Removes to the Salford Circuit—Public Distress—An Unhappy Marriage—Appointed to the Clitheroe Circuit—Prospects of Usefulness—Sudden Removal to Edinburgh—Discouraging commencement—Temperance Society—Missionary Services—Attends a Funeral—Scottish Scenery—A Brother's Death—A Sister's Death—Invited to labour in the Rochdale Circuit 42

CHAPTER IV.

Leaves Edinburgh—Arrives at Rochdale—First Sermon in Rochdale—Letter from Brother Thomas—Special Services—Letters from Brother Thomas—Death and Funeral of Brother Thomas—Death of a Nephew—Death of Brother Elisha—Reminiscences of the Rochdale Circuit—Removal to the Bury Circuit—Collision on Railway—Visit to Darlington—Mrs. Howarth's Death—Requested to go as a Missionary to Australia—Resolutions of the Connexional Committee—Preparations for going to Australia—Visit to London—Embarkation—Journal of Voyage 66

CHAPTER V.

Arrival at Melbourne—Opening of Mission—Temperance Hall rented—House purchased—Discouragements—Attacked and robbed by Highwaymen—Apprehension of the Thieves—Public Sympathy—Trial of the Highwaymen—Wages and Prices at Melbourne 117

CHAPTER VI.

Brief Description of Australia—Extent of the Country—A British Possession—General Aspect of Scenery—Varieties of the Soil, and its Rocky Basis—Supposed Inland Sea—Character of the Rivers; the Murray and other principal streams—Inundations—Interesting natural process of filling the "water holes"—Conclusion 126

Appendix 133

PART II.

REMINISCENCES OF MISSIONARY LABOURS IN AUSTRALIA.

CHAPTER I.

Discovery of Gold in Australia—Rush to the Diggings—Depreciation of Property—Influx of Convicts—Bushrangers—Increase of Population—Want of House Accommodation—Emigrants' Home—Canvas Tents—Prospect of Mission discouraging—Ministers gone to the Gold-fields—New Arrivals—English Letters—Painful Records in Diary—Public Cemetery—Struggle for Right of Interment—New Chapel—Price of Labour—Opening Services—Painful Trial on Account of Dwelling-House 139

CHAPTER II.

Congregation increases—Deaths of Henry Dent and C. Stocks—Visits Geelong—Commences a Mission at Kew and Nunnawadding—Aspect of the Bush—Yarra Bend Lunatic Asylum—Desertion of Wives—Missing Friends—Arrival of Rev. M. Bradney—Commercial Distress—Benevolent Asylum—Roman Catholic Influence—Death of Amelia—Removal of Chapel for Street Improvements—Erection of George Street Chapel—Messrs. Falkner and Batman First Colonists in Victoria—No Dominant Church in Australia—State Aid to Religion—Dissipated Life on board Ship 153

CHAPTER III.

Temperance Society—Sad Results of Drunkenness—Sunday Closing Act—Houses of Parliament—Vote by Ballot—Removes to Geelong—Marriage Law—Midnight Wedding—Arrival of Messrs. Sayer and Middleton—Opening of Windsor Chapel—Death of Mr. Samuel Heape—Returns to Melbourne—Unholy Men obtain Membership in the Church—Law Cases—Costs of Trials—Untrue Statements published in the *Wesleyan Times*—Career of Mr. J. B.—£1000 Loan to Chapels . 172

CHAPTER IV.

Division of Melbourne Circuit—Death of Mrs. Townend—Arrival of Rev. R. Miller—J. Bulmer, Missionary to Aborigines—Character of the Natives—White Man found among the Blacks—Ceremony of making the Lads Young Men—Cruelty to Natives—Climate of Australia—Hot Winds—Dust Storms—Consents to go to Queensland—Arrival of Rev. T. A. Bayley—Valedictory Tea-meeting—Letter from Hon. Richard Heales—Death of Mr. Heales 190

CHAPTER V.

Departure for Brisbane—Curry, the Murderer—Voyage to Sydney—Arrival in Brisbane—House-Rents very High—Opens Mission in Council-Chamber—Removes to the School of Arts—Purchase of Land—Building and Opening of Chapel—Erection of Dwelling-House—Bad Water—Visits to Eagle Farm—Extent of Queensland—Arrival of Emigrants—Death of Mr. and Mrs. Hawken—Disastrous Fires—Climate—Mosquitos—Failure of Health—Desire to Return to England—Arrival of Rev. R. Miller 211

CHAPTER VI.

Voyage to Sydney—Stormy Passage to Melbourne—Visits Ballarat—State of the Mission there—Is Stationed at Ballarat—Chinese Population—Labours during One Year—Desire to Return to England—Attends District Meeting—Death of the Three Carnes—Farewell of Friends—Journal of Return Voyage to England 226

THE AUTOBIOGRAPHY

OF THE

REV. JOSEPH TOWNEND.

CHAPTER I.

Parents members of the Wesleyan Society—Birth—Death of a Sister—Removal of Family to Grassington, to Linton Mill, and to Burnley—Alarmingly burnt—Attended Sunday-school—Went to work in a Factory—Benefit of Religious Instruction—Removal to Rawtenstall—Happy Death of a Brother—Subject of serious impressions—Visit to a Roman Catholic Chapel—A patient in the Manchester Infirmary—Acts as assistant-nurse—Undergoes an operation—Awful scenes in the Infirmary—Visits of friends—Beneficial effects of sympathy—Fatal effects of fruit and wine—Departs from the Infirmary.

I WAS born of poor, but pious parents, in the rural village of Cononley, near Skipton, Yorkshire. My parents were, before their conversion, sincere and well-disposed; but they were very ignorant of spiritual things. They were brought under the plain and forcible preaching of the Methodists at Glusburn, two miles from Cononley; and soon after their marriage they, both on the same day, went to a class-meeting at Glusburn. At that time they kept their shop open on the Sabbath; and it was their custom, on returning from the meeting, to open the shop for the sale of confectionery, to the young people, who stood, in groups, waiting their return. They soon found that such conduct was wrong; and, under circumstances of great pecuniary temptation, they closed the shop, invited

B

the preachers to the village, and for nine years, until a chapel was built, my father's house was the village sanctuary for the Methodists.

In those nine years, my parents had days and nights of honest toil; within that period they had seven births and four deaths. Every article which they sold was manufactured in the house, without an assistant, except during my mother's accouchement; and yet I have often heard her say, she could never remember the preacher having come when the house was not in readiness. How important the closing of that shop on the Sabbath! What fearful results were prevented; and, despite of poverty and toil, what glorious consequences followed! O Almighty God, I thank thee that thou didst enable my dear parents, at that important juncture, to make so noble a stand for Thee!

I was born October 14, 1806; and was the youngest but one of twelve, four of whom died in infancy. Ellen, who lived the longest of the four, died at the age of four years. She was remarkably beautiful, so much so that strangers passing by would stop to admire her. A short time before her death, she was upon her knees upon the bed, looking over the bed's head, when mother said to her, "Ellen, what are you looking at?" "O mother!" Ellen replied, "I have seen four pretty ladies; I should like to go with them." Soon after the lovely child died, and now she mingles with those angel forms that encircle the Eternal throne. "I say unto you, that in heaven, the angels do always behold the face of my Father which is in heaven."

Of my early days at Cononley, I do not remember anything, except a fall from off some steps, the mark of which I carry upon my chin, and also some reminiscence of my uncle Neddy's old pear-tree being richly laden with fruit. When I was about three years old, we removed to Grassington, and afterwards to Linton Mill. Of these places I know but little: the river Wharf; the shoals of trout and eels; the bridge, the houses, the factory, the churchyard, and hippins* over the river, I can now distinctly remember. During our residence at Linton, I was nearly burnt to death. One cold windy day, I had, in company with another boy, been out playing; we returned, to his father's house, very cold, and commenced mending the fire. We were alone when the dreadful accident occurred; I was lifting the kettle from off the reekon,†

* Stepping-stones. † Pot-hook.

when my apron caught fire. The boy was frightened, ran out of the house, shut the door, and looked through the window. I ran round the house several times, then opened the door, and, facing a strong wind, ran across the street, and the length of twelve houses, before I was caught and the fire quenched. I distinctly remember being laid upon the floor, and having my wounds saturated with treacle, in order to extract the fire. My right side close up to the pit of the arm, and my arm down to the elbow, were severely burnt, so much so, that all feeling for a time was gone. The doctor lived at a considerable distance; and when he came, his advice was that I should be allowed quietly to die; for he said that he was certain I should never recover. My mother said, "My child will get better; and if you will not dress his wounds, I will!" The doctor then cut away the burnt flesh, and left me to the skill and care of my best earthly friend, my mother. I was happy, and longed to die and be at rest; but it was the will of God that I should recover. What torture I endured, the twelve months I was confined to my bed! and what trouble and expense I must have been to my dear parents! The healing of the arm-pit was more than my dear mother could manage; and after many painful and unsuccessful attempts to keep the arm from adhering to my side, the struggle was given up, and the arm, down to the elbow, was allowed to grow to my side. I may here mention the kindness of two ladies, who frequently called to see me; they bought me a fiddle, that by playing it I might give motion to my arm; and when I was sufficiently restored to allow of my wearing proper clothes, they called to say that I must be measured for two suits of new clothes; but, alas! for poor Joseph, we had removed to Burnley Lane, near Burnley, Lancashire, the very day before they came to announce their kind intention.

Early in the morning of the 21st December, 1812, a cart load of goods—father, mother, and eight children—left Linton, for Burnley, Lancashire. This change proved providential; for here we had new companionships and greater privileges. I and my brothers and sisters went to a Sunday-school; and before we had been long in the place, my brother Thomas, at the tender age of fourteen, began to preach the Gospel; and he was truly a prodigy in piety, zeal, and talents. Our family pew was in the body of the chapel at Keighley Green: father sat next the pew door, mother sat at the other end, and three daughters and five sons were arranged according to their ages. Of my eldest sister Ann, I may truly say that, considering her opportunities, she was a real *gem*, in mental, moral, and spiritual culture. She died of decline at the age of twenty-three. She lived beloved and died lamented. Mother used to say of her, "Nanny never gave me five minutes' uneasiness in her life: she was more my companion and counsellor than my daughter."

When I was about seven years old, I was sent to the cotton factory, to do the best I could to make a living. My right arm was grown to my side; my jacket gave me pain, and hung upon my back as if it did not belong to me; my head was tapering and long, and altogether I had a singular appearance; and sometimes I was told that I should be rather short. These things, with what I had suffered, and the long, long dreary mill hours—thirteen and often fourteen hours per day—made me sorrowful and dejected in spirit. Still, I was fond of reading; I could sing beautifully; and mother, being a good singer, used to sing with me. I was a favourite at the Sunday-school; I often got promoted; and when a prize was offered for recitation, I with ease and modesty carried it off; so much so that ultimately I had not a competitor in a school of four hundred boys; so that, whatever my looks might be, or whatever persons might say, I knew that I was not, in the common acceptation of the term, short of sense. Yes; the Sunday-school, the chapel on the other side of the road, the benches, the pews, the tunes that were sung, the addresses that were delivered, sermons preached, and the families that regularly attended, are all written in imperishable characters upon my memory and heart. All honour to the men who took me by the hand, laid their hands on my head, and told me to be a good boy! Since then more than thirty summers and winters have rolled over my head; and not a few joys and sorrows I have experienced since then: I have enjoyed much of sacred and social friendship; and even now, whilst sitting in my study, at the Antipodes of my native land, the names of William Fishwick, James Howarth, William Hopwood, James Winterbottom, Edward Pollard, Thomas Farrar, poor Thomas Whitfield, and others, vibrate through my soul. In that part of the town where we lived, there were hordes of drunkards, blasphemers, Sabbath-breakers, and idle persons. The Bible says that, "A child left to himself, bringeth his mother to shame." Thank God I was not left to myself: had I been so left, then the evil within, the evil beneath, and the evil around would most certainly have caused me to become a drunkard, a Sabbath-breaker, a gambler, and perhaps a thief. I might ere this have been in hell. Blessed be the Lord, from these evils I was, with my dear brothers, preserved; and I here record it as my settled conviction, that, under God, the moral austerity of my dear father, the tender affection of my never-to-be-forgotten mother, the instructions and influences I received at the chapel and school—at that important period of my life—were the means of my preservation from temporal, spiritual, and eternal death. At that time, many of the leading gentry of the town were steeped in iniquity. I could mention the names of many that died awfully, during our twelve years' residence there,—of apoplexy, of *delirium tremens*, of falls from their horses when intoxicated, by being drowned in the canal which surrounded the town, and by suicide:—

> Oh, cursed, cursed Sin! traitor to God,
> And ruiner of man! Mother of Woe,
> And Death, and Hell! wretched, yet seeking worse;
> Polluted most, yet wallowing in the mire;
> Most mad, yet drinking frenzy's giddy cup·
> epth ever deepening, darkness darkening still;
> Folly for wisdom, guilt for innocence;
> Anguish for rapture, and for hope despair:
> Destroyed, destroying; in tormenting, pained;
> Unawed by wrath, by mercy unreclaimed;
> Thing most unsightly, most forlorn, most sad,
> Thy time on earth is past, thy war with God
> And holiness. But who, oh, who shall tell,
> Thy unrepentable and ruinous thoughts;
> Thy sighs, thy groans? who reckon thy burning tears,
> And damned looks of everlasting grief?
> Where now, with those who took their part with thee,
> Thou sittest in Hell, gnawed by the eternal worm,
> To hurt no more, on all the holy hills.
>
> —POLLOK.

It was not without regret that I left Burnley, the scene of so many sacred associations; and on ascending the brow of the hill which commanded the view of the whole town, with suppressed emotion I said, within myself, "Adieu! adieu!" True, Rawtenstall, to which we removed, was only seven miles distant, but all there was new to me. This change of residence proved a family blessing; and Rawtenstall was the scene of several important family and personal events. Here my brother Benjamin died. He was some eighteen months older than myself, and we loved each other indeed. Though he had been very industrious, and strictly moral, yet in his sickness he had religion to seek. I remember his struggles for acceptance with God. He had begun to meet in class with Mr. Giles Waldwark, a man full of faith and the Holy Ghost. The class met at Longholme, on the Tuesday night, and Benjamin's case was the subject of mutual and faithful prayer. One of the members was praying that Benjamin's soul might be set at perfect liberty, when Giles cried out, at the top pitch of his powerful voice, "It's done, Lord! it's done, Lord!" And verily so it was. While they were thus pleading, Benjamin found that peace which passeth all understanding, and became the subject of joy unspeakable. On my father's return from labour that night, he inquired of Benjamin how he was? The answer was, "Bless the Lord, father, though very poorly in body, yet happy in soul." My father, clasping his hands, and lifting his eyes toward heaven, said, "Let us praise God." All present rose; we sang the Doxology, and father engaged in prayer. If I remember right, we left Burnley in the summer of 1824. My brother's health failed at the Christmas of 1825. The disease, rapid consumption, made fearful strides; but God very graciously carried on his work, and Benjamin's soul was entirely sanctified. On Saturday, March 4th, 1826, Benjamin died. What a day of hallowed triumph! About six in the evening, as we were all standing round his bed, a fit of coughing seized him; he had just time to say, "Bless God, mother; this will try me!" The phlegm stuck in his throat, and his whole frame was convulsed and distorted again and again—until my sister Ellen cried out, "O God, do not let him breathe again!" It was a solemn moment; it was his last struggle: and, with a look of inexpressible serenity, he laid his head upon his pillow, and was at rest. After a silent pause, my dear father raised his hands, and exclaimed, "Bless the Lord, there's *another safe* landed!" Benjamin died in his 21st year; and his was the first corpse interred in the yard of the New Wesleyan Chapel, then not opened, at Rawtenstall. My brother's death gave me real comfort; he was safe; and had he been spared, I saw nothing but poverty and toil before him: he was, at best, a weak and sickly youth. If, during his affliction, anyone prayed for his restoration, I did not—I could not say, Amen. I was, during his illness, his almost constant attendant. When he was dead, in the house, I frequently ran up into his room, kissed his cold face, wept tears of joy, and reluctantly returned. At the funeral, when the friends were singing that incomparable hymn, "The morning flowers display their sweets," &c., it was with the utmost difficulty that I could restrain myself from singing aloud. In respect to him I could fully adopt the following lines:—

Again we lift our voice,
And shout our solemn joys:
Cause of highest raptures this,
Raptures that shall never fail;
See a soul escaped to bliss,
Keep the Christian festival.
Thou in thy youthful prime,
Hast leap'd the bounds of time:
Suddenly from earth released,
Lo! we now rejoice for thee;
Taken to an early rest,
Caught into Eternity.

Benjamin's sickness and death made a deep impression on my mind; but oh, how I trifled with those powerful calls to entire devotedness to God! I was regular at the public worship of God, was a teacher in the Sabbath-school, was strictly moral in my conduct, and in Christian theology well instructed; but my besetting sin was levity and mirth, and it was difficult for me to refrain from turning even sacred things into mirth. If in the chapel, or school, or in family devotion, there ever was anything bordering on the ludicrous, I could not suppress a hearty laugh; and there was a vein of humour in my nature, which needed to be subdued and chastened by severe discipline and divine grace. On one occasion, while resident at Burnley, through curiosity, I went to the Roman Catholic chapel, when a wicked old woman, whom I well knew, came in. She crossed herself with holy water, made a deep curtsy, walked to her place, kneeled down, and in two or three minutes was fast asleep. It was too much for me, and being at the extreme end of the chapel, I rolled my pocket handkerchief, stuck it in my mouth, and—with a loud laugh, which in vain I tried to suppress—ran out of the chapel.

I was from my boyhood an attentive and retentive hearer of the word; the men, manners, and discourses, five-and-thirty years gone by, I can now distinctly call to mind. Of all the preachers I ever sat under, the Rev. Henry Fish made the deepest impression on my mind and heart. His ability, fidelity, earnestness, and, above all, the unction attendant on his word, used to prostrate my soul in the dust, and fill me with longing desire, and, for the moment, with firm resolve to be the Lord's. It was then my settled conviction, that, if converted, I should be happy and useful. Towards the close of a powerful sermon preached by Mr. Fish, one Sabbath evening, I resolved to remain at the prayer-meeting, under the full conviction that I should find peace that night; and it was also deeply impressed on my mind that, unless I then gave God my heart, I should grieve the Holy Spirit, and destroy those powerful and hallowed feelings of which I was then the subject. But I yielded to tempation; and, by taking a quiet walk with a friend, and engaging in worldly conversation, I deliberately grieved the Holy Spirit of God: and though, afterwards, I was truly converted, those powerful and melting feelings, in the same degree, never have returned; and it was through a series of severe personal privations and sufferings that I was brought to submit to the yoke of Jesus, my Lord and Saviour.

"He that walketh with wise men shall be wise; but a companion of fools shall be destroyed," is a philosophical, historical, and biblical truth. I do not remember ever being heartily attached to an evil-disposed person; and although I have had, in my early days, several playmates, yet I never made a companion of any one, out of our family, until after the death of my brother Benjamin. In the year 1827, I became acquainted with Thomas Howarth. He was then a tall, ragged, bony, ignorant lad; but, withal, strictly moral and very quiet. Our acquaintance soon ripened into real friendship. I taught him to read; got him to go to the Sabbath-school, and to attend the preaching of the blessed word, and spent hundreds of hours in instructing him in biblical history and the doctrines of theology. His appearance, habits, and circumstances all rapidly improved. He sat with me in the singers' pew; became a teacher in the same school; was converted on the same evening with myself; he gave me the hand of my dear Sarah in wedlock; he went with me when I preached my first sermon; and when he was utterly disgusted with untoward family circumstances, over which he had no control, he went to Montreal, in Canada; and is now a successful merchant, with a wife and eight children, at Toronto, in Upper Canada.

With all my domestic, social, and religious privileges, I was not happy. I had for years resisted the strivings of the Holy Spirit; I had too much light not to see and feel my wretchedness; and I was too poor in circumstances, and too much under parental and restraining influence, to run headlong into open sin. Yet I was a poor factory lad, with no prospect of ever rising in the mill; my right arm, grown to my side, sternly prevented that; and how in the world to get out of the factory, I could not conceive. And, what was more painful than lameness and poverty, I was sincerely attached to her who now is my partner in sorrow and in joy, and she sometimes ventured modestly to hint at my gloomy prospects. About this time, while at work in the card-room, I, by some means, gave the wrist of my right hand a severe wrench. I went to the nearest doctor of any note. He said my wrist was out of joint, and he employed three men to assist him in putting it right. I waited a week, but the hand swelling, and my wrist giving me great pain, I went to the famed Whitworth doctor. He swore "the fool had broken the wrist." He then set it, and sent me home, with instructions to come again in a few days. Again and again I went from Rawtenstall to Whitworth, weeping, and sometimes kneeling down behind a wall or hedge to ask God to direct and bless me. My parents were poor, and the doctor said I must go to live for a time at Whitworth, or he would give up the case. I ventured to consult him about my arm which was grown to my side. He said he could *relieve* the case, but it would cost 100 guineas. I went home weeping, very much dejected; but my extremity was God's opportunity.

Whilst walking in the lane one day, with my hand in a sling, a woman unknown to me began to question me about my hand. She said that I had better go to the Manchester Infirmary; that it would cost me nothing, and that there I should have the best advice. I made my case and desire known to my master, Thomas Kay, Esq., and he obtained from W. Townend, Esq., a recommendation to admit me as an in-patient. On the Saturday following, with a shilling in my pocket, cleanly, but poorly clad, and with the blessing of my parents, I left home for the great town of Manchester. Going by Heywood, I spent the Sabbath with my brother Thomas, and early on Monday morning left for Manchester. I found my way to the Infirmary gates, but found I was two hours before the time to receive patients.

While I was walking about, I met with an old schoolfellow from Burnley; he was out of employ, and without money or food. I bought a pound of bread, which we ate between us, and I gave him sixpence, as I did not expect to need money. The hour came, and full of wonder, hope, and fear, I ventured amongst the crowd of halt and lame that were waiting for medicine and for the arrival of the doctors. I called that morning on

W. Townend, Esq. He asked my name? I replied, Joseph Townend. "No," said he, kindly, "my name is William Townend." I replied, "Yes, sir, I am aware of that; but my name is Joseph Townend." He then directed an assistant to go into the hall with me, and to speak for me to the governor of the house.

At length, my turn came to go in before the doctor. There sat an elderly, plain, honest-looking gentleman, with a broad-brimmed hat on his head, and minus one or two of his front teeth. He said to me—"Well, my lad, what's the matter with thee?" I showed him my wrist. He said, "You might do for an out-patient." I said, "My arm is fast to my side, sir." He replied, "What! fast! how's that? Be quick with thy jacket off!" When he saw my arm and side, he said, "Well, well! how is this?" I told him it was from a burn when I was a little boy. He inquired who was the doctor. I said, "My mother, sir." He replied, "It's like thy mother—it's like thy mother!" All the new patients were shown into an upper room, in which, when I entered, there were ten beds, and eight persons in them. The smell was almost too much for me. I thought, "Have I to live in such a place as this?" The man-nurse then came to examine our clothes, and to see if we were clean. On coming to me he said, "I see all's right with you, young man; but, as a matter of form, I must look at your shirt-neck." His kindness in thus speaking made me breathe more freely. It was just dinner time, and an old man came into the room with five cans hanging upon his fingers, half full of broth, and being subject to fits, he was seized with one, when the shaking of his hands spilled the broth, and scalded his hands. From the first the man-nurse, whom I shall call Joseph, for that was his name, showed me great kindness.

It was five weeks before I had to keep my bed, so that I had an opportunity of making myself generally useful, which was of great service to me afterwards. I lodged in the wing of the house pointing towards St. Peter's church, in a small ward with only three beds: our beds, food, and furniture were plain, but clean, and I began to feel very content. It was the business of the house-surgeon to come round to the patients every night and morning, and enquire how we did. The man-nurse, Joseph, always attended the surgeon, made plasters, dressed wounds in cases of necessity, and washed and removed the dead. There were six surgeons, who each took in patients once in six weeks, and the patients so taken in belonged to and were attended by their surgeon; and, by the good providence of God, I was under good Dr. Ransom. Each patient had his own name, and the name of his surgeon, upon a card hung over his bed's head. The removal of the card was the sign to quit the next morning, which usually was Monday morning. On the first Sabbath morning the house-surgeon examined my wrist, probed it with his lancet, the mark of which I now see as I write; he then took down my card and said, "You will be an out-patient, sir." I reminded him of my arm grown to my side; and hanging up the card, he said, "Two birds with one stone; aye?" I said, "Yes, sir." I was several times taken into the consultation-room, and before Doctors Ransom, Wilson, Thorpe, and others, my case was freely canvassed and examined. My old doctor used to conclude with, "Well, Joe, what's to be done?" my answer invariably being, "I should like to have it cut, sir." There was some difference of opinion as to whether it would be safe to operate, and also as to the mode; and the last time I was called into the consultation-room, Doctors Ransom and Thorpe got to warm words about the case. At length, the old gentleman, with his broad hat on, turned to me, and said, "Joe, thou'rt my patient?" "Yes, sir." Then turning towards the other doctors, said, "Gentlemen, you can go about your business; I will have my own way!"

I now felt myself at home in the infirmary; I could dress wounds, make plasters, administer medicines, and frequently ventured to read with and talk to the sick and dying. Some of the ministers, all of whom were of the Established Church, preached and visited like men of God; but the majority were like mere talking-machines. One case I shall never forget. Hearing that a clergyman was going into one of the large wards to visit a dying man, I followed, and sat at a distance, so as to observe what passed. The minister said to the dying man, "Do you believe the Articles of the Christian faith?" The patient replied, "I do." The minister then said to the man, "Then you must say after me." The Articles were read, and the dying man repeated after the minister, as well as he could. Several collects or prayers were read, amongst the rest, one for the king, both Houses of *Parliament,* the Lord's Prayer, &c.; then the sacrament was administered, and the minister took his leave. The next morning the poor man was dead. Alas! how many thousands have been thus officially packed up in ignorance, and sent into the presence of Him who hath said, "Verily, verily, I say unto thee, except a man be born again, he cannot see the kingdom of God."

On the Friday morning after the final consultation on my case, being in a humorous mood, with the long brush handle in my hand by way of staff, and followed by another patient, I was proceeding from ward to ward, inquiring if the patients had any complaints to lodge, as to their general treatment, diet, &c.—and having just pulled the quilt off an ill-tempered man who was confined to bed, he having hurled the Bible at me, which was upon his bed—just at that moment, the voice of the man-nurse was heard calling—"Joseph Townend!" and he, perceiving what I was about, said, "Come this way, sir; let's try to cure you of your larking!" And then, looking significantly, said, "Go into Paul's ward, and wait until I come." He stopped away a few minutes, and I was employed in looking out of one of the windows of the ward, trying to count the cabs and coaches that were standing or passing in Piccadilly, when in comes Joseph with a long thick bandage in his hand, and said, "Come this way, sir; I have a deal of trouble to make you hear this morning." He wound the bandage three or four times round my head, covering my eyes, and tied it fast; then asking me to take his arm, and the arm of the house-surgeon, I was led along the alley, up a few steps into the operation-room, was stripped, and seated upon a high seat. I could not see any one, but the voices of Doctors Wilson and Ransom were familiar. Dr. Wilson said, "Now, young man, I tell you, if when you feel the knife, you should jerk, or even stir—you will do it at the hazard of your life." My old doctor said kindly, "Joe will not stir." I replied, "No, sir." All was still: a hand firmly grasped the huge web, forcibly placing the fingers and thumb close to my side, and, with a forcible thrust, through went the knife, as near the pit of the arm as possible, and close to my side, with the sharp edge downward; the progress of the instrument I distinctly heard, and the pain was most exquisite.

I thought of home, and friends being distant. My arm being stretched in an horizontal position, I felt the weight of the web which for fifteen years had been accumulating, the smoking wound reaching better than half way towards the thigh, and very nearly to the middle of the back and breast. The web being bound round the arm, and the side plastered, the bandage was untied. The room was like a little chapel. On the floor were Drs. Ransom and Wilson, in oil dresses, attended by the house-surgeon and Joseph, the man-nurse; and the gallery full of medical and surgical students. I was then put into my bed, which I had that morning neglected to make. My arm was stretched back, projected towards the door, and supported by pillows; then, having swallowed a nauseous dose of aperient medicine, I was left to reflect on my past life, present position, and future prospects. I felt ashamed and grieved at my past neglect and wickedness in resisting the Holy Spirit. I thought of the chapel and school—I wept bitterly. I was not converted; but it grieved me to witness such deep depravity and crime in the patients. My sanguine hope was that in six weeks I should be able to return home. The Sabbath is generally the doctors' busiest day, and consequently, for the poorer class of patients, the most trying. So it was in Manchester Infirmary. Our house-surgeon had the daily dressing of all the severe cases committed to him, and the head doctor came weekly. The former was a gentleman of fine feelings, and I account for his conduct in certain cases from that fact. One Sabbath morning whilst removing the ligaments of a man's wrist, he gave the man such strong pain, that the man, stamping his foot with violence upon the floor, cursed the doctor to his face. The doctor much moved, sat down, and, in a flood of tears, said, "I wish my father had apprenticed me to a chimney-sweeper!"

The Sabbath morning after my operation, the house-doctor came up to my bed, saying, "Good morning; give me your hand, sir." And reaching my left hand across my heart towards him, he struck it back, saying, "Do you offer a gentlemen your left hand?" Then, seizing my right hand, he dragged me off the bed into the middle of the room. I leaned to my left side, and holding up my right foot, I tried to keep up my poor arm. With violence he struck at the same moment with one fist the knee, and with the other the elbow, sternly exclaiming—"*Stand up, man;* you have not your mother for your doctor now!" Immediately my leg and foot were covered with blood; and on the web being unloosed, I saw it was turned black: and my poor side was drenched in blood, and smoked almost like a kiln. The web was poulticed, and in fourteen days it dropped off in pieces. The poultices were frequently (to my feeling) scalding hot; and very often the coarse cloth in which they were put, made deep indentations in the raw flesh, and they were literally torn out drenched in blood. On the Tuesday night after the operation, I had, from ten to eleven o'clock, fallen into a gentle sleep. On awaking, the room was lighted, several doctors were moving about, and one of them bending over a man who was lying in the bed on the opposite side of the room.

As I was looking I saw the man spit a mouthful of blood and phlegm into the doctor's face; the latter slapped him in the face, and said, "Take that, sir!" They had brought in a crazy drunkard who had cut his throat, and the doctor was sewing together the terrible gash.

The operation being over, the doctors retired, and, with a light in the room, myself and a boy were left with the man. Shortly, the man began to grumble and swear, asking why they had brought him there; and jumping out of bed, off he went in his shirt up the alley. Joseph and the house-surgeon soon brought him back, put the strait-jacket on him, tied him down to the bed, and left him. He swore dreadfully; talked as if his companions were with him; then as if he were in hell, begging the devils not to run those red-hot bars into him; then he was convulsed, shouted and lifted the iron bed-stocks, making every pane of glass in our wing of the house to rattle; then he found out that he was not damned; turned religious, praised God; and, after a weary, weary night, he was taken to the *Lunatic Asylum*.

There is generally strong sympathy existing between fellow-sufferers; but especially so in a large establishment like the Manchester Infirmary. The day after the madman was taken away numbers of the patients from the other wards came to congratulate us on the removal of our troublesome guest. Several who had lost limbs, and others who had severe diseases, expressed their thankfulness that their case was not as bad as mine; certainly I was in a deplorable state.

About noon on the following Friday, a tall, bony, swarthy-looking man was brought in, and laid with his head over the foot of the bed. It was said that he was a boatman, that on the previous Sabbath he had been ruptured; but the man was so ill that he could give no account of himself. The head-surgeon stripped off his coat, and, with all his strength, pushed the part into its place. One of the doctors said, "The man is sick, bring a drop of brandy, nurse." "Brandy be d——," replied another, "the man is dead." They all left the room, and opposite my bed was the dead man, with his head hanging over the bed. Joseph, the nurse, came with the slings, and not being able to lift the man decently off the bed into the slings, he first threw the head off, and then the feet. He was called off, and left the corpse upon the floor, when Mr. Adam Kay, the superintendent of the Longholme Sabbath-school, and principal book-keeper at Mr. Kay's mill, entered the ward. He stood aghast; looked alternately at the dead man and at myself: he did not, he could not speak, neither could I. At the top of the landing he met Joseph, the nurse, who explained the case to him. The Sabbath following, Mr. Kay gave at the Sunday-school a statement of his visit, which so much affected the teachers and scholars that the school had to be closed without singing. My companion in the other bed was a sweet, intelligent, and pious lad. He was sorely afflicted with scrofula; he had a wound in his throat, out of which his breath could be felt by placing the hand over it. Early on the Saturday morning, the very day after the boatman died under the operation, the dear lad was suffocated. Joseph and the house-surgeon were called in, the window was thrown open, an instrument put down the boy's throat, but all to no effect. His spirit had fled to that "better land"

"Where sickness and sorrow,
Pain and death,
Are felt and feared no more."

Dr. Thorpe had a middle-aged patient with a tumour in the pulsation artery, between the arm and the breast. The doctor made an incision in the shoulder, removed the tumour, tied the end of the artery nearest the heart, and the man recovered. This case and mine were the most notable; so that when visitors of rank came, they were always brought to see us.

Dr. Thorpe was a clever man. A patient of his had his leg amputated between the thigh and the knee. He was taken out of bed, along the alley, over the main building, up the front of the hall into the operation-room. The wound was untied, the flesh cut round close to the bone, the bone sawed, the veins taken up and tied, the stump dressed, and the man comfortably placed in his bed again, all in twenty minutes. What a world of woe was compressed within the walls of that hospital! Fractured skulls, filmy and inflamed eyes, broken limbs, dislocated and swollen joints, purulent and fœtid sores, strictures, ruptures, cancers, tumours, jaundice, diabetes, scrofula, and even leprosy. Here a convulsive sob; there a deep groan; yonder a piercing shriek. What dreary, lonely nights! and how deep and solemn the midnight tongue of time, as heard by the agonised, wakeful patients! At length the blessed morn arrives; buckets and brushes begin to clatter; the more healthful patients to laugh and chatter, and the breakfast-tins to rattle. Bottles, pills, plasters, powders, ointments, lotions, and surgical instruments are being hurriedly handed about the wards; whilst the rapid steps of doctors, students, and nurses prevent the morning repose of those jaded patients who, from very pain, could not sleep in the night. Listen! that is the accident bell; and yonder is the rapid and well-known step of the house-surgeon, going to the accident-room. What's the matter? Some one has fallen from a building, or has been run over in the street, or mangled in the wheels, strap, or shafts of the factory, or in the stone quarry, or burnt with the fire-damp in the coal mine, or scalded with metallic liquor in the foundry, or stabbed in a drunkery.

My case was so bad that it was thought by some to be hopeless; and it was said that if my appetite failed, all was over. I drank diluted Peruvian bark like water, and ate as if I had been at hard labour in the open air. Lying flat upon my back, it was very difficult to take my food, and especially hot liquids; but necessity is the mother of invention. My shoulder blades were raw with lying upon my back; I could not wear anything in the shape of linen. My wounds had to be dressed twice every day for a long time, and the pus from the sores frequently dropped through the bed upon the floor. In this state I was visited by my good brother Thomas. A young gentleman was with him, who gave me pain of mind by frequently expressing surprise that Thomas should have a *brother* in such a place and state. My dear brother Charles, and my true friend and companion, Mr. Thomas Howarth, came to see me, and Mr. Adam Kay came every Tuesday. I knew his foot as soon as he got upon the landing. Elisha, my eldest brother, and other friends, came a long way to sympathise with me in my distress. Twenty-four years have rolled into eternity since then; but those unmistakable tokens of real kindness I shall never forget. My good old doctor treated me with fatherly affection; and the house-surgeon for six weeks dressed my sores with the greatest tenderness and regularity. I always accounted for his harsh treatment, at the first dressing, on the ground of his extreme sensitiveness. About six weeks after the operation, he had taken off the plasters, and, eyeing the sore, he exclaimed, "There, that's worth a Jew's eye." I inquired, "What is that, sir?" "Oh," said he, "there's a speck of healing in the middle of the sore, like a small island in the middle of the ocean."

How much of pleasure or pain is experienced in the aggregate of human life, arising out of the tempers, dispositions, and habits of persons with whom we have to do, and most especially with the sensitive invalid! Dr. A. Reed, in his "Advancement of Religion the Claim of the Times," states the following fact:—"A lady, suffering under one of the most severe diseases which affects our nature, was urged to see a practitioner of the first eminence. His opinion was all that could be desired. He saw through the case, and could afford her essential relief; but she could never be persuaded to see him a second time; she had rather languish on beneath excruciating pain. And why? just because he showed an utter insensibility to her sufferings." It was now deemed prudent to entrust the dressing of my wounds to Mr. Waterhouse, an elder student of my beloved and venerable doctor. His hat and coat were akin to his master's, and, to my great joy, his disposition too. He was easy, kind, careful, and communicative. Seating himself by my bed, he would place his hat carefully upon the bed, stroke his hair, turn up his cuffs, all the while talking freely; and, if in no particular hurry, he would take up one of my books, and read me half a page. I had much of what is called proud flesh, and the skin had to be twice formed before it would remain. I had large elevations of proud flesh frequently, like small hillocks on a plain. A piece of stone vitriol as large as my fist was always at hand. Mr. W. would take the vitriol in his hand, and steadily rubbing it upon the raised flesh, would say, "I will make the mountain to a plain, thou wilt see." And that he did, verily I felt as well as saw.

My bed stood under a window, and by rather inclining to my left side I had a view of the entrance into the yard, the top of Morley and Market Streets; and, on Sabbath mornings, seeing crowds of young people going to different schools and places of worship, I used to relieve my mind by weeping, and looking forward to the time when my feet would again stand within the gates of Zion. I was very cheerful, generally, and often gave out hymns, and read and explained portions of Scripture, especially historical parts, to patients who came to spend with me an afternoon or evening hour. During my confinement in bed that summer, the Methodist Conference sat in Manchester; and during its sittings, on a Sabbath evening, and through a considerable part of the night, a most tremendous thunderstorm raged all round the country. As the lightning waved along, I could see distinctly the tops of the houses, and right down Market Street. It was an awful night. My room was filled with patients, and female servants, who seemed to think themselves secure there, for they thought me very religious.

Well, I was the subject of restraining and constraining grace, and I thought my mind fully made up to be entirely the Lord's when I should return home. I was always fond of reading, and had with me my Bible and hymn-book, Pollok's "Course of Time," Milton's "Paradise Lost," Young's "Night Thoughts," and one or two other books, which frequently were taken up by the doctors and students, who seemed astonished to see me have such books.

It was the business of the night-nurse to prepare gruel, and bring it round between one and two in the morning. She was a decent, elderly woman; and, perhaps, her only fault was that she was afraid of her gruel; so that if she could catch us all asleep, gruel was over for that night. For half an hour, when supplied with gruel, all was life and stir. Smoking, snuffing, bartering with each other, and treating each other—especially after Thursday, when friends were admitted—fruits, gingerbread, toffies, wines, &c., which lay concealed from the doctors, all came out then. On one occasion I had partaken rather freely of port wine, which a friend had poured into my tin. When the wound was dressed next morning, it was very much inflamed. Mr. Waterhouse said, "What hast thou been doing? thou hast been out of bed?" He was very much grieved; and he suddenly jerked up my shoulder, which made me sweat with pain, and it cracked like the firing of a pistol. So much for wine. Several patients lost their lives by eating fruits and other things which were prohibited by their doctors. After having been full three months in bed, I began to walk about, and make myself useful to the other patients. My arm had to be kept with the elbow as high as the shoulder, as the pit of the arm was the most difficult to heal; and without my coat, with my arm in that position, I frequently went into the street, and more than once to see Mr. Kay, at the Warehouse, No. 3, Walton's Buildings, Cannon Street. At this time my two companions in the ward were elderly men, both dreadfully afflicted with stricture; the elder of the two, a recruiting sergeant, had a double rupture as well. Poor fellow! he would brush up, and walk as if nothing ailed him. I was very fond of him, waited on him as well as I could, making his bed, and keeping the door, when it was inconvenient for persons to enter, for which I was beloved, and handsomely rewarded. It was understood that if he died suddenly, I was to run directly to the Castle Inn, Dean's Gate, and inform his wife; as he had a perfect horror of being examined by the doctors after his death. The other poor man I have seen literally dance with agony, as the sweat rolled off his face upon the floor. He made me a beautiful straw hat, which I wore when I went home. My side was healed, but the pit of the arm was not. My wrist had been lost sight of; it was weak, and the bone used to ache. My old doctor said, "Well, Joe, thou's been a good patient, as patient as Job. Thou must go home to thy father and mother, and look at the green fields; and whatever *else*, don't let the doctors touch that hand, but keep it bound with the bandage, and go to Blackpool, and wash it in the salt water, and thou wilt see it will soon be well. It's a fine cure, my lad; but I'll never cut another case like thine." With the tears running off my face, I gave him my left hand, but I could not speak; and even now, whilst I record that last interview, I am deeply affected. I called in at the neighbouring wards, bidding them all good-bye; and as I descended the great staircase, with my bundle in my hand, unable to wipe the tears as they fell upon the steps, Dr. Guest, the house-surgeon, turned away much moved. I entered that hospital with fourpence, had had all my wants supplied, and received a *perfect cure*, and, with a pocket full of silver, was returning home. I here, on the 20th of January, 1852, in my study, Collingwood, Melbourne, Victoria, Australia, from the bottom of my heart, record my sincere thanks to Almighty God, and also to the subscribers and managers of that benevolent institution, for the kindness and care I therein received.

CHAPTER II.

Returns home—Maternal welcome—Visits the Manchester Infirmary, Blackpool, and Lytham—Itinerates to sell confectionery—Obtains a situation of trust—Conversion—Begins to preach—First discourse—Becomes a class-leader—Recommended to the Conference—Examined at the District Meeting—Opinions on the Divine Sonship—Distressing affliction and delirium of a female friend—Joins the Temperance movement.

WITH my hand behind my ear, the elbow nearly horizontal with the shoulder, for the arm-pit was not healed, I made my way to Hanging-ditch, to take the coach home. This was the longest and most expensive ride I had ever taken; but I was not strong, and the old sergeant had paid my coach fare. It was seventeen miles to my father's house; I was going home where I knew I should be welcome. My mother in her spectacles came to the door—for sister Isabella had seen me, and said, "Mother, this is Joseph, this is." I passed my mother, she all the while gazing up in my face, and laying down my bundle, and taking off my straw hat, sat down. "Is it my lad?" asked my mother. I said, with suppressed emotion, "It is, mother!" She lit her pipe, sat down in her chair, and took a few hearty draws of the dirty weed before she could speak again. It was her custom, when in trouble, to sit down, take the pipe, and compose, if possible, her perturbed breast. I am not a smoker, I never was, and, what is more, I believe I never shall be; but since then I have bought my aged parents many a pound of tobacco; and if they were alive now, much as I dislike the practice, I would most cheerfully do it again.

My mother had become an adept in dressing wounds, and especially burns and scalds; and after her experience in my case, she made many a fine cure, so that my arm had proper attention. As out-patient, I made one visit to the hospital in that capacity. It was seventeen miles each way. My mother gave me fourteen pence, and with brother Charles's shoes upon my feet—which, though too large and very uncomfortable, yet were, by the way, better than my own—I set off for the Infirmary. I saw a few old faces, got my salve and other little matters, and by a strange hand had my sore dressed; and in placing the pin in the bandage behind the shoulder, the stripling stuck it through the skin also. I had paid a halfpenny for coming over the bridge; I bought three-halfpennies-worth of bread, went on eating, and drank of the brook by the way; and arriving safely at home, gave back to my dear mother the shilling; when she said in her own way, "Joay, thou's very thou'tful!" My arm being healed, was yet very tender for some time, and the hand still so weak that I could not work; and as the season was far advanced, I must soon go to Blackpool, or it would be too late. My old master gave me five shillings, Miss Kay three shillings, old Mr. Hopwood, of Burnley, half-a-crown; but begging was harder work than suffering. I told my case to my brother-in-law, Richard Lupton, who was so much moved that he parted with his watch, that I might have the means to go to the salt water. With eight-and-twenty shillings, I left home for Blackpool, about the middle of September. I walked about thirty-eight miles, stopped at Martin, two miles from Blackpool, had a basin of milk and bread for supper, and the same for breakfast, paid eighteen-pence, and walked on to the place of which my old doctor had spoken. I went upon the beach with my little bundle under my arm; it was low water; I had never seen the sea before, but I heard the roar of the waves where I had slept the preceding night. I saw something in the distance, and asked a woman upon the beach what it was, who, looking at me significantly, said, "The sea! the sea!" My lodgings were plain, but clean, just like myself, for which I paid eight-pence per day, including potatoes for dinner, which I took care always to have. I remained fourteen days bathing and washing my wrist. On the Saturday I took it into my head to walk on the sands to Lytham, and stop a day or two there; I did so. On the Sabbath forenoon I went out with a view to bathe before service time: I went away from public view, stripped, and was about to go into a place surrounded by land, but near the sea. I felt very uneasy, and while sitting by the side of the pool, with my legs hanging into the water, it struck me very forcibly that the place might be very deep; immediately I rose and began to dress, and before I had finished dressing I was surrounded with water, the tide flowing at the time. A boatman asked me, what I was going to do in that pit? I said, "To bathe."

"Can you swim?" "No." "Then indeed you would have been a dead fish, for that pit is not only very deep, but very steep, it's a lucky job, my boy, you did not jump in." Ashamed at my want of caution, and very, very thankful for the care exercised over so unworthy a creature by my Heavenly Father, I then went to the church.

My visit to the sea-side was of essential service; my general health was recruited, my wrist strengthened, and with six shillings in my pocket, I walked home forty miles in one day. Still I had nothing to do, I dreaded the factory, and my parents, though very poor, were not willing for me to go to the mill again. For my sake, mother began her confectionery business again. I went round to small shops; I stood at several fairs—such as Rawtenstall, Newchurch, and Burnley—where I was well known; and succeeded very well indeed at the fairs; but I did not like it—I was truly ashamed of it. And then such remarks were made, as "A Methodist selling nuts and gingerbread!" "Well, Joe, lad! I'll spend a penny with thee for pity's sake," &c. Wearied and jaded, I resolved I would ask Mr. Kay for a situation in the warehouse, a thing I had long desired, and with some difficulty I succeeded; yes, thanks to my Heavenly Father, I succeeded. Master was sharp, and (sometimes I thought) severe; but it was just such a place as I wanted; I was not ashamed of it; I could manage it; it was trustworthy, and the company select. I got a suit of new clothes, and began to look up in the world. My friend T. Howarth was proud of me, and he was a respectable young man. My Sarah, who had never turned her back upon me, but often secretly provided me with money, would now *openly* take a walk with me. I took my place in the Sabbath-school, as teacher of one of the first classes; and, in three years after leaving the Infirmary, was united in solemn wedlock to my dear Sarah, in the parish church, Bury, Lancashire, July 31, 1830.

The Rev. W. Illingworth was instrumental in my conversion to God. Before he came, I was told by my fellow-workmen in the warehouse that I should be brought in when he came. Mr. I. was a revivalist, but I detested Methodist cant; and believed that many who professed to be converted at these excited meetings deceived themselves; and, I thought, I would never go to the penitent form. Mr. Illingworth's first sermon, under God, broke my heart; I sought to hide my tears and emotions, but could not. His text was, "Thou shalt guide me with thy counsel, and afterward receive me to glory." Psalm lxxiii. 24. He preached again in the evening, and held a prayer-meeting; and, standing on the very seat where for years I had sat (the singers' seat), he made powerful and solemn appeals, requesting the earnest seekers to stand up and decide just then. I rose the first; a hundred eyes were upon me; and I felt, as the preacher stated, "that the eyes of God, of angels, and of demons were upon me!" I was several weeks before I found peace. I had pictured to my mind how it would be, that I should feel great elevation of spirit, be filled with joy; and instead of leaving the mode to God, and simply believing the testimony of God concerning his only-begotten Son, I was practically making a saviour of my repentance, and expecting the effects before I had exercised faith in Christ as my Saviour. One Sabbath evening, towards the close of a powerful prayer-meeting, I felt very much discouraged. Many had found peace, amongst whom was my dear friend Thomas Howarth. I was weary in body because of the disquietude of my mind. Mr. Illingworth came, and somewhat sternly said, "Young man, stand up and listen to me!" I did so. He proceeded, "You are stumbling at the simplicity of the Gospel; you want the blessing before you have believed;" and then he said, "What is it you want? Do you expect God to lift you up into the air? You will have to begin over again, and learn how, as a guilty sinner, to take God at his word." He and many others went home, but I went into the vestry with a few select friends. The words, "You will have to begin again," ran through my mind. I thought, "What! all this wrestling, weeping, and praying to be done over again!" I said to myself, "You will have to believe at last—why not believe just now?" and composing my mind, I thought, "I do, I do believe!" I was then calm, peaceable, tranquil. The following day was one of severe conflict. The enemy suggested that I had not been brought in like others—I should not be able to stand fast—but I kept praying and believing, and the tempting power decreased, and I felt that "Old things had passed away, and behold all things had become new." The water as it ran down rippling, and the birds as they flew about and sung, yea, even the smoke of the long chimney of the mill, all seemed new; all praised God; and though I had no ecstacy, I had abundant sweetness and entire satisfaction.

Not long after I obtained peace, through believing, a circumstance of a painful and dangerous character occurred. We had been very busy preparing a load of goods for market, and the carter was waiting to take them off the premises. It was three in the afternoon when he left the ground, and he had a very heavy load. The carter desired us, three warehousemen, to go and give him a thrust up the hill; we did so. Behind the hill there was a public-house, and the man urged us to go to the inn, and said he would pay his footing. We went, and, as we learnt after, the carter privately saw the landlord, and stated that he had "brought three Methodist devils, and he should like to see them all glorious drunk." And he ordered whiskey, but we were to be told it was common gin. We got a quantity, I cannot say how much; and from having it upon empty stomachs we were more or less intoxicated. The eldest of us was the leading man in the warehouse, and the superintendent of the Sabbath-school; and it was pitiful to see him stagger home, running against the rails of the master's house, and thus cutting his face. I went home and laid down a few hours, got a cup of tea, and went to work. Sabbath came, two of us, with grief of mind, took our places in the school; but he who was the superintendent never took his place again; and from that time to this never recovered from the sense of shame which he experienced. Mr. Kay, hearing the whole case, never mentioned it in our hearing—but turned away the carter; and very soon after the landlord died. At that time the Temperance Society did not exist. I felt no guilt upon my mind; but I was sorry for what had taken place, and from that time was very careful about such matters.

When I began to think about being more extensively useful, I was sincerely afraid that I should feel it to be my duty to call sinners to repentance. The responsibility I saw to be great, and to have my name on the plan, and to take the sacred place, without benefiting the people, I viewed with abhorrence. Besides, I had little time, few books, and it would be such a task, that to have been satisfied that the Sabbath-school and the prayer-leader's plan was all that I was called upon to attend to, would have removed a heavy burden from my mind. The impression deepened, and I got very uneasy. One Sabbath evening, being planned, at an obscure place, to assist in carrying on a prayer-meeting, at six o'clock, I resolved, on my way, to attempt talking a little to the people, and fixed in my mind a few plain thoughts. When my turn came, I gave out the page, and whilst the people stood finding the hymn, I began to talk. The old man of the house said,

"Sit you down, folks, this lad will talk to us a bit!" I staggered, I was fairly committed. I proceeded until my voice became natural, and for about ten minutes, with pleasure to myself and profit to the people, spake of the necessity of personal religion. It was reported that I had begun to preach, and being urged to preach the next Monday evening but one, in a large house in Rawtenstal Fold, I reluctantly consented. I made what preparation I could, but at the same time I was in hopes that I should not be able to proceed, and if so that I should take it as an indication that I was not called, and that so my mind might be at rest, and the matter would end. The night came, the house was full of people, all of whom I knew. I stood behind a chair, on a log of wood, and gave out my first hymn, "O God, our help in ages past," &c., and before the hymn was gone through, I felt as certain that I *must* preach as I felt certain of my conversion to God. It was a solemn meeting. I did not take a formal text, but stated as my subject, "The shortness of time," which I proposed to illustrate and improve.

SUBSTANCE OF MY FIRST DISCOURSE—"ON THE SHORTNESS OF TIME."

Time, observes a certain writer, is one of the most undefinable and paradoxical of things; for although it assumes a variety of terms and positions, yet it cannot by those names and positions be explained. If we speak of time past, we say it is gone; of the future, that it is yet to come; and as to the present moment, it becomes the past even while we attempt to define it, and, like the flash of the electric fluid, no sooner exists than expires. Time is the measure of all human things, but is itself immeasurable; and the grand disclosure of most things, but is itself undisclosed, and although it is the present ally of death, yet it will ere long prove his conqueror. But it is not to the nature, but to the brevity of time, and its solemn connecting circumstances, that we wish to draw your attention. We shall, by the blessing of God, and reliance on your prayers, attempt, First, An Illustration of the fact asserted; and, Secondly, An Improvement of the same. In the illustration of this subject we remark:—

1st.—That time is short, when taken in its most extensive sense, compared with *eternity*. True, we cannot comprehend the range of time, but this does not so much arise from the length of its duration, as from the hidden limit of its termination; were the exact period known when time would cease to be, the probability is that the arithmetician, with his numbers, would easily compute its ample range. But as, when the destruction of our planet and the end of time will be is unknown—let us, for the sake of illustration, suppose a period when time will cease to be, and then, calculating from the period when, at the formation of our planet, "the morning stars, exulting, shouted o'er the rising ball," to that period when "the mighty angel shall stand with one foot upon the sea, and another upon the land, and, lifting his hand to heaven, shall swear by Him that liveth for ever and ever, that time shall be no longer; and then bring our hundreds and thousands, or hundreds of thousands, and as many more as you please, of years, and place these under the line of *Eternity;* then begin the process of subtraction, draw the lesser number from the greater, in order to show the difference of the two. Who does not see the absurdity of the proposition? for, in order to draw a lesser number from a greater, you must of necessity know both the numbers. But what do you know of eternity? Go back in search of its beginning, pass the time of the formation of our planet, the creation of chaotic matter, the creation of angels, and, as far as our shallow conception of the subject can go, when nothing existed but abstract deity. Let the mind dart backward and backward, and still farther; we have to come back to the Bible for a solution of the problem. "Before the mountains were brought forth, or ever thou hadst formed the earth and the world, even from *everlasting* to *everlasting* thou art God." On imagination's pinion bring back the mind, pierce the vista of time, pass the general resurrection and conflagration, the final destiny of man and demons, and darting onward and onward, until imagination begins to reel and fancy to lose herself in the labyrinths of eternity—even then, with mighty force, mind shoots forward, and arrives where thought cannot follow and bold fancy dies. There is some proportion between a single grain of sand and the largest mountain in the world—because the mountain is composed of so many grains, were it possible to count them. There is some proportion between a single drop of water and the unfathomable ocean—this is accounted for on the same obvious principles. There is some proportion between the light of a candle and the effulgence of yon bright orb of day, but there absolutely is not any proportion whatever between time and eternity. Time only recently commenced, and it will soon terminate. Eternity, as to

God, never began, and eternity, as it regards your existence and mine, will never end. But in the illustration of this important fact we remark—

2ndly,—"That time is short," if we think of it as the period allotted for human life. Ever since the fall, the laws of decay have been in operation; then was issued the edict which we must all obey: "Dust thou art, and unto dust shalt thou return." True, the lives of the antediluvians were protracted to a considerable extent: some of them lived six or eight hundred years. Of Methuselah, the oldest man, we read that he lived nine hundred and sixty-nine years. But after the flood, human life was considerably shortened; and ever since the days of the composer of the ninetieth Psalm, the age of threescore years and ten has been regarded as an old age—and if, in cases of more than ordinary constitutional health, a few persons have reached fourscore years or more, yet have their days been labour and sorrow. We know it is difficult to impress the brevity of life upon the mind, and most especially on the minds of the young; arising from the fact that we do not measure time prospectively as in the retrospect; and so time plays the cheat with us: for whilst in her approach she imitates the slow imperceptible tide, yet in her retreat she is like the swiftest torrent; whilst she approximates, her tardy wheels move slowly on, yet when passed by there is then nothing observable but her broad pinions swifter than the wind. Let us seek experience in this matter. When the venerable patriarch Jacob stood before Pharaoh, and was asked, by that monarch, his age, he answered—"The days of the years of my pilgrimage are an hundred and thirty years: few and evil have the days of the years of my life been, and have not attained unto the days of the years of the life of my fathers in the days of their pilgrimage!" Job says, "Man that is born of a woman is of few days and full of trouble. He cometh forth like a flower, and is cut down; he fleeth also as a shadow, and continueth not." The Psalmist says, "Behold thou hast made my days as an handbreadth, and mine age is as nothing before thee: Verily, every man at his best state is altogether vanity." "The voice said, Cry. And he said, What shall I cry? All flesh is grass, and all the goodliness thereof is as the flower of the field: the grass withereth, the flower fadeth; because the Spirit of the Lord bloweth upon it; surely the people is grass. The grass withereth, the flower fadeth: but the word of our God shall stand for ever." Isaiah xl. 6, 7, 8.

Unto what in Scripture is the life of man compared? Is it compared to the everlasting mountains—so called in reference to time —which are the same to-day as they were a thousand years ago? No; but unto the grass; which, though now beautiful and healthful, will ere long be scorched by the heat, withered by the drought, blasted by the storm, or cut down with the scythe. "All flesh is grass." Unto what, in this blessed book, the Bible, is the life of man compared? Is it compared to the stately oak, which hath long survived the angry pelting of the winter's storm? No; but unto the leaves which adorn that tree. We see them in all the verdure, beauty, and freshness of the spring, in all their strength and summer maturity; but they wither in autumn, and, falling from the trees, they rot under our feet in winter. "We do all fade as a leaf."

See how quick that shuttle glides across the loom; "Our days are swifter than a weaver's shuttle." How oft, seated by the fire listening to the artless tale, has the winter's eve passed imperceptibly away, when the tongue of time has told us it was midnight. "We spend our years as a tale that is told." Yes, but here we learn from this blessed volume, as well as from daily observation, the fleeting brevity, the fading glory, the frail uncertainty, and the certain mortality of our earthly pilgrimage. We remark—

3rdly and finally,—That time is short, if we think of its great uncertainty—we repeat, its great uncertainty—which assumes so many forms, wears such a variety of aspects, that we scarcely know how to illustrate it. For brevity's sake we name the two general features of uncertainty—accident and disease. It is the property of an accident to come unforeseen; it takes its victim ere he is aware, and—alas! we fear, in many cases, when he is unprepared—hurries him into eternity without a moment's warning. How many whom we have personally known have met their death in such a way. And had we the omniscient eye of Jehovah, what a spectacle would, this instant, be present to our view! Here is a man tumbling from a tremendous precipice, and he is dashed to pieces at the bottom; yonder is an individual buried under the ponderous load which was suspended over his head; and another is struck dead by lightning, the awful artillery of heaven. The raging dog, the furious bull, the galloping steeds, the swelling torrent, the sweeping winds, the raging ocean, the dreadful explosion destroy men's lives. Yes, in a hundred ways men have been taken suddenly, by accident, to their account. Our poet justly says—

> "Dangers stand thick through all the ground,
> To push us to the tomb."

Yes; the traveller on the coach, the driver by the team, the farmer in the field, the miner in the pit, the mariner on the ocean, the merchant in his counting-house, the weaver in the loom, and the maid in the kitchen—all, more or less, are exposed to danger.

As to the second feature of uncertainty—*Disease*—he devours his millions at a meal. Not satisfied with victims from the aged and infirm, he seizes the young, the thoughtless, and the gay. What is the language of observation? Whilst we see here and there a solitary aged person, how many of the young are wasting with consumption, burning with fever, strangling with quinsy, suffocating with the asthma, stabbed with the knife of luxury, or poisoned with the cup of excess. How many in our different neighbourhoods, who were our former companions and acquaintances, are now no more; persons who were our associates at the Sabbath-school, in the solemn temple, or at the nightly revel or midnight debauch. We think of one, gone; another, gone; and another, gone;—verily, we almost stand alone!

Did I speak only of neighbours and acquaintances? has Death come no nearer? has he not also entered our own abodes?

> "Has not the monster played his deadly weapon,
> In the narrower sphere of our sweet domestic comfort,
> And cut down some of the fairest of our sublunary joys?"

Yes; a brother, sister, parent, child, husband, wife. We marked the progress of consumption; stood appalled at the dreadful fever; were confounded at the unexpected accident. How many can adopt the language of the impassioned poet, Young—

> "Insatiate archer, could not one suffice?
> Thy shaft flew thrice, and thrice my peace was slain;"

and some of you can go on and say,

> "And thrice, ere thrice yon moon had filled her horn."

> "Death more than causes sorrow, he confounds;
> And ere we cease to weep for one, another falls."

I think I hear some one say, "Yes, it's all very true; but I have a good constitution; I need not fear, I wish while young to enjoy myself, and shake off such gloomy thoughts." My friends, listen! Your departed friends, some of them at least, thought as you now think, spoke as you now speak, acted as you now purpose to act; their sparkling eyes, healthful countenances, and active limbs all spake of years of pleasure yet to come. Oh, with what tenacity they clung to life; with what reluctance they marked the power and progress of disease; and when convinced they must go,

"How the conscious tears stood thick
As the dew-drops on the bells of flowers: honest effusion;
In vain the swollen heart works hard
To put a gloss on its distress."

O ye gay triflers, ye simple souls in quest of butterfly enjoyments! ye who, waking, dream that religion and melancholy are the same thing; ye who dream of passion, pastime, and mirth as the elixir of human bliss, come with me and visit the graveyard where your friend lieth. Remove that earth, take off that lid—see, on that once fair and damask cheek,

"The high-fed worm, in lazy volumes roll'd,
Riots unscared. For this was all thy caution?
For this thy painful labours at thy glass,
T' improve those charms and keep them in repair;
For which the spoiler thanks thee not? Foul feeder!
Coarse fare and carrion please thee full as well,
And leave as keen a relish on the sense."

"Boast not thyself of to-morrow; thou knowest not what a day may bring forth." Come, let us ponder over the lines on yonder tomb—

"Pause here, and think; a monitory rhyme
Demands one moment of thy fleeting time.
Consult life's silent clock; thy bounding mien
Seems it to say, Health here has long to reign.
Hast thou the vigour of thy youth;
An eye that beams delight, a heart untaught to sigh;
Yet fear; youth ofttimes, healthful and at ease,
Anticipates a day it never sees;
And many a tomb, like Hamilton's aloud
Cries, Prepare thee for an early shroud."

Having thus endeavoured to Illustrate our proposition, we

proceed, Secondly, to Improve the subject. In doing so, we shall not bring the light of philosophy, or the dim taper of infidelity to shine upon our subject, but our statements and reasonings shall be from, and in accordance with, the revealed word of God.

1st. We remark, if it be true that time is short, it is also true that eternity is at hand—

> "If death were nought; and nought after death ;
> Then might the debauchee untrembling mouth the heavens ;
> Then might the drunkard reel o'er his full bowl,
> And when 'tis drenched fill up another to the brim,
> And laugh at the poor bugbear death."

But *eternity*, *eternity* is at hand! Close at the heels of death is an everlasting state of being. There is no intermediate state in which the sinner's polluted spirit may be purged; none except in the dogmas of deluded and deluding men. "If the tree falls to the north or to the south, so it lies"—

> "So man departs to heaven or hell,
> Fixed in the state wherein he died."

Whilst we cheerfully admit that there are degrees of character, and, if you like the phraseology, good, better, best; bad, worse, worst; yet let it be remembered that there is an essential difference betwen right and wrong; between righteousness and unrighteousness; between the saint and the sinner; the child of God and the child of the devil; the converted and the unconverted; so that it is the being born again, or the not being born again; the being holy, or the not being holy; the belonging to the sheep, or the goats; the belonging to the family of God and household of faith, or the not so belonging, that will, *at death, seal our eternal doom.* Does Lazarus die? he is carried by the angels into Abraham's bosom. Does the rich man die? In hell he lifts up his eyes, being in torments. "To be absent from the body," said Paul, "is to be present with the Lord." "This day," said Jesus to the penitent thief, "shalt thou be with me in paradise." "*Whatsoever* thy hand findeth to do, do it with thy might; for there is no work, nor device, nor knowledge, nor wisdom in the grave, whither thou goest."

Eternity, O eternity! who can define, explain this inexplicable term. The venerable Harvey has said, "astronomers have instruments by which they can measure the distances and magnitudes of the celestial orbs; arithmeticians have numbers by which they can calculate the lapse of ages;" but, he asks, "what line can guage, what numbers can state the lengths and breadths of eternity?" "It is high as heaven; what canst thou do? Deeper than hell; what canst thou know? The length thereof is longer than the earth, and its breadth broader than the sea." Here is a mighty mysterious existence, a sum not to be lessened by the largest deductions; a period not to be diminished by the most prodigious lapse of ages; for when ages, numerous as the bloom of the spring, increased by the herbages of summer, augmented by the leaves which fall from the trees in autumn, multiplied by the drops of rain which drown the winter; when these, and ten thousand times ten thousand more, have run their ample rounds—it is still *eternity*.

2ndly, We further remark—That this is not an eternal state of dormant feeling or inactivity. It is not annihilation or an eternal sleep. I know there is a sleepy, dreamy, easy way of disposing of these things, so as not to alarm the conscience, or awaken the careless sinner; but if there be one truth more clearly stated in the Bible than another, it is this—that our eternal condition will be one of unspeakable happiness or of unspeakable woe; of ineffable pleasure or exquisite pain; of everlasting salvation or of eternal damnation. Yes; while eternity turns on its ever-turning axis, I, as an individual, shall be sinking deeper and deeper in the darkness of eternal despair; or rising higher and higher in the heights of everlasting joy and rapture. "In thy presence is fulness of joy; at thy right hand there are pleasures for evermore." Psalm xvi. 11. "Depart from me, ye cursed, into everlasting fire, prepared for the devil and his angels. And these shall go into everlasting punishment, but the righteous into life eternal." Matt. xxv.

What, brethren, is the very next thought that would strike the attentive mind? Why, this—that our eternal state depends upon our use or abuse of our precious time. Surely we are something higher than the mere animals; we are not here merely to eat and drink, and toil and rest our jaded faculties, and then perish like the brutes. We are here on trial for another state of being; probationers for eternity; with the line of duty marked out by the revealed will; with capacity to understand that will; with the guide-posts distinctly pointing the way to Heaven, and the way to Hell. Those who have lived are now reaping the reward of their doings; millions are saved, for ever saved; or eternally undone.

> "There rolls the rattling chain,
> And all the dreadful eloquence of pain;
> Black fires' malignant light, the sole refreshment of this doleful sight;
> Hope never comes, that comes to all while here;
> But torture without end still rages, and a fiery deluge,
> Fed with ever-burning sulphur, unconsumed."

Did they repent, believe, obey, and continue faithful to the end of their probation—

> "Above yon angel powers,
> In glorious joy they live;
> Far from a world of grief and sin,
> With God eternally shut in."

But now is my state of trial, and now is yours also. It has been stated that what can only be done once ought to be done well. Apply this to human life, and, oh, how forcibly it cries, "Live well! live well!" Youth once wasted can never be brought back. Opportunities once neglected will never return. The day of life once gone by, unimproved, ten thousand voices from the pit say, "Gone for ever! Gone for ever!"

Our time is short; but, oh, what a work we have to do! the sinner has to repent. Can he do it when he will, where he will, how he will? Oh, sinner! this is not work to be put off to a day of sickness—to the hour of death. What will God say to thee, when, after wasting thy time, health, and opportunities in the service of Satan, thou shalt come to Him with thy emaciated body, with thy crocodile tears, with the mere snuff of life's candle? Will He not say, "I called, but thou refused; I stretched out my arm, but thou regardedst it not; I also will laugh at thy calamity, I will mock when thy fear cometh."

Are we the servants of God? Our time is short: what personal and relative duties devolve upon us. "Let us work out our own salvation with fear and trembling." Let us guard against ease, effeminacy, sloth, and making provision for the flesh. See what God has done for us in the gift of His Son, who lived, laboured, suffered, and died, and in the gift of His holy word. Oh, friends, it will be well if, when retiring from the stage of action, we can say with the Psalmist, "Thy statutes have been my song in the house of my pilgrimage."

Oh, Christian men and women, take care of the Sabbath; its hours are sacred. What! are not six days sufficient, without unnecessary encroachments on the Sabbath? Do you lounge in bed longer, and retire earlier, on the Sabbath? Does your wife or servant keep back from the house of prayer, to prepare you a feast, and that feast to prepare you for drowsiness and stupor; and that on the Sabbath! It is not true that three or four persons cannot have a comfortable Sabbath dinner without one person being robbed of the best half of the best day of the seven. Time is short; parents and children must soon part. What vigilance, care, industry, prayer, and faith are needful to make a deep, a lasting impression! If not done speedily, the opportunity will be for ever lost. What a state the world is in! and the Church is to witness for God. His servants are to labour in this vast field. Oh, how many souls perish, partially through the idleness of professors! Thank God, there is a noble race of noble men—aye, and women too—that have done nobly; and the result, by the grace of God, stands out in bold relief in our country, in schools, chapels, libraries; and we have an able, active body of religious men.

Finally, are you afflicted, poor, distressed with the ills of life? Endure a little longer, hold fast the beginning of your confidence, look to the strong for strength,

> "And watch a moment to secure
> An everlasting rest." Amen.

Since the delivery of my first discourse, I have never had a doubt but that I was called of God to preach His word; and I should as soon think of ceasing to eat my daily food, as of ceasing to distribute the word of life; unless I should be prevented by sickness, or overtaken by sin, and disqualified by delinquency.

The members of the Bacup Circuit, its chapels and societies, are embalmed in my memory and heart. Many of the dear people who smiled on my weak, but sincere, endeavours to spread the Saviour's name, are now no more. The Dawsons, Earnshaws, Kays, Whiteheads, Hargreaves's, Parkinsons, Moorhouses, Heyworths, Grimshaws, and others of those days, I cannot forget—with them I hope to spend a happy eternity.

When old James Moorhouse left Longholme for Brooks-bottoms, his Tuesday-night class was without a leader; and, by the unanimous voice of the Leaders' Meeting, I was appointed to succeed him. To take any class, would have been, at that time, no ordinary trial to me; but to succeed an aged veteran, who had for many, many years enjoyed entire sanctification—an individual dearly beloved by all—a class, too, every member of which was older than myself—was the greatest trial I ever had, so far as labour and office in the Church were concerned. In the cross there was a blessing. Our first and only child died when she was eight days old. She was a lovely babe, early transplanted to bloom in a fairer Eden. It was thought by some, that I should be wholly engaged in the ministry; but I was married, and the Conference law prohibited my having a home circuit. I was therefore asked, whether I was willing to leave country, parents, and friends, and go to wherever the Missionary Committee would send me. I was so willing; and was recommended from the Bacup Quarterly Meeting to the District Meeting. The day before the District Meeting was to be held, my superintendent called, and said, "Joseph, you will not forget the District Meeting to-morrow!" "No, sir!" "Are you prepared for your examination?" "I hope I am, sir." "What is your opinion on the Sonship question?" "I have no opinion; I know nothing about it." "Well, that is something; no opinion, Joseph, on that subject! they will squeeze your very soul out about it. I know some of them are great sticklers for the Conference view: as for myself, I believe with Dr. Clarke. I have read every line that has been written on it, but to my mind they all make the subject muddy except the doctor. Whatever will you do? When I passed it was not a test, but it is now; and I dare not speak against the law. On this question, I hold my *status* by being silent; and you know my family claims." On seeing my aged superintendent affected to tears, I said, "Do not let it distract your mind, I will take the straightforward course, and you will see we shall come out right in the end." The next morning I walked over to Burnley; for, although in the Bolton district, the District Meeting that spring was held in Burnley. I took a little dinner with my dear father and mother, who then resided in Burnley. Mother was troubled at the thought of my leaving my native land; and as I took my hat to go to the meeting, she said, "Well, Joseph, I will go and pray all the afternoon that thou may not pass." I said, "Do, mother; and I will go and do my best to pass, and the will of the Lord be done." On passing the Sabbath-school, and entering the chapel-yard, I was deeply moved: there were the scenes of my former years. I entered the vestry; it was full of experienced divines. I, a poor ignorant youth, who had never in my life been a day in any school but the Sabbath-school, had to stand with a preacher's son, who had been trained at Kingswood or Woodhouse Grove. The Rev. Philip Garratt was chairman. I raised my heart to God, and became calm and collected. With ease the examination proceeded, until we came to the knotty question. The Chairman said: "Brother J————, do you believe in the eternal Sonship of Christ?" Mr. J.: "I do, sir." Chairman: "How do you prove it?" Mr. J.: "Unto the Son he saith, Thy throne, O God, is for ever and for ever." Chairman: "Do you believe in the deity of the Lord Jesus, brother Townend?" I replied, "Yes, sir." Chairman: "To what extent?" I answered: "That he is co-equal and co-eternal with the first and third persons in the Godhead." Chairman: "But do you believe in the eternal Sonship of Christ, brother?" I replied, "I cannot say that I do, sir, and yet I have no reasons for disbelieving. The truth is, I do not understand the question: I have had to work hard, and have had but little time and few books. I have not read Clarke or Watson, or any one else, on the subject. I give out Mr. Wesley's hymns bearing on the point without any scruple, 'The Father's co-eternal Son,' &c.—believing him to be a wiser and better man than ever I shall be." Chairman: "Don't be alarmed, brother; we do not want you to believe *how* it is, but that it is. Why did the Jews stone the Redeemer? They stoned him because he said he was the eternal Son of God. Don't you see?" I replied, "My mind is open to conviction, and I shall be glad to receive further information." The Chairman then spoke of his personal friendship with, and the high estimate he held of the piety and learning of Dr. Clarke; but said that on that question the good doctor had got beyond his depth; he had recourse also to some other statements or illustrations which I did not understand; and, pausing for an answer, I said, "I shall feel obliged for further information on the subject." The Rev. Mr. I. said, "Mr. Chairman, we cannot stop here all day bothering with this brother. My conviction is that he does not believe the doctrine. If he does believe, why not say so at once!" Mr. B. said, "Mr. Chairman: I am ashamed of the conduct of brother I.; did he not hear brother Townend state his openness to conviction—that he had no opinion on the subject—that he had not read Clarke or Watson, or any one; he (Mr. B.) would take the liberty to say, for the information of brother I., that from what he knew of brother Townend, by the time he had read as much as you and I have read, he will know as much. Would you have him to lie to get into the ministry? I tell you, he will not do that. I am ashamed of such treatment." By this time, the preachers were talking one to another; when the oldest man in the meeting came towards me, and kindly said, "My good brother, read the Epistle to the Hebrews. Although I prejudge the matter, I will say that you will pass this meeting with credit: and you will also pass the Conference: but as you offer for foreign service, you will have to pass the Missionary Committee in London, and I tell you as a friend, if you then have a shade of a doubt upon your mind on the doctrine of the eternal Sonship, Dr. Bunting will send you home in a moment." All this being over, the young man and I walked into the chapel-yard, until the meeting decided on our cases. "I am sure I shall pass," said my companion; "I have given them Wesley's definitions of doctrines *verbatim*, and I am sure that will please the old gents." After a full hour's conversation, we were called in. The chairman said, "Brother J., in the opinion of this meeting, you are not a fit and proper person to take a circuit in our Connexion. Brother Townend, this meeting has pleasure in recommending you to the next Conference, as a fit and proper person to take a Mission Station in our Connexion."

I sincerely tried to take the Conference view. I read "Pearson on the Creed": compared Scripture with Scripture: I read "Richard Watson," but I could not comprehend all his meaning; but the arguments of Dr. A. Clarke made a deep and favourable impression. I was grieved that such a subject should be made a test: and, besides, some other matters occurred at that time which made me dissatisfied with the proceedings of the Conference. Our Circuit Quarterly Meeting wished to memorialise Conference against some of its proceedings on the College question. When the motion was to be put, the superintendent vacated the chair, stating that he durst not allow the motion to pass, as he knew it would be obnoxious to certain persons in power. The meeting proceeded to elect another chairman, one of the local officers, when the superintendent said it would be of no use in the world, for in the absence of the superintendent, the meeting was illegal.

When clearly convinced that it was my duty to leave the Wesleyan community—though it was very, very painful—I resolved, in the fear of God, to do it. I sent a note to the preacher resident at Longholme, a month before the plan was out, desiring him to leave my name off the next plan. And when we had a personal interview, he wept with me; said it was a hard case; and were he in my place, he would act as I was doing. There was no stir; the people wondered at my name being off the plan, and I received a new plan from the resident minister, with my name only on the outside.

A short time before I left the Conference Wesleyans, a circumstance of a very painful and impressive character occurred in my class. Mrs. —— had been confined, and, after three months' absence from class, came. She spoke most feelingly of her state of mind, as not being happy, and of having long trifled with her soul, but said she was resolved to begin afresh. At the close, she engaged in fervent prayer, being led out to pray for pardon for herself and husband. She was very weak in body, and could just manage to walk home, only a few yards from where the meeting was held. On the following Sabbath evening, several prayer-meetings were being held, the singing in which she could hear in her own house. She began to be quite excited about her soul; she said persons were praying all around, and she, a member of the Society, was without religion; and she was going to die, she knew. Mrs. Townend went into her house, when she insisted upon her going to prayer, as she was about to die, and she was not ready. The neighbours got alarmed, and a messenger was despatched to Newchurch to tell me of the case, that I might come in haste. On my arrival she had been put to bed, looked distracted, and, as near as I can remember, said, "O Joseph, I am going to die, and I shall be damned! yes, I shall. Oh! you know how my husband and I have been professing religion, with our hearts stuck full of pride; and you know, you all know that we have no religion! Ah, to go to prayer-meetings, and never pray at home!" And, looking at her husband, who must have felt it keenly, said, "O ——, you know that what I say is true! Oh, hypocrisy, hypocrisy! But God will—yes, He will, ——, make an example of us! Pray, pray, or I shall drop into hell!" Several persons engaged in fervent prayer, and the moment we ceased, she sat up, and shouted, "Only prayer keeps me out of hell!" We continued until midnight, when she seemed to get a little ease of mind, and I left for the night. The night following she was in a dreadful state. I went and got in all the most pious persons in the neighbourhood, and requested all others to retire, and we began praying with all our might. She insisted upon it that it was a judgment from God: appealed to those present that knew them best, whether she did not speak the truth; and calling her husband to the side of the bed, spat in his face. It seemed as if, for a few moments, the devil raged in her. I was holding her head from behind the bed, when she made a desperate attempt to bite a female present. At that moment the friends all fell upon their knees, and mightily cried to God. She was calm; and, looking at me as I held her head, she said, "I am a brute, a devil; did I attempt to bite?" "Yes, you did; but you did not know what you were doing." "No, no, I did not know what I was doing. Oh, pray for me. Do you think I shall be saved?" "Oh, yes, you will be saved. See, they are all praying people, and Jesus lives to plead for you: I feel you will be saved." "Oh, I feel a little better; there is a light like a single star. Oh, how sweet is hope!" We prayed, and she wrestled until she cried out, "I am saved, I am saved!" She desired her two children to be brought, that she might kiss them; then, in the most affectionate and faithful manner spoke to her husband, and then turning to her friends, thanked them for their sympathy and prayers. She spoke of her parents departed, and said how delightful it would be to meet them there. Then she was apparently exhausted, and we all expected every moment would be her last. At one time we all thought she had departed; and I was leaving the house, when I was called back. She said, "I thought I was gone; what is it that keeps me here? Oh, friends, stop with me until I have crossed the gulf! Oh, the gulf of death!" She then repeated, in the most touching and correct manner—

"Vital spark, of heavenly flame,
Quit, O quit, this mortal frame;
Trembling, hoping, lingering, flying,
Oh! the pain, the bliss of dying;
Cease, fond nature, cease thy strife,
And let me languish into life.

"Hark! they whisper: Angels say,
Sister spirit, come away.
What is this absorbs me quite—
Steals my senses, shuts my sight—
Drowns my spirit, draws my breath?
Tell me, my soul, can this be death?

"The world recedes, it disappears;
Heaven opens on my eyes; my ears
With sounds seraphic ring.

Lend, lend your wings; I mount, I fly;
O grave! where is thy victory?
O death! where is thy sting?"

I had often before read and heard these verses; I could even then repeat them. I had heard them sung in company with the solemn tones of the organ; but never before, or since, did I feel their force as uttered by that dying, sensitive, intelligent woman. She lingered; and about two on the Tuesday morning I retired to my home. Reader, can you anticipate what I am about to state?—from that moment poor Mrs. ——— was literally mad; what I saw, heard, and felt that week, I will not attempt to describe. Shouting, screaming, laughing, taunting. She would only have a certain class of persons in her room. It took five strong men to hold her in bed; and before the madness she was too weak to walk alone. What a sight! Shaven head, rolling eyes, wild countenance, bitten lips, and chewed tongue. Poor, poor, poor Mrs. ———; Thursday evening she was much weaker, and it was arranged that I should take my rest; and she was left in the care of two men and a strong, spirited woman. At four in the morning I was called up in haste, Mrs. ——— was on the floor. In company with a female, I was there in three minutes, and walked carelessly round the room. She was sitting by the bed, her attendants rubbing her hands and feet. There were five of us; we seized her; it was a terrible struggle, but we bound her fast; when, with a laugh that made us shudder, she said, "You have beat me at last!" While shouting, and calling on a dear friend by name, she struck into a well-known tune; I took the bass; and, as if in perfect health, the insane woman sang it through, and said, "There, we have done that well!" She then screamed so as to be heard all round the neighbourhood; and did literally bark like a great dog. She grew weaker, and on the following Monday, *dumb*, *deaf*, and *blind*, the young, the handsome, the intelligent, and the never-to-be-forgotten Mrs. ——— expired.

The doctor stated that her strong mental exercises were too powerful for her weak state of body, and had brought on fever on the brain, of which she died. Our young minister was utterly appalled, and begged most tenderly that I would attend to the case. All the shocks I sustained in Manchester Infirmary were not to be compared with that of this one case. My nerves were so shattered that when the poor creature had been several weeks in the grave, I ran from my employment to hide myself amongst the piles of goods, fancying I heard her scream, and that she was coming into the warehouse.

January, 1832, in the Methodist chapel, Longholme, after hearing Mr. Livsey's Lecture on Malt Liquor, I with much fear took the teetotal pledge; and from that day to this, February, 1852, I have been a consistent teetotaller. Teetotalism is not religion, but a handmaid to it. It has been of essential service to me. First, in preventing me from unnecessarily wasting either my own or other people's money. Secondly, in preventing me from setting a bad example, as a minister and a Christian; but contrariwise, showing to the young, and others, that persons may be healthful, social, active, and useful, without strong drink. Thirdly, in enabling me to be useful to an extent, and to persons with whom I should never have come in contact had I not been an abstainer. I would not barter the clear, calm, constant, sense of the rectitude of my proceedings in this matter for all the hilarity and glee produced from the fumes of alcoholic liquors; and I here record it as my solemn, settled conviction that if I were to use intoxicating liquors as a mere beverage, I should sin against my judgment and best moral and religious feelings, against society at large, and against Almighty God. That there are good men who use intoxicating drinks as a beverage, I cheerfully admit; but, query, are they as good and as useful as they would be were they abstainers? The sacramental and medicinal use of these liquors are other questions altogether.

CHAPTER III.

Leaves the Conference Connexion—Becomes a salaried Local Preacher at Burnley—Examined at the Leeds Annual Meeting—Appointed to the Keighley Circuit—Removes to the Hull Circuit—Visits an Afflicted Family, and the Hull Infirmary—Father's and Mother's Death—Leaves Hull, and goes to the New Mills Circuit—Evils of Drunkenness—Temperance Meeting—Victims of Intemperance—Removes to the Salford Circuit—Public Distress—An Unhappy Marriage—Appointed to the Clitheroe Circuit—Prospects of Usefulness—Sudden Removal to Edinburgh—Discouraging Commencement—Temperance Society—Missionary Services—Attends a Funeral—Scottish Scenery—A Brother's Death—A Sister's Death—Invited to labour in the Rochdale Circuit.

On the last Sabbath which I spent with my old friends, the Conference Wesleyans, I was planned in the Haslingden Circuit. I preached in the morning at Hippins, from Heb. ii. 10; at Accrington in the afternoon, from Mark xvi. and last clause in 16th verse; and in the evening in the Haslingden chapel, from Luke xvi. 31. It was Easter Sunday, 1835, a day I shall never forget; a day of sorrow, but of power. I was blest in my work, and at night I was ready for rest, having walked above twenty miles, and preached in the three principal chapels. The Sabbath following I preached the school sermons for the Primitive Methodists at Rawtenstall; and the next Sabbath for the Protestant Methodists at Burnley. About seventy persons had left the Wesleyans at Burnley, about the manner in which the Rev. Philip Garratt had been removed from that circuit; and these seventy united with the Protestant Methodists of Leeds,* who had left the Wesleyans on the organ question. The small society at Burnley had called out as their pastor the Rev. W. Incé; and at the time I was invited to preach for them, they were making great

* The Protestant Methodists were united with the Wesleyan Association in 1836.

progress. I preached to three numerous congregations, especially in the evening, in the large room in Mr. Pollard's new factory. It was well filled, some seven or eight hundred persons must have been present; and several souls found peace in the prayer-meeting after the evening service. This people invited me to join them, many of whom I knew very well. I united with them, and the Monday night after that Sabbath I was appointed to be leader of a class of three members at Newchurch, in Rossendale. I commenced preaching in the writing-school at Newchurch; and in three months I was called out to labour as a hired local preacher, and recommended to the Annual Meeting to be employed as a travelling preacher.

I was happy in the work at Burnley, the friends were kind, and there was a blessed work in the circuit. I can never forget the good that was done at Gisburn, and the blessed seasons I had with those simple-minded people. I was very comfortable with my colleagues, Messrs. Ince and Robinson. Scores of souls were brought to God that summer. The Annual Meeting was held in Leeds, in September, and opened its sittings on the Monday morning. Brother Robinson and I had to go to be examined for admission into the itinerancy, and to preach our trial sermons. We had each a hard day's work the Sabbath previous; and without going to bed, we left Burnley about one o'clock in the morning to meet the coach at Crosshills, about half-past five; some fourteen miles we had to walk. This journey was very trying to brother Robinson, for he was not strong. We took some refreshment at Mr. Joseph Smith's, Glusburn, who walked on with us to meet the coach. At Keighley, Mr. John Smith took his seat with us, and this was the first time I ever saw that good man.

Next morning at five o'clock I had to preach my trial sermon in Stone chapel; I was on my way to the chapel by half-past four, but being an entire stranger, I was late, and when I got to the chapel, Brother Cruickshank was reading his text. "There," said he, "he is come;" and giving out a verse, invited me up, saying "You have just half an hour for a sermon." I told in few words the cause of my being late, and preached from "This I say, brethren, the time is short," 1 Cor. vii. 29. That day I stood for examination with Messrs. Worrall, Woolstenholme, Robinson, and J. R. Roebuck. Dr. Turton of Sheffield was present. Brother Roebuck was by far the youngest who had to be examined. Mr. Sigston conducted the examination; and on his asking brother

Roebuck, "Do you believe in the divinity of the Holy Spirit?" the stripling answered, "I object to the term divinity, sir, I think it ought to be deity of the Holy Spirit; we call ministers divines; we speak of John the Divine; even a Socinian would grant you divine influence, but would deny you either personality or deity." I need scarcely say that the meeting was astonished at the clear statement, bold and independent conduct of that wonderful lad.

Brother Robinson was to have preached that evening, but being very poorly, I was requested to take his place, which I did. We were all received on trial, and I was appointed to the Keighley Circuit. I write it with feeling of gratitude to God, and deep self-abasement, and sincere respect for the departed, that, of the five persons who stood for examination that day, I am the only one left alive. Robinson, Roebuck, Woolstenholme, and Worrall are all gone. My parents were much pleased with the openings of providence for me; and with about two pounds worth of books, and much fear, Mrs. T. and I left Longholme in Rossendale, for Keighley in Yorkshire. The first Sabbath I preached twice, led the lovefeast in the Town Chapel, had a good prayer-meeting in the evening, and was kindly received. Monday was the day for the quarterly meeting, and there was a warm debate as to where I should live. The country members contended that they had most places, and that a place in the country would be most central for the preacher; while the town members pleaded usage, the importance of a thriving town, and also the sum they raised. The brethren got warm, and, not in measured terms, some of them contended that travelling preachers, and a paid ministry, had upon the whole been a curse rather than a blessing; and it seemed doubtful, at times, whether that meeting would recognise me or not. True, the contention was not about me personally, and I also knew that considerable harshness, if not cruelty, had been practised by Wesleyan ministers in that neighbourhood. I said nothing about the matter, but, in the best way I could, I attended to my duties. It was a laborious circuit: the week I was in the country I preached eight times, and the week I was in the town three times to the same congregation. I fondly thought if I could compose as many new sermons as would see me to the end of one year, then I should be removed. I was invited to remain, yet I thought that the Annual Meeting would remove me; but I was appointed to Keighley a second year, and I had only one sermon which I had not preached. The people were very kind, and I laboured hard in visiting, reading, and studying; and God Almighty gave me favour with the people, and blessed my feeble efforts; and I was invited unanimously to remain a third year. The Lord gave me a few souls in this circuit; some of them are gone to glory, and I hope to meet them there.

APPOINTED TO THE HULL CIRCUIT.

The leaving of my first circuit was a very great trial; I was in deep trouble, so much so that I was taken very ill in Leeds, and confined to bed two days. I was very happy in my soul, and thought that it was very opportune to die before I had reached my new sphere of labour. The kindness of Mr. and Mrs. Rinder, with whom we were lodging, and of the medical attendant, was very great indeed; and we were able to proceed on the Friday. The sail from Selby to Hull was very pleasant and bracing. The sight of Hull made me tremble; such a large town, such a large chapel. Our Hull friends rented the Tabernacle at £90 per year, besides paying for its being cleaned and lighted. The trustees received only about £60 per annum by pew rents. Their late minister, Mr. Kennedy, a learned and pious man, had been voted away, after being with them only nine months; and four of the officers and about forty members had left the Society—all this was very discouraging. Saturday night we had a sweet and promising band meeting. On account of my weak state of body, one of the town missionaries preached in the morning, and I in the evening. Thank God, this is the only Sabbath service I have had to omit from that day to this—Feb. 4th, 1852—on account of the want of health. The friends in Hull rallied around me; they bore with my weaknesses, and admired my sincerity, zeal, and diligence. The congregations improved, souls were brought to God, and the people had a mind to work. In the spring of 1838, the Tabernacle was given up, and a neat chapel holding 700 and upwards was purchased. All the seats were let, and some £30 more per year was realised for sittings than in the Tabernacle. We had a blessed work; souls were awakened and converted. We had a mighty praying force always at hand. Oh, what prayer-meetings in the bottom of that chapel, and in the vestry behind the chapel.

My brother Thomas came from Leeds, to preach on the Sunday our missionary sermons; and on the Saturday before, I walked to

Beverley, nine miles distant, to prepare the way for my preaching on the Sabbath. I had the address of the town crier, who it was said was friendly to our cause; I had never seen him, and knew no one in that town. I found the man in a drunkery, half intoxicated, with a long pipe in his mouth; he acknowledged that he had taken too much liquor, begged that I would excuse it, assured me he was a sincere friend of the cause, and took my money for crying the services which I was to hold at the Cross the following day. He told me where he had spoken for lodgings for me; and on asking a decent woman who had seen us talking what sort of place it was, she told me it was one of the worst houses in Beverley; invited me to make her house my home, which I did; and for which she would not have any recompense. I preached twice, standing upon the elevation in the large area in the centre of the market-place. My dear friend, Mr. Maynard, walked over from Hull, stood by me, and led the singing. We had very good congregations. Thus we began our mission to Beverley, where good was done; but our falling perpetually into bad hands was a most serious evil, and prevented our success.

Receiving a hearty invitation to remain in Hull a second year, I most cheerfully accepted it, and God Almighty crowned my feeble efforts with abundant success. When in this circuit, I became acquainted with the friends in Louth, York, Scarborough, and Whitby. In one of the back alleys in Hull, I found a young man in the second stage of consumption. He resided with two sisters, one a mere child, and the family were maintained by a mangle. They were very, very poor; the father had run off to America, and subsequently the mother had died of decline. The young man was profoundly ignorant, but very willing to be taught. I made the case known to our active and influential friends, who regularly visited the family, and provided them with needful things. The young man was savingly brought to God. I saw him about an hour before his death, but I could not hear him articulate. When dying, he sat up in bed, and, as if in health, with a firm, clear voice, said, "Now they are come; now I am going;" and with a loud voice, that brought the neighbours out of their houses, he shouted, "Glory! glory!" and, with uplifted hands, made a pause and said, "One more glory!" sunk down, and in a moment expired.

In Hull, I frequently visited the infirmary, going from bed to bed to speak with the patients, and then kneeling in the middle of the rooms engaged in prayer. One of the town missionaries requested me to accompany him to a house of ill-fame, where a young woman was lying in a state of putrefaction. The house was kept by an elderly woman. We found the person dead, and were admitted into the house by the sister of her that was dead, who was following the same dreadful course of life. While we were endeavouring to point out the direful results of such conduct, a very decent young woman came in, and accosted us as follows—"Gentlemen, I am pleased to meet you here. I am in service at the Rev. ——— in this town, and a member of his church. The young person who lies dead, and this young woman sitting beside me, are my own sisters. We were brought up in the same family, and why they should have taken this wicked course I cannot tell. Accept my sincere thanks for your attention to the departed, and for the advice to my sister yet alive." She could proceed no further. We prayed, and left them. I never remember being insulted in the streets or in the docks of Hull. Our open-air services were always well attended, and crowned with success. Oh, it is balmy and pleasant to think of those happy days! and since then I have been privileged in making several visits to that dear people.

While stationed in Hull, my dear parents both left the shores of time for a blissful eternity. The last interview I had with them was when I left the Keighley Circuit. Having urged the reception of temporal aid, my father requested me to engage in prayer. I did so, until, being deeply affected, I could not proceed; and, with deep emotion, I left their humble dwelling, never more to see them again in the flesh. On leaving, Mr. William Chaffer said: "Well, Joseph, it's a long way to Hull; I think your father may die suddenly, and if so, you cannot well attend the funeral. However, I will write if anything happens." The first letter I received from Burnley was the following, from the pen of Mr. Chaffer, not two months after—

"Burnley, October 2nd, 1837.

"Mr. J. Townend—Sir—By request of your mother, I have to inform you of the death of your father, this afternoon at five o'clock, after a few days' illness. If you could make it convenient to come over, they think of interring him on Friday next, at Longholme chapel. Your mother is as well as can be expected under present circumstances.

"I remain, yours respectfully—W. CHAFFER."

This letter filled me with sorrow. I felt as if I had never before loved him. Now I had no father to pray for me; I had sustained a heavy loss. I could not go to the funeral, but kept the day sacred, and in mind was present. On the following Sabbath I preached on appropriate subjects, and gave a short sketch of his life to the congregation. This I found to be much better, for all parties, than shutting myself in the house, and disappointing the people. My dear father died in his 70th year; had been a consistent Wesleyan forty years. He was a man possessing genuine piety; of few words, clear views, and peaceable disposition. One of the superintendents of the Burnley Circuit gave it as his opinion that Thomas Townend, sen., had as clear views of Christian theology as any man in that society.

The following letter was an announcement of my mother's death—

"Burnley, June 11th, 1839.

"My dear Brother,—This comes to inform you that mother was taken seriously ill on Wednesday last, and continued so until last Monday night, when the weary wheels of life stood still. We hope to see you at the funeral, which will start for Longholme next Friday, at two o'clock in the afternoon.

"With love to sister Sarah, I remain, dear brother, yours affectionately—ELISHA TOWNEND."

Mrs. Townend accompanied me to the funeral, and we arrived in Burnley about an hour before the time. A few select friends were invited; and before the corpse was removed, brother Elisha gave out, "O God, our help in ages past," and set mother's favourite tune (Tabernacle), which she had often requested us to sing at her funeral. Brother Thomas engaged in prayer; and my dear mother's corpse was followed by her six surviving children to the grave. It is the custom of the country for the nearest relatives to lift the corpse from the gates into the inside of the chapel, or church, and from thence to the grave. The Rev. T. O. Booth conducted the service, and it is said that he could not refrain from tears when he saw four sons, all preachers, carrying their mother to the grave. My dear mother was an active, honest, economical, cheerful, and pious little woman. She died in peace, in the 71st year of her age. Her husband and six of her children went to heaven before her. Since then, four more have died in the faith.

My sister, I expect, is still living in the town of Burnley, with her face toward Zion,* and I am at the antipodes of my native land, preserved by the gracious providence of Almighty God, to pen this simple tribute of respect to the memory of my best earthly friend—my mother.

NEW MILLS CIRCUIT, DERBYSHIRE.

The parting scene at Hull was deeply affecting. A chaise, with two grays, conveyed us from a friend's house down to the pier, where a great portion of the society stood waiting with their tokens of affection. It was gratifying, but very trying to our feelings; and when the steamer put off into that fine river, such waving of hats and handkerchiefs I never on such an occasion witnessed, either before or since. Our removal to New Mills was a great change. We found the country bold and romantic, and the people less polite than in Hull. We had some difficulties, arising out of the house being badly finished, which very much endangered our health, and also on account of the New Mills Chapel being on the shareholding plan. It was however upon the whole a comfortable circuit, presenting a wide field for usefulness; plenty of places, good Sabbath Schools, and an active and talented staff of Local preachers. Drunkenness was the crying sin of the neighbourhood. I was, so far as I could ascertain, the only abstainer in the neighbourhood, and I resolved to advocate my principles. My first attempt was upon a young married man, the son of one of our local preachers, a confirmed Saturday night and Sabbath sot. I went on a Sabbath morning, roused him from his slumbers; got him upon his knees, and that morning he took the pledge, and became a changed man. I resolved on having a meeting in the chapel; got the Independent minister to act upon the principle, and to take the chair. The difficulty was to get at the people, and the town-crier was a victim to the bottle. I offered him money to lend me the bell, that I might get a sober person to cry the meeting. "He would not lend his bell to the Queen; he was sober, and if I would give him a shilling, he would soon make the people hear." Off he set, commencing just opposite our chapel. Having jingled his bell, he began, "Temperate Meetings, Sociable Chapel, Mr. Townend will address the chair. Three times three; God bless the Queen and me!" In a few months we had two hundred pledged teetotallers, and crowded

* Since died in the faith of the Gospel.

meetings were held alternately at the different places of worship. We soon dispensed with the drunken bellman, and those hills and dales resounded with teetotal melody. Several young men were reclaimed from the very verge of hell, and since then have been consistent members of the Temperance Society. We had some good congregations, and, I believe, souls were saved by my feeble but sincere efforts in Macclesfield, Bollington, Glossop, Hayfield, and New Mills. While in this circuit, I had frequently friendly communication with Mr. Ince, my friend and brother in the ministry—he having been my predecessor in that circuit, and he was much beloved by the people.

In this circuit, I witnessed the direful effects of strong drink upon educated, pious, and useful men. Before I arrived, the young Wesleyan minister, the son of an influential aged Wesleyan minister, lost his *status* and influence through drinking. He commenced business as a grocer; but his habits were such that they involved him in debt: he abandoned the trade, and began to teach a school in our chapel. I got him to take the pledge, and he gained ground a little, but his health had materially suffered: and while he was heavily afflicted, he was taken out of bed and committed to the county gaol for debt. I was deeply afflicted to see him dragged from his couch to prison. I wrote to his father as follows—

"Rev. and dear Sir—I feel bound to communicate to you the mournful tidings, that your son is a prisoner for debt in the county gaol at Derby; sent by a grocer in Stockport, with whom he transacted business after leaving the ministry. He has been very bad of rheumatism most of the winter, and when taken he was very ill, under the care of Dr. H.—I am, &c.

"———."

Having written to the young man, I received the following letter—

"Derby Gaol, Aug. 1, 1840.

"My dear Friend,—I received your kind epistle, and will most cheerfully answer it according to my present views. When I arrived here my state of health was most alarming. I was, in fact, deprived of reason, and my companions expected to hear of my departure every day. In this state I remained for fourteen days. My appetite failed, but I cannot remember any circumstance that transpired. Through the *mercy of my God*, and the attention and skill of the doctor, I gradually recovered. At present I enjoy a good state of health, and if I had more exercise, should be more active and cheerful. I pant for liberty, which I shall value more than a little bird which has been confined to its cage many months. I long to visit Mount Pleasant chapel, and to have a friendly chat with you and your kind, though reserved lady. There are about 160 prisoners, some of whom are in for murder. The judge enters Derby on Monday next, hence some of these poor creatures will suffer the penalty of the law in a very short time. One interesting young girl is in for wilfully murdering her infant. I have taken great notice of some of the prisoners' conduct; they are a naughty race of beings. Transportation, imprisonment for twelve months, hard labour, and the like, are regarded as trifles.

"There are several lads in, not more than nine years old, for stealing. Sin is of a hardening nature. Happy is the man who feareth the Lord in all places and at all times. Religion is most certainly the only and best preventative against sin of any description. 'The fear of the Lord is the beginning of wisdom.' I feel thankful for the religious impressions which have been made upon my mind during my residence within the lofty walls of this castle. I hope that the lessons which have been taught me during my affliction and confinement, will be of a permanent nature. I still believe that the star of Divine Providence conducted me to Derby gaol. My afflictions were of such a character as to require special help. In future I shall take care of the farthings, remembering that two make a halfpenny. As it regards my future prospects, I know not what to say: some of my friends wish me to take charge of a National School in New Mills, but when I visit you we can talk over the matter. My objection to beginning again in the old school arises from its peculiar position to the minister's house. I feel this, and so do you; and it is a great objection to all of us; and the only plan is to remove. I shall never be happy but in one place—namely, the pulpit. I long to preach again, but I must wait the openings of Divine Providence. I must pray much, think much, and consult my friends. You know that I am poor, and cannot begin business. I should like to go abroad, and distribute Bibles, or tracts, or anything, so that I may be useful. My mind is so constructed, that I must be actively engaged in something.

"I must conclude, hoping to see you and yours. I hope you are not removing, as you are so beloved and useful. May God bless you and yours! Give my love to all friends, and excuse all errors, as I have written this letter surrounded by my noisy companions on this busy day. I cannot write as I would wish.

"I remain, yours affectionately,

"——."

Ten years after, I again saw this person; but he was so bloated and disfigured with intemperance, that I did not know him. In the interim, he had for a short time been the pastor of an independent church, but his besetting sin slew him. One evening, in the dusk, while I was resident at New Mills, a rather tall, genteel-looking young man, came to our door, and inquired for the individual just referred to. I replied, "He is not at home." He then stated that they were educated together at Woodhouse Grove; that he had come on his feet all the way from Manchester to see him, and that he was without money or friends. His black clothes, hat, and boots, had all, like himself, seen better days. I invited him to take a bed with us, and while at supper, he told me his name, and the name of his father; that he had been a travelling preacher, but, like his friend before referred to, and many others of that class, he had been ruined through drunkenness. A third victim from the same school of the sons of the prophets, fallen from the same *status* in the Methodist Society, I became ultimately acquainted with while resident in New Mills. One Saturday afternoon a calico printer, about sixty-five years of age, was returning from his labour with his wages to New Mills. On his way he went into a drunkery, and got intoxicated, and swore, and used other filthy language too bad to mention. On having reached the top of a flight of steps which led to his dwelling, he fell over the railing and broke his back. After a day or two I was told of this awful case, and I visited the man. There were several persons standing round the bed. I said, "Well, my poor fellow, you are in a sad state." "I am, man!" "You were drunk when you fell over the rail, were you not?" "I must tell no lies; I had had ten pennyworth upon an empty stomach. I have been a wicked sinner sixty-two years to my knowledge; and now I am going to die with all these sins upon my conscience." He was then seized with a paroxysm of pain, and cried out, "O God, hell cannot be worse than this; let me die and know the worst of it!" I said, "My poor fellow, you must not speak in that manner; hell you will find to be worse than anything you can suffer here; you must pray for God to have mercy upon you, and spare you until you are pardoned." Here the clock struck three p.m. I said, "If you cry to God, He can save you before six o'clock this evening." He then said, "O God, I shall die before six o'clock." I asked him, "Must I pray?" when he said, "Yes, if you will not be long." Immediately he was seized with dreadful pangs; he shook his head in the most frightful manner, with contortion of visage, uttered a heavy groan, and expired. His sister, a tall, heavy woman, stood by, and on seeing that he was dying, screamed aloud, and fell senseless upon the floor. Another man in that neighbourhood, upon his dying bed, I visited frequently; but it seemed as if he could not lay hold on God for mercy. At length he sent for me to have a private interview. On attempting to speak he seemed almost choked with grief, and then burst into a flood of tears. I encouraged him to speak his mind in confidence; then he made confession of having been guilty of one of the most degrading and brutalising sins that ever stained poor, fallen, degraded humanity. The particulars of that case I shall never, never disclose. The man became calm, and I hope died a penitent believer.

Though requested by the vote of the quarterly meeting to remain a third year, I thought it best to remove, and accepted an invitation to become superintendent of the Salford Circuit. Since I removed from the New Mills Circuit, I have paid several refreshing and profitable visits to the beloved friends in that circuit.

SALFORD CIRCUIT.

In the year 1841 I removed to the Salford Circuit, and, for the first time since I became a travelling preacher, I there had a colleague. In this circuit there were some good preaching places, many respectable families, and a dense population. During my sojourn with this people the times were very hard; but the leaders' meeting voted large sums of money to the needy members, and, generally, the preachers had the privilege of distributing the aid, according to the votes of the meeting. By this means our visits to the poor of the flock were sweetened, and made balmy. There was also, in connection with Bury-street Chapel, a Good Samaritan Society, out of the funds of which I had to bestow largely; and thus I was, in two or three instances, instrumental of saving life. I was punctual in my visits, and often received the blessings of them that were ready to perish. There can be no doubt in my mind that, at that time, some persons did lose their natural life from lack of food. I and a benevolent individual connected with the society, one evening went seeking out some of the worst cases. We found two females, from twenty to thirty years of age, making boys' cloth caps, at threehalfpence per cap. They could not earn more than two shillings per week, one of which went for rent. The place in which they lived was one very small room—no furniture or bed, but an old pan, pot, and spoon. Their aged mother was in the Salford workhouse. They were intelligent and amiable women. We found one old man, in a cellar, lying upon straw, and that straw moving with life; and the place had not been whitewashed for seven years. The old man was very deaf, and almost as ignorant as a beast, and he cursed in the most awful manner. Perceiving his wife to be more intelligent, and younger in years, I turned to her, and said, "Mistress, how came you to be married to this man?" She replied, "It was one of the most foolish things in the world. That she had seen better days, and had had for years a seat in, and attended, an Independent chapel." Oh! how many young women have I seen utterly ruined by their violation of that command, "Be ye not unequally yoked together with unbelievers." In such cases, one wrong step may involve ruinous consequences. Query?—Are parents, class-leaders, teachers in our schools, and, above all, ministers of the Gospel, clear in this matter? On this subject they ought to give "line upon line, precept upon precept." Take one case—A young female, of more than ordinary piety and accomplishments, was insulted by an offer from a profligate young man. She sternly rebuked him. Again and again he applied, and at length she began to listen. Her leader and parents expostulated, and she again refused the man. He then reformed, professed to be religious, and again applied to the young woman. She was told that his religion was all hypocrisy, but she gave him her hand. In a few weeks he became the drunken, blaspheming, unclean person he had been before; and in two or three years, this poor young woman died a mass of putrefaction, brought on by the impure habits of her husband. One man in the Salford Circuit, who attended upon our ministry, was addicted to drunkenness. He would weep under the word, and it was clear that nothing but abstinence could keep him from ruin. At length he launched into sin, and instead of giving up his trade as a brewer, he left the chapel, became a confirmed sot, and died of *delirium tremens*, and was over head and ears in debt. Some years before this, during the ministry of the Rev. H. Breeden in that circuit, one Sabbath evening a public brewer took his place on the free seats. He had recently buried a child, and was under the strivings of the Holy Spirit. Mr. Breeden's word was with power, and the brewer resolved to live a new life. He left his brewing establishment, and commenced another business, was converted, and now he is one of the most useful members and officers of that church; has a large family and flourishing business.

Manchester is a very busy town, and there are many calls to tea-meetings and committees; and upon the whole my mind got dissipated, and too much drawn aside, so that my religious experience was not what it ought to have been. Still the Lord was gracious to me, and gave me seals to my ministry and souls for my hire. While resident in Salford, I became acquainted with many friends in our other circuits in that town, whom I love and esteem. I was urged to remain a third year; but I parted for more rural scenes, and accepted an invitation to the rural and beautiful town of Clitheroe.

CLITHEROE CIRCUIT.

August, 1843, we removed to the ancient town of Clitheroe. There was a good house; a beautiful chapel, close to the house; a first-rate Sabbath school; a good congregation and society; and a very energetic Teetotal Society; the surrounding country picturesque and inviting. The town-castle stands nobly on the fragment of a huge limestone rock. Old Pendle Hill rears its majestic summit at a distance of two miles from the town. Opposite, at double that distance from the town, may be seen, glittering in the sunbeams, the towers of the ancient Roman Catholic college at Stonyhurst; while the river Ribble, with its pure stream—as yet untainted with factories, print-shops, and dye-houses, meandering between the sloping banks of those fertile meads, gives to the whole an air of rural simplicity, beauty, and grandeur. If I looked from my study window, and glanced over the beautiful landscape, my eye rested on a full view of the largest elevation in the country, reminding me of the everlasting mountains—emblems of the majesty, power, and faithfulness of God, our Father. If I looked from the front window, there stood the noble castle, reminding me of the castle of David, erected on the mount, which he took from the Jebusites. If I looked from the end window, there was the place of our Sabbath solemnities, in utility and elegance not surpassed by any in the town; here our tribes came up to worship; and as I was the individual who had chiefly to offer to them the bread of life, the very sight of the place often filled my soul with strong desire that at our next gathering I might be the instrument of good to the people; and that God, even our own God, might bless us. The truth is, my heart was in the right place, and everything around seemed to chime in with the sacred melody and hallowed feelings within. Our Young Men's Mutual Improvement Society was well attended, and was the means of much good. Our Sabbath-school was a nursery for the Church, and many of those tender plants are now pillars; and then our vigorous and uncompromising Abstinence Society, like a great moral bulwark, shielded our people from the withering influence of tippling. I reserved my most awakening sermons for Sabbath evenings; and a few of our most tender friends—and some sleepy, dreamy professors—were dissatisfied with their frequency. Some who neglected the week-night, and frequently the Sabbath morning's discourses, would fain have received some cordial to their minds on an evening. I felt their remarks, but durst not, did not, alter my modes of procedure; and ultimately it was clear that I was right. God was in the work—there was a regular breaking down—and some scores of souls were quickened, and brought to a knowledge of the truth. In this place our Amelia, Mrs. Townend's niece, about nine years of age, was very nearly burnt to death. Her neck and arms were dreadfully burned; and for three months, night and day, she was confined to an easy chair, with her head stretched, and tied to the back of the chair, to prevent contraction in healing. It was a painful and expensive matter, but God was with us and brought us through. How well it would be, if, when persons take fire, instead of beating, running and fanning the flame, they would just lie down, and roll themselves upon the floor, which would most effectually smother the flame.

One Thursday morning in March, 1845, I had been looking over our Circuit accounts; and finding God had blessed us with a considerable increase upon the quarter, whilst upon my knees returning thanks to Almighty God, the postman came to the door, and on opening the letter I read as follows—

"Dear Sir—Our preacher at Edinburgh, having gone over to the old body, the Committee have resolved upon your going there forthwith, if you are willing; and the Revs. J. Molineux and D. Rutherford, are appointed to visit your Circuit, with a view to your immediate release: the Committee will appoint a suitable supply for your Circuit, until the next Annual Assembly. You will oblige by having the brethren together to meet the Deputation on Friday evening next. "Yours truly,

"H. BREEDEN, Cor. Sec."

I was surprised! "Go immediately to Edinburgh! A meeting to-morrow night!" Again I read the letter: but it was true! The meeting was convened, and the deputation came and were heard. All was silent. It was an urgent case; and, finally, it was moved and seconded, by two of our most aged and beloved leaders, both weeping as they rose, "That this meeting comply with the request of the Connexional Committee."

EDINBURGH CIRCUIT.

At half-past five, on the Wednesday morning after we had received the letter from the Committee, we were seated upon the coach, and off for Edinburgh. To what changes of scenes and persons are itinerant ministers subject! Having arrived in Manchester, a few of our Salford friends accompanied us to the Liverpool railway. As my brother Thomas was then in Liverpool, he and a few friends took tea with us at Mr. D. Rowland's, where we were commended to the care of Almighty God; and by seven in the evening we were on board the steamer which was bound for Glasgow. We had the state berths, but as we were sea-sick until noon the next day, when we got into smooth water, it was to us a weary, uncomfortable passage. We arrived at Glasgow, and were surprised with its magnitude and grandeur. By half-past six in the evening, on the wings of steam, we were ready to be borne along the iron road to the capital of Caledonia; and about nine in the evening, on Good Friday, March 21st, 1845, we were put down by the cabman, at the mouth of . . . . . . Close, Grass Market, Edinburgh: and having found our way up the darkest alley we were ever in before, and groped up a winding stair to the third flat, we found ourselves in the comfortable apartments of, and met with a hearty welcome from, Mr. Jonathan Bladworth and family.

On the following Sabbath I opened my mission in Wesley Chapel, North Richmond Street, in the old city of Edinburgh. I had seen, on the Saturday, advertisements that I should be there, and preach morning and evening; and to my bitter disappointment, there were only forty persons present in the morning, and about sixty in the evening. Sabbath after Sabbath rolled away, and scarcely a new face could be seen in the chapel. The former minister had got into unpleasant circumstances with some of the church officers, had made a party, and he and they had gone to the Conference Wesleyans, with a view to his becoming a circuit minister in that body. Poor, silly man! he met with bitter disappointment; and if the Wesleyan superintendent, who advised the good man to take such a rash and foolish step, intended thereby to close the chapel belonging to the Association, he also missed his aim. I commenced street-preaching on Wednesday evenings, and Sabbath evenings, and the season being very dry, I kept to the work, and frequently preached to large and attentive congregations. Six, seven, or eight stories high, the windows along each side of the street would be thrown up, and scores of the sick and indigent in this way heard the word of life. Sometimes, when it was moonlight, crowds would come round, and the high buildings acted as enclosures to my voice, and I could continue my discourse for an hour with liberty and power.

There was in this city the most efficient Teetotal Society I ever met with. Its officers were men of moral and religious influence in the city. I was waited upon and requested to speak at the next Tuesday night meeting; which offer I gladly embraced; and here I had the ear of 500 persons, who received my speech with hearty applause. In this cause I laboured hard both in Edinburgh and Leith, which brought around me a large circle of valuable friends, and gave me an extensive field of usefulness. Persons taking the Temperance pledge in Edinburgh, had first to provide themselves with a card, which cost a penny; then the person had to attend the weekly meetings in the hall. After the speaking, the president for the year would request those persons, who would that night take the pledge, to stand up. He then, after having read distinctly the pledge, requested them to signify their assent by holding up their right hands, until he counted them. Then these persons had their cards filled up by the secretaries, each person paying twopence; so that it was a matter of care, solemnity, and expense; and from December 1845 to December 1846, the average signatures thus taken were one hundred per week. Oh ye brave, disinterested, moral reformers of Caledonia! I am glad that I ever saw your faces, and witnessed your zeal in this great cause; and though so far removed from you, I am still of the same mind, and engaged in the same work. Oh ye dwellers in that

> "Land of brown heath and shaggy wood,
> Land of the mountain and the flood;"

how long will you refuse those soft and balmy waters which roar from your sublime cataracts, or roll from your magnificent lakes, or glide from your perennial fountains! And prostrate in body—in soul—in circumstances—drink of the burning, reddening, deadening river of Death; produced by the maltreatment of the good grain, sent for other purposes, and clearly intended to be used as food, and not to be changed into alcohol! O ye standard-bearers of Emmanuel! Ere this, we trust many of you have ceased to sign the annual certificates of those who obtain their living by serving at the soul-stained altars of Bacchus! Surely ere this, you have ceased to press to the bosom of your churches those iron-hearted men who, for sordid gain, hold their bottles to the mouths of the fathers, and mothers, and sons, and daughters of your victimized, whiskey-stricken, and dying population! In Edinburgh, I found that we were not despised on account of our obscurity and feebleness as a Church. Seeing an advertisement of a biennial Sabbath-school meeting, to be held in Mr. McGilchrist's church, and to be addressed by some of the stars of the city, I went, with no thought beyond that of taking my seat, and listening to the speakers; when, lo, I was forced to ascend the platform, and second a resolution. With freedom and simplicity I detailed my own experience of good received in Sabbath-schools; gave an outline of their operations in England, and related two or three very striking anecdotes, and sat down; and the meeting was much moved with the statements I made.

Shortly after, we held our anniversary for Missions, and I resolved to try the strength of the Evangelical Alliance principle. We first waited upon Dr. Alexander, and requested him to preach in the morning. He told us that last night he had denied the Wesleyans for that day on which they intended to reopen their chapel; that they were having Drs. Beaumont and Candlish, and that they had strongly urged Dr. Alexander; but, said he, "I thought they were doctoring the thing too much. Now, we sympathise with your church polity, and believe that you with us are contending for Christian liberty." Then looking at me, he said,

"Well, my Brother Townend, if you will take my pulpit that morning, it will afford me much pleasure to take yours." I could scarcely credit my own ears, but replied, "If you dare trust me, sir, I will." He said, dryly, "I'll trust you." The Rev. Mr. Watson, Baptist, preached in the evening, and I in the afternoon. And for the Missionary meeting and soirée, we had plenty of help from the various Dissenting ministers. These things were very healing and balmy to the members of our little church; and we raised upwards of 40*l.* to the Missionary funds that year. A Mrs. Binney, an elderly lady of but small means, contrived to spare me a considerable sum, which I distributed amongst the sick and poor as opportunity and necessity dictated; this enabled me to visit in quarters where otherwise I could not have found access; and frequently I received the sincere benediction of the afflicted and the dying, who otherwise would have been neglected. An old gentleman, near our little kirk, used to be very social and kind to me, but he was a sot. He used every argument to get me to take wine with him, until I told him he must cease to ask me to drink or I should cease to call. He tenderly begged my pardon, and promised never to ask me again; and stated, that he had many Christian friends, who called in the evening, but without exception they all drank with him; that it was such company that had frequently lulled his guilty conscience. He then said, "Oh, my dear, dear friend, you are come here too late; I feel that wine will prove my ruin!" He was a fine, intelligent, generous man, and I entreated him as a son would his father. Poor Mr. A ——, he had occasion to go to Dalkeith on business; late in the evening, he was brought home in a cab very drunk, and next morning he died. As minister and chief mourner I attended his funeral: relatives he had none: his pot companions seemed abashed: his housekeeper was drunk; and that evening, his desk and drawers were broken in quest of the will and money.

On one occasion, I was invited to the funeral of a heavy whiskey drinker, and on entering the room, an elderly man, the brother of the deceased, said, "Come, Mr. Townend, take a wee drop of the crathur; my brother is gone, and we cannot bring him back ye ken, so it's na good being melancholy." I said, "Yes, Mr. ——, your brother is gone, and I fondly hoped his death would have been a warning to you; as to myself, I never drink whiskey, much less at a funeral."

His son, an intelligent and pious young man, said, "O Mr.

Townend, nothing will take hold of father! I can prove that during the last twenty years, uncle has drunk as much whiskey as would float a seventy gun-ship." The Rev. Dr. Ritchie, at a meeting held in Dr. Alexander's church, stated that a friend of his was once at a highland funeral, when all parties got so drunk that they had got two miles towards the kirk before they discovered that the corpse was left behind.

"There is a stream whose ceaseless flow
Has curs'd our land, and marr'd its peace,
And borne away to worlds of woe
The myriad slaves of dark excess.
Black as the grave, its waters roll,
And roll unfathomably deep;
And hourly some immortal soul
To everlasting ruin sweep!

Once at the fountain-head they stood,
And thought the stream was pure and fair;
Now they have grasp'd the fancied good,
And found the sting of death is there.
And ever and anon some wretch
Will struggle to the burning sand,
And vainly his wild eye-balls stretch,
And sorrow for his fatherland.

Oh, short regret! too proud to hear
The whispering voice from reason's throne,
They plunge again to deep despair,
And with the crowd rush madly on.
Soon, soon their little life is fled,
And raised by sin's all-blasting breath,
The threat'ning wave has swiftly sped,
And borne them to eternal death."

Our little church now began to thrive, the congregations were doubled, the prayer-meetings, class-meetings, and lovefeasts—which we called experience meetings, and held, after preaching, on Sabbath evenings—were all well attended, and we were very happy. Edinburgh, with its suburbs, is enchanting beyond description, uniting within a circle of four miles, the sea, the land, the city, the country,—the beautiful, the magnificent, and the sublime. And then, if you wander off as far as Roslin Castle, through Hawthornden, or down the serpentine Frith of Forth, to Stirling, on to Callander—and take a survey of the Lake district, make the "bristling pass" between the perpendicular rocks, on the dark still waters of Loch Katrine, rapidly borne on with the oars of some eight highlanders, accompanied with the echo and yell of a highland song; then you will have a key to Robert Burns' and Sir Walter Scott's writings, and no longer deem Scottish history, Scottish scenery, and Scottish song a mere romance. Whilst resident in Edinburgh, I visited some of these scenes, in company with dear friends, who are gone to higher and nobler scenes, Mr. W. Horner, of Manchester, and my dear brother Elisha. On ascending the Radical Road, along the edge of Salisbury Craigs, just at one point, there is a natural opening in the rocks above, giving the brow, nose, and chin of a celebrated English duke. On making this point one fine morning, in company with Mr. T. Schofield and my brother, I stopped them, and asked, "Whose physiognomy is that you see in the rock?" They previously knew nothing about the thing. After a pause, Elisha said, "Take off your hats, gentlemen." We did so; then he began an apostrophe with "Venerable Sire: they call thee the Iron Duke," &c. These visits I shall long remember; they are green spots in this wilderness.

While resident in Edinburgh I lost a brother and a sister by death. Dec. 11th, 1845, I received the following letter from my dear friend, the Rev. J. W. Gilchrist, then stationed in the Bacup Circuit.

"Bacup, December 11, 1845.

"Dear Brother Townend,—I am sorry to have to inform you that your brother Charles was suddenly taken ill on Tuesday evening, I think about ten or eleven o'clock. The doctor came about twelve, called again early yesterday morning, and again about noon, and prescribed, I suppose, what was most desirable. Being at Newchurch yesterday morning, I was informed of his illness, and about midday went to Longholme. I found Charles very ill, and suffering great pain. He remarked that the doctor had intimated that he was in a very dangerous state; but said that he was not alarmed or terrified: he rested on the Lord. He requested me to write to Elisha by first post, that he wished to see him. Before going to the meeting at Newchurch in the evening, word was brought to me, that, after I left Charles in the afternoon, he continued to get worse, and that about seven in the evening he expired. After the meeting I went to Longholme: the poor widow and children were much afflicted by the loss they had sustained. I cannot state the particulars of the disease, not having heard them exactly. The doctor spoke of the pleurisy fever; still I apprehend there was something besides. He was sensible to the last—often saying, as he rolled in agony from one side of the bed to the other, 'O Nanny; it's a rough sea, but I shall land safe.' Just before his exit, his wife asked him if he felt the Lord precious to him then? He said, 'Yes, yes; glory! glory!' The funeral is fixed for Monday afternoon next. You cannot be here: I have written to Elisha and Thomas, who will no doubt both be present. I need not tell you any other matter, the preceding is enough for you. My esteemed friend! may I say to you, 'Rejoice for a brother deceased in the Lord!'—My respectful compliments to Mrs. T.

"Yours truly,

"Rev. J. Townend. "J. W. Gilchrist."

With this unexpected news I was deeply afflicted. We had a passionate regard for each other, having been together from our childhood, up to the period of my marriage; and to never, never see him more on earth wrung my soul. As to his eternal safety, I had not the least doubt. I received the letter on the Saturday, altered my selection of subjects for the Sabbath, and brought the case before the congregations; deep sympathy was manifested, and good was done. How frequently, when death enters a family, he takes from its embrace more than one. In the spring of 1846, I received the following letter from the pen of my dear friend:—

"Bacup, May 9th, 1846.

"Dear Brother Townend,—I am sorry to have occasion to communicate intelligence that will again make you grieve. Your sister Ellen died this morning at an early hour. A few weeks ago, she was confined, and had partially recovered. About a fortnight ago, when I saw her, I expected she was well again. But she became worse; I cannot tell from what cause. I was informed on Monday last of her indisposition, and have seen her every day since, yesterday twice. The child is put out to nurse, the rest of the family are as usual. Her husband is gone to Rochdale, to consult with Elisha. I suppose Elisha will write to Thomas when they have fixed the day of the funeral. Being Saturday I cannot write much—I hope your sister lifted her heart from earthly things to things above. She was sensible of having had her affections and main anxieties too little on the concerns of grave solemnity; and she seemed to turn her soul at length to the refuge. Elisha is not well: on Thursday he was in bed; I have not heard since. I think Thomas is more feeble than formerly. I hope you keep hearty and strong. I sympathise with you in your troubles. Trust in God! He is an abiding and joyful portion; all beside is passing away. My regards to Mrs. Townend; also, when you see them, to the Bladworths, Crooks, and all friends.—I am, yours sincerely,

"Rev. Jos. Townend. "J. W. GILCHRIST."

Poor Ellen! she did not marry a converted man, and though he was steady and industrious, yet he had no soul for religion. They had a numerous family, and struggled hard for a living. Ellen was a beautiful singer and had a vigorous intellect. Not long before her death, her eldest son, a careless lad, aged fifteen, fell upon his head from a trap-door in the factory at Bacup, but was unable to speak after, and in fifteen minutes was a corpse. She never recovered from this shock. She left her husband with seven children, the youngest only a few weeks' old. Again I was unable to attend the funeral. Brother Thomas was stationed at this time, his second year, in Liverpool, but, not being strong, he had resolved to try another circuit, and had accepted an invitation to superintend the Rochdale Circuit. Between the March and June quarterly meetings, he got worse, and consequently had declined the offer of the Rochdale people; and, in consequence, I received the following communication—

"Rochdale, June 25th, 1846.

"Rev. Joseph Townend,—Dear Sir,—We beg to hand you, as annexed, copies of resolutions adopted by our quarterly meetings; and, in accordance with the same, we respectfully invite you to succeed Mr. Smith, as Superintendent of this Circuit. We may also add that Mr. Gibbons consents to remain with us a third year; and that Mr. Chesson has consented to labour with us next year. An early reply will oblige,

"Dear Sir, yours respectfully,

"Thomas Shaw,
"James Hoyle, } Circuit Stewards."

"Rochdale Quarterly Meeting, March 25th, 1846.

"Resolved—That the Rev. Thomas Townend be invited to succeed Mr. Smith.

"Resolved—That, in the event of the Rev. Thomas Townend declining, the Rev. Joseph Townend be invited to supply the place."

"Rochdale Quarterly Meeting, June 24th, 1846.

"A communication having been made to this meeting, from the Rev. Thomas Townend, through Mr. James Hoyle, that the state of his health is such as to afford no expectation that he will be able to take the superintendence of the Rochdale Circuit—

"Resolved—That this meeting deeply sympathises with Mr. Townend in his affliction, and fervently prays that he may soon be restored to health."

I felt myself in trying circumstances. Rochdale was the leading Circuit in the Connexion; and "to be the *Superintendent!* and then brother Elisha would never endure my weakness before such a people!" Then, again, on the other hand, as I had never even dared to think of such a thing I thought that my going there would not be of my seeking, and brother Thomas urged me to go, that I might take oversight of the orphans and widows in our family, and that he might be allowed perhaps to die under my roof. As to Edinburgh, I could cheerfully consent to end my days there, and the church there I loved and its members loved me. Still it was composed of heterogeneous materials, and I had fairly tested the leading men as to some changes, which, in my opinion, were required, if we were to enjoy permanent peace and success; to which they would not listen. I therefore accepted the kind invitation to Rochdale, and subsequent events have demonstrated that I took the right course. It was a great trial to leave Auld Reekie. In that city I had more friends out of our little church than I had enjoyed in any previous circuit. When I was leaving, the Temperance people held two soirées: one public, in Adam's-square Hall, and the other private, in the large room in Mr. Johnstone's Temperance Hotel; and a church soirée made me a presentation of Horne's "Introduction to a Critical Study of the Scripture." While resident in Edinburgh, I also became sincerely attached to several friends in Glasgow and Paisley.

CHAPTER IV.

Leaves Edinburgh—Arrives at Rochdale—First Sermon in Rochdale—Letter from Brother Thomas—Special Services—Letters from Brother Thomas—Death and Funeral of Brother Thomas—Death of a Nephew—Death of Brother Elisha—Reminiscences of the Rochdale Circuit—Removal to the Bury Circuit—Collision on Railway—Visit to Darlington—Mrs. Howarth's Death—Requested to go as a Missionary to Australia—Resolutions of the Connexional Committee—Preparations for going to Australia—Visit to London—Embarkation—Journal of Voyage.

ROCHDALE CIRCUIT.

We left our comfortable dwelling at Wights Place, West Newington, early on a Tuesday morning in August, 1846. I was very sorrowful: the thought of that morning even now fills my eyes with tears. Our favourite puss came to the carriage door, and, putting up her feet, mewed most plaintively. Poor Mrs. Whitford, a widow to whose family I had been useful, stood wringing her hands, exclaiming, "O Mr. Townend, dinna gae an' leave us!" and I must say that that morning I felt heartily sick of an itinerant life; and, as the snorting steam bore us along the iron road, and the majestic castle and glittering spires of that modern Athens retired from our view, I said within myself, "Farewell! farewell! Auld Reekie! I should like to have spent my days in thee." We were soon in the city of Glasgow, and dined with Mr. and Mrs. Cochrane, whose kind attention somewhat healed our lacerated spirits; but my dear wife at these times always displayed more magnanimity of soul than I could. We had a comfortable sail from Ardrossan to Fleetwood. We remained at Fleetwood five days; there were many Lancashire people there, and compared with the people in Scotland, we were much struck with their coarseness of language and manners. We landed safe in Rochdale, Wednesday, August 19th. It was Bagslate races, and not a 'bus or cab at the station. No one knew that we were coming that day; and with as much of our luggage as we could carry, we stole along the skirts of the town, to No. 12, West Street; there we found a beautiful house, well furnished, a servant maid waiting our arrival; and my dear brothers, Thomas and Elisha, sat down to tea with us. Thomas was looking better, but his cough and shortness of breath were ominous; the Annual Assembly had given him, in the balmy atmosphere of Penzance, a year's respite from labour. Elisha was not strong, but went about his work as usual. The magnitude of the Circuit, Society, Chapel, and Congregation, almost overwhelmed me. I had left a small pastorate; one little chapel, about fifty members, and one hundred the average congregation; and in the Rochdale Circuit, there were eighteen preaching places, and forty-eight names upon the Local Preachers' Plan, above three thousand Sabbath-school children, and one thousand and sixty-six church members. Sabbath came: I had to preach in the large chapel in the morning: I was very modest, indeed, I was frightened: in the afternoon and evening I was all right, and soon gathered confidence, and felt glad to be once more among the factories, schools, and sanctuaries of Lancashire. On my second appearance in Rochdale pulpit, I was quite at home; I spoke with freedom, and the word was with power. Elisha said to me, as he wiped the tears from his face, "O brother, let us thank God; I listened to you last night with unmingled pleasure." This to me was a cordial, it placed me on vantage ground.

Brother Gibbons heard my first sermon in Baillie Street, and he said that I did not read the text properly; I read it thus—"Deliver me, I pray thee, from the hand of my brother, from the hand of Esau; for I fear him, lest he will come and smite me, and the mother with the children." "Now," said Mr. G, "you ought to have read—'Deliver me, I pray thee, from the hand of my brother, from the hand of *Elisha*, for I fear him, lest he will smite me, with his penetrating criticisms." I was never afraid of Elisha after, and my residence in Rochdale with him, proved our mutual solace and comfort. The Rev. John Gibbons was a sweet and powerful preacher: but his health failed almost as soon as I and brother G. Chesson got to the circuit; and it was thought best for him to winter with his father-in-law at Penzance. On writing to brother Thomas, I received the following reply—

"Bellevue Terrace, Penzance, Nov. 16, 1846.

"My dear Brother,—You ask me whether Samuel has returned; he is at present with us, and likely to remain for some time to come.

I am much obliged to Julia for her affectionate solicitude for our welfare. Sin and death have cursed the earth with mourning. The amiable and excellent Mr. Rich, of Worle, you say, is no more. Well, he did not set his heart upon that shadow, that floating vapour, *the world.* He had chosen a better portion, one which death could not touch. He has not left his riches behind; he has taken them with him to that world where 'the inhabitants shall not say, I am sick, and where there is no more death, neither sorrow nor crying; for the former things are passed away.' Jonathan will not be out of his time until a year come next March, and, owing to domestic affliction, his master would be badly off without him. I feel the importance of that good advice, 'Trust in the Lord with all thine heart, and lean not to thine own understanding. In all thy ways acknowledge Him, and He will direct thy paths.' I am sorry that brother Elisha remains in comparative weakness; still the gold loses nothing by being cast into the fire, that is, nothing of its sterling excellence; the dross may go, but the gold is purer and brighter without it. It is natural for children when they are in trouble to run to their fathers; and God has said, 'Call upon me in the day of trouble, and I will hear and deliver thee, and thou shalt glorify me.' Then, I am not to be without a companion in tribulation! Well, I shall be glad to see brother Gibbons, though sorry for the occasion. 'You don't know what you are to do without him.' But if we so lean upon creatures as to imagine that we cannot do without them, God takes them away, that we may learn to lean upon *Him:* he removes them that he may show himself: he takes away intervening objects, that our eye may rest immediately upon himself. Thus, when in our extremity we are brought to trust entirely in God, we feel that his grace is sufficient for us, and that he can do 'exceeding abundantly above all that we ask or think.'

"The widow and the fatherless find mercy. Brother Charles and sister Ellen still live in their posterity, and the God of Abraham still lives to take care of them. When you see them again, tell them that uncle Thomas often thinks of them, and loves them. I am glad that your chief anxiety is to be useful. A man may be popular, he may be a master of eloquence, he may be able to attract and charm large audiences, and yet he may not be useful. Sinners may not be awakened, penitents may not be justified, and believers established. It is one thing to please, another to profit: the former without the latter is a vain thing, and becomes important only as it leads to the latter. It is therefore not to be sought for its *own sake;* but if we seek to please men, it must be to do *them good to edification.* You will want to know how my health is getting on. Upon the whole I am better; and were it not for the distance, I might be tempted to slip over and see you, and try, in some small measure, to supply brother Gibbons' lack of service. Perhaps it is well I am where that temptation cannot reach me. Brother Gibbons will no doubt be followed by the earnest prayers of an affectionate people, and I hope their intercessions will avail for his perfect restoration to health—accompanied with an abundant increase of the Spirit's power. Mrs. Townend and Samuel desire to be remembered to sister, to Amelia, and to yourself. Remember me to your colleagues, and all inquiring friends—From your affectionate brother,

"T. TOWNEND.

"P.S.—Remember me specially to George Howarth and family."

The Ladies' Dorcas Society, for making garments for the poor of the town, was a powerful means of good; and as brother Elisha was the missionary for our Society, and general distributor of charitable funds, he took a lively interest in the Dorcas Society. All the preachers, and the missionary, took tea with the ladies on the sewing day once in the month, when subjects which had been announced at previous meetings were discussed; and these meetings were of a most social, interesting, and useful character. Special subjects were announced by small hand-bills for the Sabbath services in Baillie-street Chapel; and prayer-meetings, and protracted services, and open-air services were held, and the Spirit of God was poured out abundantly upon us. I cannot forget the feelings which agitated my bosom, when I had to stand before two thousand people, and to speak on special subjects: such as "The Nature and Consequences of Infidelity"; "The Existence and Influence of Evil Angels"; "Unscriptural Marriages"; "Belshazzar's Feast"; "The Causes, Crimes, and Consequences of David's Fall"; "All War condemned by the Saviour, and the Spirit of New Testament precept and practice"; &c. Oh, the weight of responsibility which, before I entered the pulpit, used to almost crush my spirit! I never ascended that awful place in my own strength; and to the glory of God's grace I deliberately declare, that on these very trying occasions I was never confounded, but had surprising self-command, and liberty of speech. My colleagues, the local preachers, and the leaders, were most of them under special influence, and we had a considerable in-gathering of souls; several hundreds were brought to God, and have maintained their connection with that energetic church. The Temperance Society, and Peace Society, in the town and neighbourhood, were vigorously advocated and maintained; and on looking back on those scenes of excitement and labour, in connection with the regular calls of duty in the circuit, and frequent visits to other circuits, I wonder that my health did not fail. Thank God, I was willing and able to work in his vineyard; and he did abundantly bless and refresh my spirit.

My brother Elisha was now evidently very feeble, and I could plainly see he was unfit for his labour. It gave me melancholy pleasure to assist him in any way possible. On writing to Thomas, I received, without date, the following letter—

"My dear Brother—I am much obliged by your kind letter, and for the information which it contains, respecting those in whose welfare we feel a more than usual interest. Am sorry to hear that brother Elisha is looking so poorly, I should like to have a line from him. You wish me to write more for publication, but you do not know how much I am averse to that sort of thing; being deeply sensible that so many are better qualified to write for the press. How is it that the sermons preached at the Annual Assembly are not forthcoming in the Magazine? I have received a circular from brother Saul, making a demand upon me for 3*l.* 11*s.* 2*d.* Of course you will fulfil your engagement of paying the subscription due from me to the fund for the present year: I having continued my subscription to sister on the strength of that engagement. I cannot say that I am improving in health; have been very feverish to-day; pulse this afternoon 116—and that when sitting calmly in the house. I trust I do not call in question the wisdom and kindness of God's dealings with me. My only quarrel is with myself: I want a greater measure of the spirit of prayer, of faith, and of watchful care, to improve the time. But it is amazing how the infirmities of a sickly body draw the attention, and engross the thoughts. Let me have an interest in your most earnest prayers. My dear Samuel is leaving us for Liverpool. He is but young to be at his own disposal in a great town like Liverpool, where every kind of snare is laid for unsuspecting youth. I think his health is so far recovered, that he will have a chance of overcoming his tendency to consumption. My dear wife has got a cold, and is rather low-spirited at parting with Samuel. She would like much to be back in Lancashire, where she would be nearer her sons, and in the bosom of her friends. You have brother Gibbons back, but I fear not in a state fit to enter upon much labour in the way of preaching, &c. Give my kind love to Sarah and Amelia, to brother and family, to Mr. G. Howarth and family, and, if not too great a burden, to all enquiring friends.—I am, my dear brother, yours ever,

"T. TOWNEND."

Disease was making melancholy havoc with my dear relatives, but my mind was cheered with the enjoyment of personal religion; with the revival of true and vital godliness in the societies and schools in the circuit; and the well-grounded-hope that those already departed—sister Ellen Baxter not excepted—were safely landed; and that Thomas and Elisha were ripening for a better world. Still, when I thought of their being amongst us no more, with the loss of their counsel, I reeled at the thought, and fondly hoped that their lives would be protracted. Elisha could scarcely move about the town; and on a Thursday, when he usually called towards noon, I used to prevail upon him to take a rest upon the sofa, have a little dinner and tea with us, and allow me to go to Spotland poorhouse and preach for him; he would sometimes say, "O brother, you're very kind; what a mercy it is that you are stationed with us at this time."

It was a melancholy pleasure for us to read the letters from my brother Thomas. Early in 1847 I received the following—

"Penzance, Feb. 18, 1847.

"My dear Brother—I was comforted and refreshed by your kind and welcome letter. I trust I am not insensible to the tenderness of your sympathy, and of the churches you mention. If the sympathy of friends be sweet and kind, what must that of our Great High Priest be!

With joy we meditate the grace
Of our High Priest above;
His heart is made of tenderness,
His bowels melt with love.

Touched with a sympathy within,
He knows our feeble frame;
He knows what sore temptation means,
For he hath felt the same.

But why should I be at the trouble of writing down these lines—since you have probably known them for many years? Why, just because their beauty, their poetry, their pathos, and especially their Scriptural truth, give them a resistless charm, particularly to a tempted and tried Christian: so that though they may have been read or heard by us a hundred times, they still strike the eye and ear with grateful delight. Your letter calls up the endearments of the past—father, mother, brothers, sisters—but whilst I write these words, my eyes fill with tears. Ah! they sleep in Jesus; their spirits are with God in joy and felicity. They are waiting, you say, to welcome me when I am called hence. And what a welcome will that be! What a meeting! What must it be to see them there, with every tear wiped from their eyes, and their faces radiant with glory, and hearts overflowing with pleasure! What will it be to look down from the heights of that glory on all the way in which our Heavenly Father led us; and then to join with them in the song and anthem, which shall swell with all the voices, and all the harps of the heavenly host. I am glad that brother Elisha is better, and that there is some hope of his life and health being spared to his family and the church. It is also pleasing to hear that your health, both of body and soul, continues good; and that you have the satisfaction of knowing that your labours in the circuit are both acceptable and useful. To God be all the glory! I am greatly obliged by your kind invitation to come over during the summer months. I doubt not I should meet with every kindness both from you and the friends; and it would be very gratifying to me to see all your faces, and enjoy your company again. But Graham, in his 'Domestic Medicine,' says, that invalids improve more here in the summer, than in the winter months; so that it will be proper to try its effects, should Providence permit. My health has been better these last few days. Last Sabbath was a very warm and sultry day; I remained up a short time after the rest were retired to rest; I went into a back room, where the coals are kept, and where there is a hole in the wall to admit air; a piece of beef hung up in the place, and I heard a voice in it, which was the cause of my taking a candle and looking in, being anxious to ascertain the occasion of the noise. What was my surprise when I was attacked by a large snake or adder (I know not which, but from its size I should suppose a snake); it got hold of my leg, but I succeeded in throwing it off before it could bite me. I fled from the presence of his majesty with all convenient speed, called up

Samuel and Mr. Miller, who dressed and put on their boots, and, armed with sticks, went in search of the intruder, but he had made his escape. I suppose the bite of these venomous reptiles is fatal in twelve hours, unless the part is immediately cut out. How often may it be said, that there is but a step between us and death. And how little we know of what shall be on the morrow. My Mary Ann has not been so well lately. Samuel is better. If all be well, we intend to send him back to Liverpool in April; but if my health does not recruit, or if I am taken hence, of course he cannot be maintained in that situation. But these are matters I must leave with God; being 'careful for nothing, but in everything, by prayer and supplication with thanksgiving,' making known my 'requests unto God.' Mary Ann and Samuel join with me in kind love to you, to Sarah, and Amelia, also to brother Elisha and family.—I am, my dear brother, yours most truly,

"T. Townend."

At the March quarterly meeting, 1847, I received a unanimous invitation to remain a second year, which I thankfully accepted; resolving to give myself fully to the Lord. Brother Gibbons' appointments having to be supplied, I preached frequently, four and five times in the week—and preached for Elisha at the poor-house—and very frequently three times on the Sabbath, beside meeting classes for tickets and the like: still my health continued good. I was happy in God, and in my work. Having written to brother Thomas, I received the following reply—

"Penzance, April 5th, 1847.

"My dear Brother,—I was much pleased with your letter, notwithstanding its brevity. You think I should write often; but as you were keeping up a regular correspondence with brother Gibbons, it was natural to suppose, that you were almost weekly hearing of my state. I rejoice that you are happy in God, and happy in your work, and that you see some cheering measure of success. To God be all the praise. I don't wonder that you should tremble under the responsibility of having to declare God's message to such a company of immortal beings as assemble to hear the word in Baillie-street Chapel. The importance of the work of the ministry made an apostle cry out, 'who is sufficient for these things?' All those, however, whom God has called to this work, may, and ought to rejoice, that their sufficiency is of Him; and that he has said, 'Lo, I am with you always, even unto the end of the world.' I was very glad to hear once again intelligence concerning uncle Elijah Townend. The very mention of his name in your letter, called up, as by a magic spell, the scenes of bygone days. I always had a strong affection for him, and also for his son Enoch. It is but as yesterday, since father and all my uncles were in the prime of their days: but the rush of years has borne some of them and their partners to the grave, and those who remain are tending to its margin, and will soon lie down amid the clods of the valley. Well—

> 'Let sickness blast, let death devour,
> If heaven must recompense our pains:
> Perish the grass, and fade the flower,
> For firm the word of God remains.'

Brother Elisha it seems is recovering his strength. We ought to give special thanks to God on this account; I hope that his improvement will be permament and complete. Brother Gibbons returned to Penzance on Saturday; he was up at our house to-day, and appears to be much improved. I hope that, with care, he will again become an efficient man. Brother Miller is in good health. He declined an invitation from this circuit to remain another year, on the ground of the uncertainty of our remaining; it being probable that if we remove, the Annual Assembly will send a married man, on account of the house and furniture. He has accepted an invitation to Helston, being anxious to remain in Cornwall on account of his health. Mr. Reed stays a third year in Helston, and Mr. Sayer is likely to stay a third year at Redruth. They have had a glorious revival there the last few weeks. In this, and the Helston Circuit, the societies are drooping. We are to have Mr. Darke next Lord's day twice, preaching Missionary sermons, and the Missionary meeting the Wednesday night following. You enquire kindly concerning my health. I cannot say that I am improved since I wrote last, though I expect I shall be better in a few weeks, as the weather gets milder. I cannot stand the north-east wind, nor the east winds; when they prevail I have to keep within doors. My bowels are very irregular, generally in one or other extreme. My breathing—on ascending a hill, or any motion requiring exertion—is exceedingly short and laboured. My cough and expectoration are very bad, and yet I have a good appetite, and am not conscious of being much weaker than when I came here. I think that my complaint is a slow asthmatic consumption, that it is beyond the power of medicine to cure it, and that possibly it may be several years before it strikes the final blow which will end the painful strife. My dear wife and I talk about the ways and means, by which we may gain a little bread, should my affliction continue for some years; but we are obliged to come to this point, 'take no thought for to-morrow, sufficient for the day is evil things.' Samuel should, according to arrangements, go to Liverpool at the close of this month, but during the past week his cough has returned with so much obstinacy as to give us great uneasiness. Mary Ann is quite well; all join in love to you, to Sarah, Amelia, brother, and family: we were glad to hear of sister Lupton.

"T. TOWNEND."

Poor Thomas! one other short note terminated our earthly correspondence. How little we know of the future; indeed, how unwilling and slow we are to read the signs of approaching dissolution. These signs were apparent in the case of both my dear and honoured brothers; as well as in the case of my noble, cheerful, pious, and accomplished nephew Samuel.

The Annual Assembly of 1847 drew on, and was held in Leeds: the representatives for Rochdale being myself, the Rev. G. Chesson, and brother Elisha. It was a pleasant and painful meeting to Elisha; pleasant for us to sit and represent the same society, and lodge together at Mr. Porter's; painful to listen to letters on behalf of, and from, our absent and dying brother; and besides, Elisha was far from being well: the internal abscess, which finally terminated his mortal existence, was even then making fearful havoc in his constitution. The Rev. W. R. Brown was invited, and was put down for Rochdale. And we reported 163 members on trial, with the same number of full members as in the last year. I was very happy with my colleagues. The local preachers and other officers had a mind to work: during that summer, scores of sermons were preached in the open air. Our Saturday night band-meeting was well attended, averaging two hundred and fifty. And the chapel was frequently filled on a Sabbath evening. We had some painful matters between some of our principal families, which almost distracted the Leaders' meeting; but by the gracious protection of our Heavenly Father, these things were not allowed to stop the blooming work of grace. In this respect, Satan was defeated and God glorified.

On arriving in Leeds, for the Assembly of 1847, I received a note from Thomas as to a matter of business, which he requested me to attend to for him. In regard to his health, he stated,—" The doctor examined my chest last Saturday afternoon by stethescope. He stated that there were tubercular deposits in the lungs; but that the right lung was much the worse. He however thought that he might succeed in arresting their further spread, relieve the chest, and so prolong life. I asked him concerning a change of air, but he said this air is the best for my case that the kingdom affords; and that I had better not go further north. I have been much relieved by his medicine. Give my best love to Mr. and Mrs. Porter and family. I hope God will be with you in the Annual Assembly.

"I am, my dear brother, yours truly,

"T. TOWNEND."

By the time I had got fairly into the work of the circuit, after the Assembly, I received the following letter from the Rev. John Gibbons.

"Penzance, September 6th, 1847.

"My dear Brother,—The melancholy task devolves upon me, of informing you that your dear brother Thomas is no more. He died last evening, about ten minutes past seven o'clock. His end was triumphant. We scarcely expected that he would be gone so soon. He was up a short time on Friday, but on Saturday and Sunday he kept his bed. I spent an hour or two with him, very profitably, on Saturday evening; but did not expect it to be our last interview on earth. I did not think he would remain long, and yet I was not prepared to hear on Sunday evening that he was dead. He died while we were at chapel in the evening service. It was your brother's dying wish, that you should come down and be present at his funeral; and also take his poor widow back with you to Rochdale. The timed fixed for his funeral is Saturday morning next. In order to be here in time, it will be needful for you to leave Rochdale as early as possible. You will have to come by railway to Exeter, and from thence to Penzance by the mail coach. Mrs. Townend wishes me to say, that nothing must prevent your coming, as there are matters which cannot be settled without you.

"I am, dear brother, yours affectionately,

"JOHN GIBBONS."

As soon as I received the letter, which was on the Wednesday morning, I hastened to brother Elisha. I met him in the street, and told him of the letter. He lost all command of himself for a few minutes. I had not read the letter right; and yet he was so agitated that he could neither read it himself, nor listen to me. At length he relieved himself by a flood of tears. In two hours I was off for Penzance, and lodged in Birmingham that night. Thursday night I lodged at Exeter; and at five next morning was upon the mail for Penzance. I arrived safe that evening in Penzance, kissed my nephew Samuel, his disconsolate mother, and the cold, cold lips of my dear brother. The funeral was unpretending, but respectful; and on the Sabbath evening I preached from, "But this I say, brethren, the time is short!" And on the Tuesday evening following, from the Transfiguration. My journey to Penzance was pleasing and melancholy. Samuel took me to all the private and beautiful walks he and his father had often taken; and on the Saturday evening we all arrived safe in Rochdale. Mrs. Townend remained with us, and Samuel returned to his master in Liverpool; and in about six weeks he was ordered away from Liverpool. He had been spitting of blood, and was very much debilitated. He with his mother wintered at our house; the young man devoting his time to books and study, until he sunk under the weight of disease. His brother, Jonathan Townend, was just out of his apprenticeship, and came over from Darlington, and was with me in the room when Samuel died. The following is the entry I made at the time—

"Samuel Townend died on the 13th day of March, 1847, in the 19th year of his age, at his uncle Joseph's, 12, West Street, Rochdale. He was a gifted, accomplished, and pious young man. He literally 'fell asleep in Jesus,' for he departed this life, whilst asleep in an easy chair. I here record my sense of gratitude to our friends in Rochdale, for their kindness to this youth, and his widowed mother, during their residence in our house." Brother Elisha had just strength left to attend the funeral of Samuel. It was a very mournful and melting scene; and the grave of Samuel was close to the one, soon to be opened to receive the remains of my much esteemed, and only surviving brother Elisha. Amid these mournful scenes, the revival in the circuit steadily progressed, and almost all places on the plan partook more or less of the good work.

Mr. Brown was very delicate when he came amongst us; but his health improved, and he laboured with great acceptance and profit. I was in a fix as to my stay in Rochdale: I had never remained a third year before; and to remain where there was a little more in the way of salary I felt looked very selfish. I consulted my brother, who said, it would be cruel to think of leaving, when the work was going on; that the Rochdale people would feel insulted by my refusing to stop; and then he touched a tender chord, by saying, "Stay, brother, and see what will be the end of my affliction!" Brother Brown, brother Chesson, and myself were all invited to remain, which invitation we cheerfully accepted. Oh what days of power and gracious influence were those! What Saturday evening band-meetings, open-air services, protracted meetings, and blessed Sabbath services! Brother Chesson, myself, and Mr. Oliver Ormerod were intrusted with the representation of the circuit at the ensuing Annual Assembly, to be held in Manchester; when we had the pleasure to report an increase upon the year of 235 full members, leaving 157 on trial.

Elisha's end now drew near—he could no longer go about the town, distributing the alms of the rich, and succouring the poor who were rich in faith, and leading others to the Redeemer for salvation. What painful hours, weeks, and months he suffered, ere he was confined to his room. His labours in planting churches at Whitworth, Shaw, Crompton, and Bowers Row—when, at a late hour in the night, he passed through Rochdale to his house in Heywood—laid the foundation of his last sickness. How often did I hear the good people, of those isolated parts of the circuit, speak of his untiring efforts to do good.

Painful were my feelings during the months of June and July, with the reminiscences of recent deaths around me: yet I almost daily found time to see my dying brother. Frequently, he could not speak, and sometimes he could not open his eyes. His desire was that I should always sit where he could see me. His last effort was to write the memoir of our dear brother Thomas. The first part came out in the July number of the Wesleyan Association Magazine, in the very month in which he took his flight to join those who had gone before. On taking the number into his chamber, I said, "Thomas is come, brother." "Is he?—let me look." I showed him the page, and holding it so as he could see, his lips moved a moment—"Memoir of the Rev. Thomas Townend!" He then said, "That will do, brother. Mr. Schofield said it would read well."

On Wednesday, July the 26th, 1848, the Thirteenth Annual Assembly commenced its sittings in Lever Street Chapel, Manchester. Elisha, with one exception, had never before this time been absent; and Thomas, up to his affliction, had always taken an active part in the proceedings of our yearly gatherings. I took my seat, and, when my name was called, I could scarcely answer. Thomas was in the grave, Elisha was dying! Only a solitary widowed sister, besides myself, left of a large and healthy family, who only a few years ago filled a large pew: I sought where to weep, and thus relieved the anguish of my spirit. Still, I was happy: I would not, if I could, call back the dear departed—

"Those unbound spirits into bonds again;"

and as to Elisha, I felt reconciled to the will of Heaven. My feelings laid hold of my body, and I became very unwell; and on the Sabbath morning, at half-past ten, I had to preach in the Lever Street Chapel, where many distinguished persons would be present; and in the evening in Bury Street Chapel, amongst my old friends. The Bury Street Chapel pulpit was then in mourning for the eldest circuit officer, Mr. W. Matthews.

On the Saturday evening I had my last interview with my dear brother. I said, if it were his desire, I would remain with him, and write to Manchester to have my appointments for the coming Sabbath supplied. He was much moved; but insisted on my return to Manchester by the next train. "O brother, go," said he, "and do your work like a man, and in the name of your God, and He will bless you." Though very weak, I preached in the morning, my subject being the Transfiguration; and in the evening I had a blessed time, from Isaiah xl. 6, 7, and 8. The day following was the last of my dear brother's earthly existence. He was very poorly but very cheerful, and while his friends were trying to put him in an easier position, he said, "O if I could slip out of your hands, into the arms of Jesus, it would be a blessing!" And, after extreme suffering, he calmly expired on the evening of the 31st of July, 1848.

The following notice appeared in the August number of our Magazine for that year:—

"Died in peace, at Rochdale, July 31st, 1848, Mr. Elisha Townend, in the forty-eighth year of his age. His long and painful affliction was borne with Christian submission and fortitude. He had for many years held the offices of leader, preacher, and missionary, with the Wesleyan Methodist Association in the town and circuit of Rochdale. His mortal remains were carried to the peaceful grave surrounded by a crowd of sympathising spectators, led on by the preachers, leaders, and stewards of the Society, and were followed by his sorrowing widow, three fatherless children, and other relatives and friends."

Further particulars concerning my brothers are in the "Wesleyan Methodist Association Magazine:" as to Charles, see the year 1846, page 334; as to Thomas, see the year 1848, page 321; and as to Elisha, see the year 1849, page 457.

In the churchyard, Kildwick, Craven, Yorkshire, there is a headstone bearing this inscription—

"Here lieth the remains of John Townend. He was a sincere Christian, a faithful servant, and an honest man."

That is the grave of my grandfather; and in the same rural and beautiful graveyard rest the remains of the four infant branches of our family. Sister Ann sleeps alone in the churchyard at Burnley, and brother Thomas in the cemetery at Penzance; Elisha and Samuel, side by side, in Lady Huntingdon's chapelyard, Rochdale; and father, mother, Benjamin, and Charles, with my infant daughter, in the Wesleyan burying-ground, Longholme, Rawtenstall, Rossendale. What of human friendship! what of all the endearments and tender ties of father, mother, husband, wife, parent, child, brother, and sister, if after this momentary existence, with its hopes and fears, joys and sorrows, we sink into annihilation!

"They who with smiles lit up the hall,
And cheer'd with song the hearth,
Alas! for love, if thou wert all,
And nought beyond, O earth!"

Thank God there is something beyond! "Life and immortality are brought to light by the Gospel." Jesus said to Martha, "I am the resurrection and the life; he that believeth in me, though he die, yet shall he live; and he that liveth and believeth in me shall not die eternally": though their bodies moulder in the silent grave—

"Yet these, new rising from the tomb,
With lustre brighter far shall shine,
Revive with ever-during bloom,
Safe from diseases and decline."

My third year in Rochdale was attended with circumstances which made me feel solitary and pensive. Elisha was no more. His familiar rap at the door no longer cheered me. In passing through the streets, no longer did I meet him with, "Well, brother!" When I entered his house, there was his vacant seat; and when in the pulpit, the presence of his widow and orphans would fill my eyes with tears. No longer did the postman leave me letters from an absent brother; letters full of breathing thoughts and burning words, the reading of which enkindled within my breast feelings the most sacred and hallowing. Then, in our large society, affliction and death were ever making inroads into the domestic enclosures in our Sion, which gave a tinge of the pensive and melancholy to my general habits and public ministrations. I was, however, cheered by the possession of personal religion and the healthy state of the circuit, and enlivened with the hope that, if faithful, we should all meet again, where pain and parting will be no more. I felt a lively interest in the services held in the poorhouse at Spotland. I was glad that the service was not paid for out of the rates, or monopolised by the clergy of the Establishment, and anxious that, as a society, we should do our duty in the matter. The local preachers supplied on the Sabbath evening, and, after my brother's death, the travelling preachers on the Thursday afternoon. What a motley group assembled in that room! the major part wrinkled, and bending with age, most of whom were ignorant and wicked. Here and there might be seen a lean and careworn widow, with her cluster of fatherless children; then, among the mass of children, many might be found who were destitute of either father or mother; and, last of all, the different grades of idiotcy in its vacant laughing, moping, and revengeful aspects.

One Thursday afternoon, whilst conducting worship there, an alarming thunderstorm broke over Rochdale and its vicinity; on account of which my discourse was very short. For a few minutes it seemed to have spent itself, and just as we were singing,

"Because thou didst for sinners die,"

whilst the word "die" was in our mouths, a terrible flash of lightning, with an immediate peal of thunder, such as I never heard before, caused us to cease singing; and instantly all present fell upon their knees, when I said, "Lord, save us!" There was a spontaneous "Amen!" Having pronounced the blessing, I left, and was anxious to see if any serious damage had been done. A short distance from the poor-house, the electric fluid had done considerable damage in two cottages by the road-side. A woman and her daughter had called for shelter, and in the interim before the last blast, the mother went to the porch of the house to see if she might venture out, when the electric fluid, rushing in, struck her, and she fell dead upon the floor. She looked as if she had died of fright: a small prick or cut was to be seen upon her forehead, where the lightning had struck her, and a small streak of blood had run down her face. That evening I preached in the open air at Smallbridge to a large concourse of people, and referred to what had occurred.

I feel thankful that Providence directed me to the Rochdale Circuit, at the very time when I could render a little assistance to my afflicted and dying relations; and also for all the kindness we received from that society. Should my life be spared, and I be permitted, in the order of Providence, to visit my native land, it would afford me great pleasure to stand once more in Baillie Street Chapel, and look round on the soul-stirring spectacle of two thousand immortal beings assembled to worship Almighty God. Should that ever be the case, what changes will have taken place! how many, removed from the militant to the triumphant church, will be missing! Some, it may be, ere then, may have "returned like the dog to his own vomit, and the sow that was washed to its wallowing in the mire." Of all the changes that ever occur in a Christian church, backsliding is the most to be deplored. My removal from Rochdale was very trying and painful, arising from the many pressing invitations I received from other circuits, and most especially from the Grosvenor-street and Lever-street (Manchester) Circuits. After much thought and prayer, I accepted the invitation to Bury, Lancashire, only six miles from Rochdale.

After the close of the sittings of the Annual Assembly of 1849, held in Liverpool, Mrs. Townend and I had a pleasant sail to Menai Straits, we remained all night in Bangor, and returned to Liverpool the next day. In the night, a dreadful thunderstorm visited the place; several head of cattle were killed with the lightning; and a lady, who sailed with us from Liverpool the previous day, was either struck with the electric fluid, or was frightened to death. Her husband was unhurt.

BURY CIRCUIT.

It is a wise arrangement in the itinerant system for the circuit to provide furniture, so that on removing, only books and clothes have to be taken. On the 16th of August, 1849, a post-chaise drew up to No. 12, West-street, Rochdale. I and my family stepped into the chaise, and in little more than an hour, we were put down at No. 32, North-street, Bury, just opposite our commodious chapel, school, and public burying-ground. We met with a kind reception from that modest, unpretending, but intelligent people; with whom I lived and laboured, with great pleasure and some profit, for eighteen months; and, so far as that society was concerned, I was sorry that we had to be so soon separated.

On November the 16th, 1849, early in the morning I left our new, sweet residence at Seedfield, near Bury, to attend missionary services at Darlington. When I was travelling by the East Lancashire railway, at Cross Hills, Mr. Hailey, an intelligent local preacher in the Leeds circuit, took his seat by me. When we were a little past Keighley (my first regular circuit), we had a rather serious shock; our train ran violently against some carriages that were on the same line, unlading lime. The passengers were all much shaken, but I was struck almost senseless; I remember asking what was the matter, and Mr. Hailey walking me about at the next station, where we exchanged carriages. When we were off again, I began to weep, and asked Mr. Hailey whether he knew what I was about? and where I was going? when he told me that I was going to Darlington; had to preach there that night; three times on the Sunday; and attend four missionary meetings the following week. My recollection had completely left me. My hat was broken; my face bruised; and my right eye almost swollen up. I wept like a child that had lost its mother, and begged Mr. Hailey not to leave me. Mr. Hailey had to leave me before we arrived at Leeds, but another gentleman kindly saw me safe into the Leeds and Thirsk railway waiting-room, where I rested two hours and a half, awaiting the next train. I got a cup of tea, bathed my face all the time with warm water, and when I arrived at Darlington, Mr. H. Tarrant was waiting my arrival. He said that it was half an hour past the time, but that his colleague, Mr. Keene, had commenced the service. We took a coach, and soon were at the chapel. The service was held that night in their beautiful school-room, which gave an air of comfort and simplicity to the gathering. My limbs shook, and with difficulty I took the desk, and read for my text, Rev. iii. 20. The service was the last of a series of protracted meetings. I told the good people what had happened to me on the way, and spoke with freedom. After preaching I retired to rest; but the prayer-meeting continued until eleven o'clock, and good was done. It was some time before I could again travel by rail without fear.

The Annual Assembly of 1850 was held in Rochdale, and I was intrusted with the representation of the Bury Circuit. Brother Thomas had made his home in Rochdale at Mr. Howarth's; and after my brother's death, I was requested to occupy his place; and after leaving the circuit, Mr. Howarth's was my home when visiting the circuit. Mrs. Howarth was a woman of superior mind; and at the Christmas, 1850, the family sustained an irreparable loss in her death. On New Year's Day I had the melancholy pleasure of conducting the funeral service of this estimable individual, in the Wesleyan Chapel, Rochdale; and ever after, on entering that domestic circle, there was an involuntary feeling of sorrow, arising from the absence of one so dearly beloved. There were five interesting children, whose first look used to say, "Mother is gone!" The dejected mien, and pensive looks of good Mr. Howarth were unmistakable. On being seated, the vacant chair of Mrs. H., and the likeness of my dear brother Thomas, which hung upon the wall, greatly affected me. Seldom did we speak of the departed; and as the waters of the deep river glide silently away, so the deep current of feeling prevented anything bordering on loquacity. On an evening I used to take the hymn-book, Mr. Howarth his violin, Mr. Henry, or Miss Jane the piano; and, weeping, we made melody in our hearts unto the Lord, and thus anticipated that day—

"Which shall our flesh restore,
When death shall all be done away,
And bodies part no more."

In the bosom of this interesting family it was my privilege to lodge during the sittings of the Connexional Committee, and the last Annual Assembly that I attended before leaving the shores of my native and beloved country.

The autumnal sittings of the Connexional Committee of 1850 were, for the first time, held in Bury; at which time we held our missionary anniversary. It was at these sittings that my name was mentioned as a fit person to send to Australia. Having occasion to be absent for half an hour, on returning, Mr. Breeden whispered, "The committee will feel obliged by your retiring a few minutes." I went into a corner of the school-room, and poured out my soul in prayer, that we might all be directed; for my impression was that the brethren were thinking and talking about my being sent to Australia. Presently, John Kipling, Esq., came for me, and, much agitated, I entered the committee room, when the President rose and said: "Brother Townend, before I read to you a resolution passed in your absence, I beg to state, that so far from any one voting against the resolution, every person in this full committee held up his hand in its favour."

RESOLUTION OF THE CONNEXIONAL COMMITTEE.

"The committee having been informed that there is reason to believe that Brother Joseph Townend would be willing, if it were the desire of the committee, to labour in Australia; this committee deems it proper to declare it to be its opinion, that brother J. Townend is a suitable man to labour in Australia; and this committee would feel great pleasure in receiving an intimation from him, of the willingness of himself and wife, to devote themselves to the important work of establishing in Australia a mission in connexion with, and on the principles of, the Wesleyan Methodist Association."

In reply, I said, "I am happy in my work, and perfectly content to dwell in my native land: that when I was a Conference Wesleyan I offered myself to the mission work, but not being allowed to be neutral on the question of the eternal sonship of Christ, I felt it my duty to leave that community: that I felt interested in our missions, and especially the Australian: that if favoured with a copy of the resolution, I would consult my wife, and would talk, and think, and pray about the matter." Two of the brethren then earnestly prayed that we might be divinely directed; and in company with the Rev. W. R. Brown, my late colleague, I went to consult my wife. At first, she said she would not go: but her aged mother, then living with us, having stated her conviction that we ought, and her willingness that we should; and, after due thought and earnest prayer, my wife said, "Tell them, Joseph, that we will go cheerfully." In conducting family worship, the first time after our decision, Mrs. Townend could not proceed in the reading of the appointed portion, it seemed to bear so decidedly upon our case; and in prayer I was so affected that I could not proceed. After communicating our decision to the committee, the following resolutions were passed unanimously:—

"Resolved, that this committee is gratified at having received from brother Joseph Townend an expression of his willingness to accept an appointment to Australia."

"Resolved, that the offer of brother Joseph Townend, to labour in Australia, be accepted, on the conditions which have been resolved on by the committee. That it be referred to the Connexional Officers, to solicit the concurrence of the Bury Circuit in this appointment, and to arrange for obtaining a satisfactory supply for that Circuit, and that the Connexional Officers be empowered to make such other arrangements as they may deem advisable."

It was with great difficulty that the deputation, Messrs. Molineux and Peters, succeeded in obtaining my release from the circuit. During the ensuing six months, in visiting different circuits, and attending missionary and other meetings, I passed through a series of labour and excitement which threatened me with mental and physical prostration. My visits to Ickornshaw, Clitheroe, New Mills, Hull, Rochdale, Darlington, and the Manchester circuits, with the solid tokens of real friendship and kindness—by which, at the antipodes, I am surrounded—made an imperishable impression on my mind and heart.

As our vessel sailed from London and Southampton, we had an opportunity of visiting the great metropolis. Its magnitude, grandeur, and traffic, exceeded all my conceptions. We visited the principal buildings, and spent one day at the world's fair, held within the precincts of the Crystal Palace; and in surprise, astonishment, and wonder, gazed upon the countenances, costumes, productions, and manufactures of the world. For more than three weeks, while in London, we were hospitably entertained in the domestic circle of the Rev. Robert Eckett; and had opportunities of social and religious converse with many of our friends of the Association in that city. I here record my feelings of respect and esteem for the talents and probity of that gentleman; and also the grateful feeling which will ever be cherished by myself, Mrs. Townend, and niece, towards his amiable and benevolent wife, and the other branches of that interesting family. Our stay at Mr Eckett's formed a kind of breakwater to the deep and rapid current of sorrow and excitement.

On my last Sabbath but one in England, I preached three

times in the Bury chapel, to overflowing congregations, and made collections for the school; then came the valedictory service in Lever-street Chapel, Manchester, Monday night; and the farewell tea-meeting at Grosvenor street Chapel, Tuesday night; and the leaving next morning pierced my soul. Still, we were going to London, and our home was to be at Mr. Eckett's house; and even the journey by rail was made pleasant, by persons in our society being in the same carriage with us. On Friday, May 9th, 1851, we bade farewell to Mr. Eckett and family, and on the wings of steam we had a pleasant and pensive ride to Southampton. What a change from a commodious house to a narrow berth, in the thronged and dirty ship; in our berth of which there was not room to kneel or sit, except upon the bed! We soon, however, got accustomed to the change. On the next Sabbath we worshipped in Southampton; and in the evening, at the Wesleyan Chapel, Mr. Leigh, a returned missionary, preached; and in his opening and concluding prayer mentioned our ship "The Asia," and in the most earnest and feeling manner commended us to God. We retired to our floating home, having been much blest by the service in which we had been engaged.

JOURNAL ON BOARD SHIP.

May 12, 1851. Monday morning, quarter past nine—amid the clatter of ropes, shouting of sailors, removal of breakfast tins, and adjusting of boxes—our ship, loosed from her moorings, slowly moved out of the Southampton Docks. Some were weeping, waving hats and handkerchiefs, but the major part were full of bustle. Though much excited at the thought of leaving my native country, and casting a prospective glance at a three or four months voyage, yet the scene was enchanting, the sea calm, and the morning fine. Three or four of the passengers, contrary to orders, had strolled into the town, and were left behind; who at some risk, in an old leaky boat, and at considerable expense, were brought after us. Mr. Hall, one of the owners, accompanied us as far as the Needles; also the Rev. Mr. Faithful, father of our chief mate, and another gentleman. After shaking hands, these gentlemen got into the pilot boat and returned. I stood much affected at this last farewell scene; and the little boat soon disappeared. I felt happy though sorrowful, and said within myself, "God bless Old England." We soon passed St. Alban's Head, and saw only, here and there, a vessel on the wide expanse.

Tuesday 13. Second day at sea. We had a good night; I rose at six, and shaved with great ease. This operation at sea I had much dreaded. A fine morning and favourable breeze. Many are sick, but most are able to go on deck. We have forty-two children under ten years of age; their crying, laughing, and tumbling, with the grunting of hogs, barking of dogs, bleating of sheep, and the cackling of poultry, give an air of rural life to the scene. Mrs. Townend and niece are squeamish, but I am regularly sea sick.

Wednesday 14. Third day. Last night cold, not much wind, a good night; this morning fine breeze, six knots (miles) an hour. There is something to do, especially for the mess mate; fetching water, food, washing dishes, &c., and preparing, carrying, and fetching the meals from the cook's galley. Our ship is like a bee-hive. Spoke a vessel bound for England. Rather better of sea sickness.

Thursday 15. Fourth day. On the poop at six; rather cloudy; many are quite sick; and the messes broken up. We are, for convenience, divided into messes, eight or more in company. In this respect we are very comfortable. There are our three selves, two young ladies from Scotland, the Rev. J. Tester, and granddaughter. I am happy in God, but pensive, and bowed down with sea sickness. Oh how I should enjoy a cup of tea with a friend in England. Sea sickness, sea biscuit, and a rocking table, are sorry things. Such utter prostration and loathing! Yet we have many things on account of which to be thankful.

> "There's mercy in every place,
> And mercy, encouraging thought,
> Gives even affliction a grace,
> And reconciles man to his lot."

Friday 16. Fifth day at sea. Rose early; a fine morning; spoke a steamer to starboard, and a bark to larboard, both bound for England. A decided improvement in the health of the passengers. Some are indulging in levity, wine, cards, songs, and dancing.

Saturday 17. Sixth day. Rather cloudy, wind unfavourable. Some were frightened in the night by the changing of the position of the sails. A fine day, but little progress. We are much amused by the appearance and playfulness of porpoises gambolling round our ship.

Sabbath 18. Seventh day. Our first Sabbath at sea. A steady

breeze: most seem to know that it is Sunday; better clothes, less levity. At eleven A.M. the union-jack was spread, and the bell tolled the hour for prayer. At the tolling of the bell, and muster for worship, I wept. We have a clergyman of the Established Church on board, with his wife and nine children; and he, in his clerical robes, conducted worship. The singing of the morning hymn, and the entire service, I very much enjoyed. It was announced that I should preach at three P.M. There was a good attendance; the high church party, as if from fear of taint, keeping at a respectful distance. I spoke with freedom from "But this I say, brethren, the time is short." O blessed Sabbath! O delightful worship! We should have had prayers in the evening, but our cook filled his boiler with salt water instead of fresh, which was not discovered until we were all seated for tea. What pulling of faces, and what a stir with the captain and our ill-tempered cook. That evening I saw a whale.

Monday 19. Eighth day. Rather sick; fine morning, and steady breeze: six knots per hour during night. The sea looks grand: beautiful variegated colours from the bursting crescent. Porpoises play cheerfully around our floating dwelling. Our neighbour, yesterday a-head, is now astern, scarcely discernible. How gallantly our ship rides the foaming waves. All looks well. "O that men would praise the Lord for his goodness, and for his wonderful works to the children of men!"

Tuesday 20. Ninth day at sea. Last night a very strong breeze from the north-west: such rolling and heaving; many of us were not a little disturbed. It seemed as if we were about to be tumbled out of our hard and narrow beds, and the vessel thrown on one side. About one in the morning, one of the sails was split with the violence of the wind, and the vessel rolled from side to side, upsetting our plates, pannikins, barrels, &c.: such rolling, jumbling, tumbling, rattling, so as to keep awake most of the passengers; some laughing, others crying and screaming, and a few raising their hearts to God for his protection. Afternoon. The breeze continues; the day very fine. The last twenty-four hours we have made 212 knots. Glory be to God!

Wednesday 21. Tenth day. Last night we spoke the "Marian Watson," bound for England. She would report, "The 'Asia' off the coast of Spain: all well." A good night. Mrs. Townend rather sick; a nice breeze; very pleasant sailing. Boxes brought upon deck, that what is wanted may be got out. We are like a company of gipsies. At four P.M. we spoke by trumpet a small craft from Alexandria, bound to Londonderry. She would report "The 'Asia' all well." Weather warm and beautiful.

Thursday 22. Eleventh day at sea. We have had a good night; some have been free with the fire-water; on account of which the captain has locked up the wine and spirit stores. A petition is being handed round, to the effect that the petitioners hate drunkenness as much as the captain, but wish the stores to be opened. I and my friend Mr. Brown refused to sign. A young clerical student is very active, and other influential passengers, who pant for the burning liquor. I find teetotalism to be very useful at sea. We are almost becalmed.

Friday 23. Twelfth day. A good night. Up early; fine morning, but little progress. Thermometer 68° in the shade. Called together by the captain; who complained, that a senior and influential passenger had been teaching insubordination to the passengers. He, as *commander* of the ship, whilst upon the high seas, was determined to punish all offenders. Drink is the cause of these disturbances. I am reading the "Seventh Vial." What a monster is popery! Hallelujah! her days are numbered.

Saturday 24. Thirteenth day. A most beautiful day; not much wind, but plenty of grog. In the night, two of Neptune's sons refused to obey the second mate, and had to be bound and confined. We have made Madeira, but it was not visible. Much disturbance through the rites of Bacchus. I here enter my solemn protest against the sale and use of alcoholic liquors, as social beverages, on board a ship. Here are sailors and passengers staggering, swearing, and smoking: some of them creeping into their berths, with lighted pipes, while in a state of intoxication, surrounded with combustible matter. Under such circumstances, what security can there be for life or property? We have a doctor who can administer medicine when called for; but the secret is, men like strong drink, and the sale is lucrative. Our third mate has been confined since the third day of sailing. "The way of transgressors is hard."

Sabbath, May 25. Fourteen days at sea. A most delightful day. What a stir last night upon the poop! glee-singing and dancing. It is eleven o'clock, Sabbath morning; the bell tolls solemnly. Our six midshipmen having adjusted the seats, and spread the British flag, stand three on each side of the braces, neat and clean. Our card-playing, dancing, and swearing student, clerks for us out of *the* book; and our clergyman, whom no one charges with being righteous over much, reads the prayers, and maintains his dignity at the hour of prayer. This solemn mockery is sickening to a pious mind, and is a burlesque to our crew. In the afternoon I spoke from Lamentations iii. 24; a good time, and numerous attendance. The Rev. J. Tester read the Scriptures, and offered prayer. At evening prayers, our clergyman read part of a sermon from "What must I do to be saved?" but it got dark, and he had to stop until a light could be brought. Upon the whole, this Sabbath passed pleasantly and profitably over. In the evening, whilst sitting on the stern of our floating home, I cast my eyes over the blue waters towards the land we had left. Sorrowfully and pensively I mused on the Sabbath scenes, and hallowed associations there. Tears rolled down my face, but no murmuring thought escaped my breast, believing that I was in the way of Providence, and of some service in my present position.

Monday 26. Fifteenth day. Beautiful morning; steady breeze; five knots per hour. Expecting soon to meet with the trade winds. What a magnificent firmament we beheld last night! I stood for some time alone on the forecastle, musing on the scene. Only a little past eight, and quite dark. It seems strange for the weather to get hotter as the days get shorter. I am happy in God my salvation.

Tuesday 27. Sixteenth day at sea. This morning I spoke to our young clergyman about his polka dancing with other of our fine folks last night in the dark upon the poop: I told him he had better give up his frolics, or else cease to take a leading part in our Sabbath devotions. He excused himself by saying he was not in *holy orders*, and that an ordained clergyman ought not to act as he did. I told him, he and others were making our Sabbath prayers contemptible. We sail most delightfully. The weather is very warm, and the sun is nearly vertical. At twelve at noon, my shadow is about a foot long.

Wednesday 28. Weather fine and warm. Our gallant ship, in full sail, glides imperceptibly upon the glassy ocean. We are now off the Canary Islands, but have no land in sight. Through mercy we are all well. I have finished the "Seventh Vial." What scenes and sufferings have God's saints endured! But they looked for a better inheritance; and upon the mother of harlots, God will avenge their blood.

"Rome shall perish; write that word
In the blood that she has spilt:
Perish, hopeless and abhorred,
Deep in ruin as in guilt."

I long to be holy and useful; that when my pilgrimage on earth shall cease, I may meet with martyrs, confessors, friends, and relatives in that better country. North lat. 27° 13'; west long. 22° 15'.

Thursday 29. We are sailing on, and getting into the trade winds, and near the tropics; not a sight of land since we left St. Alban's Head, and not likely to see any until we get near Adelaide. Heaven speed us well!

Friday 30. Nineteenth day at sea. A strong breeze carrying us on seven knots per hour. Just entering the tropic of Cancer. Many are drunk; how unthankful, wicked, and debasing! It is very wrong to sell strong liquor on board, or, indeed, anywhere else, merely as a beverage. How thankful I feel for true religion and teetotalism. Our water is very bad and scarce. Filters, oranges, lemons, figs, cheese, jams, and oaten bread, are very useful.

May 31. Twentieth day at sea. A good night, and fine morning: splendid sailing—eight knots per hour. We spoke a ship to larboard—the "Columbus," bound to South America, out from London twenty-five days. We generally speak by signals. Many are squeamish, and some very sick: my dear wife is poorly: I am sick, but just able to write a line. Happy in Jesus.

Sabbath, June 1, 1851. Twenty-first at sea. Propitious gale. Prayers, and short sermon from the Storm on the Lake. Not much point. "Good men have difficulties and troubles, they must look to God." No caution to our wicked passengers, or reference to our voyage! Evidently written for landsmen. Service at three P.M.; captain and lady present. Mr. Tester led the devotions. I spoke from 1 Peter iv. 17—A solemn time. There is some improvement in morals; the captain says I am right, and he will put down the night dancing. In the evening we had prayers. A very good Sabbath. Thank God.

Monday 2. A very good breeze—eight knots per hour; we made Cape de Verde at five this morning, but it was not discernible. A fine ship is passing. Flying-fish and porpoises in abundance. Our water is bad. Some have filters; others drink it mixed with vinegar and sugar. All well, and in good spirits. Three weeks at sea.

Tuesday 3. Twenty-third day at sea. Very hot; last night tossing and broiling—not much sleep; we are weak and sickly. A sea-voyage like this requires fortitude. Some on board would be glad to be back in England. A brisk and favourable wind. Hoping in a week to make the *line*. Thermometer 78°. We are in good company at our end of the ship.

Wednesday 4. Twenty-fourth day at sea. Another tropical night is past. A fine breeze. I have just had a misfortune: having taken a tin of ox-tail soup to the cook's galley, by the lurching of the ship, the tin was upset, and the contents lost. Our cook is a saucy fellow, and insisted on my cleaning it up; but the first mate taught him better. Mrs. Townend has just had a heavy fall, but, through mercy, is none the worse. We have passed a French brig, probably laden with sugar from the West Indies. We have many Irish passengers, who behave better than the English. A strong north-east wind bears us on gloriously. My head is too hot to read much.

Thursday 5. Twenty-fifth day at sea. A fine wind in the night. I have slept well, and have not any sickness. Boxes up and opened. What a scene! Very hot and little wind. Mrs. Townend is better. We seem all in better spirits.

Friday 6. Twenty-sixth day. How beautiful the moon and stars were last night! Not much wind and very hot—nearly becalmed. 7° North latitude.

"O for a prosperous breeze,
To waft us o'er these burning seas."

Saturday 7. Twenty-seventh day at sea. How rapidly, towards evening, the sun, as if tired of his own heat, hastens to dip in the ocean! And how little twilight compared with what there is at home! Tropical heat is very trying to some constitutions. This morning, at six, a splendid rainbow and teeming shower.

Sabbath 8. Twenty-eighth day. Slow progress and intense heat. Another noise last night about twelve o'clock; the captain struck one of the sailors, who in return knocked down the captain; the chief mate and others knocked down the tar, and the captain gave him several severe blows in the face. Some of the passengers think themselves insulted by the captain. Many of the passengers were much alarmed by this drunken nocturnal skirmish. I have just returned from church, as we call it; thin attendance; no sermon. The sailors are in the dumps, respecting the skipper's conduct last night towards one of their number. I spoke in the afternoon from Peter's Deliverance out of Prison. The few that fear God were encouraged.

Monday, June 9. Twenty-ninth day. Almost a dead calm and very hot. Some 2000 miles from land, with anything but a good understanding between captain and crew; and a number of drunken, gambling passengers. One of these sons of the ocean came the other Sabbath devoutly to prayers; and not being able to find the place in his book, soberly asked of his comrade, "Where the ——— is it!" And not hearing an announcement, in true sailor style, asked, "What did the —— fool say!" Poor Jack!

Tuesday 10. Thirtieth day. Four weeks at sea. No wind, the sea like a lake. As some of our male passengers were sleeping on the poop last night, a rude young fellow diverted himself by pouring water in their faces. He has just been tried on the forecastle for his offence, and condemned to sit until some dozen buckets of salt water were dashed in his face. He came off the forecastle, like a drowned rat, professing to have enjoyed the sport.

Wednesday 11. Thirty-first day. Cloudy and rain. Shouts of "Squall! squall!" Two conflicting winds in the north-east; the sea is black and high—"There! there it comes!" And just as the reefs were finished, we were in the storm. Our gallant ship was driven out of her course for a short time. Such rain I never saw before: immediately the atmosphere was cooled. It is a humorous sight to see tars and gentlemen clad in southwesters, dabbling in the rain like ducks. Now we have a gentle breeze in the right direction. We are yet six degrees from the line.

Thursday, June 12. Thirty-second day. We were awoke this morning and ordered to close our port-holes; a heavy squall was upon us: for two hours we had heavy rain but not much wind: a heavy swell a-head, caused our vessel to pitch: headaches and sickness prevailed. We hope to fall in with the trade-winds to take us across the line. What with cooking, washing of utensils, nursing, and cleaning of children, we are a noisy community. I often commune with myself on privileges and friendships gone by. O God, bring us safely to the land we seek; that we may love, and be beloved; do good, and get good: Lord, bless our churches!

Friday 13. Thirty-third day. Still three or four degrees north the equator. Thermometer 83°, but the air much cooled by the heavy rain. The squalls from the south-west, just give time to reef top-sails. Our old ship pitches so as to turn many sick, as bad as at first. Pots, tins, water-barrels, &c., continually tumbling and jumbling: I am very sick, throwing off my stomach all I take. My dear wife is unwell, but very cheerful: I am surprised and comforted by her fortitude. Amelia, Messrs. Brown and Taylor are well. Last night, with an empty stomach, and grieved with the levity and utter lack of morality on the part of our two Sabbath officials, I returned to my cabin. Having committed myself and all on board to God's care, I fell asleep. About three in the morning, I awoke out of an awful dream. I thought I was at Rawtenstall, all our family then alive: an awful thunderstorm swept over the country: I saw the chapel fall, and heard the terrible crash, and awoke in terror; when the vessel was pitching awfully. I sat up, looked round, and considered whether I should wake my wife, and prepare for the danger; thinking that the dream might be sent as a warning. Suddenly I felt calm, as if in the arms of Jesus: I laid down again, and fell asleep. I am happy and confident I am in my providential path.

Saturday 14. Thirty-fourth day. A beautiful day, fresh breeze, not so hot. We have now passed the variable winds, and region of squalls. Still three degrees north the equator. I have sat several hours on the poop to-day, pensively nibbling some of the nice things our good friends in England gave us. Shall we ever meet again on earth!

Sabbath, June 15. Thirty-fifth day at sea. Delightful sailing, seven miles an hour. At eleven the capstan was covered with the British flag, and the bell tolled for church. Our ocean sons not present, the captain having closed the grog stores. At three P.M., I preached from John v. 28, 29. Solemn time. I could be distinctly heard in every part of the ship. I am not nice about introductions: speak about forty minutes: I am said to be the only preacher on board. God is with me. Prayers, and a short sermon in the evening, from Mr. P*****, our clergyman, who treats me kindly, only keeps a respectful distance during our service. The day was very pleasant, not a sail was touched. Sabbath is my best day; still, I sigh when I think on Sabbaths and privileges at home.

Monday 16. We slept well last night, a good wind and pleasant day; flying-fish, and here and there a nautilus, or "Spanish man-of-war,"—so called—a curious little fish, riding upon the wave with its sails spread to catch the breeze. At ten this morning we made the equator without having any nonsense amongst the sailors, about old Neptune and his sons, We had got fourteen knots into the tropic of Cancer before we knew that we had crossed the line. Summer being now north the equator, we have now comfortable weather. There is gladness amongst us, now that we have made the line so soon, and that without any serious accident or death. My head is bad, sickness scarcely kept off: I am weary of sitting, stand long I cannot, and walking turns me giddy: cannot read much; pensive, but not fretful; I look backward toward England—forward toward Australia—and upward toward heaven—then, wiping the scalding tears from my face, say, "Thy will, my God, Thy will be done."

Tuesday 17. Thirty-seventh day. We have had rather a tossing night; but now we have a beautiful day and good wind; we are three degrees south latitude; warm, but not hot. Passengers' health much better: much talk about how long the passage is likely to be.

Wednesday 18. Thirty-eighth day, Another beautiful day, with moderate breeze. I am languid, but not sick. Our ship's company are seated in groups, reading, writing, knitting, sewing; small schools superintended by parents, governesses, and others. There is far less finery than at first; and real worth begins to be appreciated. The evenings are long, quite dark at seven. The stars and planets seem nearer than they do in England. We have left the North-star below the horizon, and the "Great Bear" will soon disappear in like manner. The chambers of the south are being unlocked, and constellations more numerous and more brilliant invite our gaze. When tired of star-gazing, we lean over the bows and sides of our floating house, and behold the beautiful phosphorus light, in its wonderful variegated hues, fantastically playing on the ocean.

Thursday 19. Thirty-ninth day. I am better; fine sailing. We have had a sham duel, creating senseless mirth. I am reading the life of the Rev. H Moore, in which are some very affecting relations. What numbers are gone to glory! Oh, may I live and die in Christ's cause, and spend a blessed eternity with them in the better land! Amen, amen!

Friday 20. Fortieth day at sea. A very strong breeze from the south producing a head sea; vessel lurching and pitching, and lying on one side; it is very difficult to move, such tumbling and upsetting of dishes; some laughing, others crying; indeed, we have here a sore life. I have just read the last book in Pollok's "Course of Time," beginning with—

> "God of my fathers! Holy, just, and good,
> My God, my Father, my unfailing hope!"

It has proved a cordial to my spirit, and inspired me with the fortitude to endure, with cheerful submission, all the ills of life.

Saturday 21. We have a head wind, tacking to keep off the American coast, being only ninety miles from land. Ship's motion very trying. I am languid and poorly to-day; rather disposed to be fretful. My Father, help me! South lat. 10°; west lon. 37° 20′.

Sunday 22. Last night was very wet: fine morning, a dead calm; very unusual in these latitudes: numbers of sharks, whales, and grampuses, play about our ship. When under the water and near the surface, these monsters of the deep look very beautiful. Occasionally they roll their huge carcases upon the surface, and, snorting, send up a volume of water, as from a large water engine. We were cut short in our morning prayers by a sudden squall of rain and wind. I spoke in the afternoon from Rev. iii. 20, a very solemn service, but cut short by the near approach of the Naiad, from Liverpool, forty-five days out, bound for St. Francisco. It was quite a treat to see the little bark hoist our national flag, and speak to her floating neighbour. The night was squally and the tea late; so we had no evening service.

Monday, June 23. Forty-three days out at sea. Six weeks upon the deep. Thank God, He has been with us in our trials, and many are past. We have had a very uneasy wet night, the poor tars are tired out. Now a change; wind south-west-south: we are all pleased: I am better: Mrs. T., niece, Messrs. Brown and Taylor, well.

Tuesday 24. Forty-fourth day. A beautiful day, not much wind, and too much from the quarter towards which we wish to steer. Just spoke a small merchant vessel, out sixty-three days from Boston, bound for Buenos Ayres. Poor fellows! they have been three weeks becalmed upon the line. She came very close to us. We have had our bed and cabin well drenched, by the water washing in at our porthole, left open to air the place. I have had several foul falls: it is very dangerous: God be gracious to us all!

Friday 27. A fine windy day with a little rain: our course east by south; much cheered.

Saturday 28. Forty-eighth day. A very fine day and favourable wind; our course being almost direct east: south lat. 12° 41'; west lon. 30° 42'. It seems we went a little north yesterday, but gained considerably in longitude. The extra motion has upset me again; violent vomiting; so weak I can scarcely walk. The doctor has ordered me arrow-root with a little brandy in it. Upon the whole, so far, to me the voyage has been painful. God help us past the stormy Cape!

Sabbath, June 29. Forty-ninth day out. A fine day, good wind; prayers morning and evening. I preached in the afternoon, from "Which is Christ in you, the hope of glory?"

Monday 30. Seven weeks out. A long time to be out of sight of terra firma. Lovely morning. In all our trials the Lord has been gracious. We are sailing direct south; I am better. South lat. 14° 48'; west lon. 31° 21'. Thermometer steady at 76°. At a distance of some 400 miles we are passing St. Helena, to which island Napoleon was banished.

Tuesday, July 1, 1851. Fine sailing. Boxes up; what a stir! some of the boxes are damp, clothes spoiling. Most of the passengers in health and spirits.

Wednesday 2. Sailing steadily due south, five knots per hour. South lat. 18° 29'; west lon. 32° 9'. Again I am very sick; but cheered with the thought that we are half way.

Thursday 3. Very fine and good wind. South lat. 20° 49'.

Friday, July 4. Fifty-fourth day out. Since twelve o'clock yesterday a splendid breeze: south lat. 23° 7'; west lon. 30° 45'. Praise the Lord, we are now leaving the tropics; it is light in the morning at half-past six, and dark about the same time in the evening. The moon, three days old, looks very beautiful. The sun sets grandly; a light purple sky, with the deep red in the horizon, and the variegated clouds in grotesque figures, make the scene truly enchanting. Whilst I am writing, our water is being measured out; the water smells very badly. We have a great deal of nonsense; this evening we are to have a play. Our clergyman and student swear when irritated. Petty thefts are not uncommon.

Saturday 5. Fifty-fifth day. Though here it is now winter, it is warm; we put on our upper coats to sit on deck in the evening only. Albatrosses and Cape pigeons are occasionally to be seen. South lat. 24° 50'; west lon. 30° 39'.

Sabbath 6. Another fine day; midshipmen, mates, and sailors clean: a good wind, right course: south lat. 27° 4'; west lon. 28° 17'. Prayers, morning and evening. I spoke in the afternoon, from

Isaiah xl. 6, 7, 8. Mr. S. Taylor of Manchester led the singing: I had great liberty in speaking, and the service was numerously attended. Bless the Lord, he gives me favour with our floating community! but whilst we enjoy these privileges, Oh, how we pant once more to enter the sanctuary on terra firma.

Monday 7. Fifty-seventh day. Not much wind; rolling waves; expecting a breeze from the west. We are within the influence of Cape Horn. Oh, for a prosperous sail round the Cape of Good Hope. South lat. 28° 38′; west lon. 26°.

Tuesday 8. Almost a calm. South lat. 30° 8′; west lon. 26° 40′.

Wednesday 9. Fifty-ninth day. Weather fine, breeze springing from the north-west, just what we want. South lat. 30° 48′; west lon. 25° 48′. This morning, a beautiful brig, a slaver (most likely) from Rio Janeiro, bound to the Cape Coast, passed under our bows. Thank God! our country does not now deal in human flesh. We are all well. Our floating community presents a busy scene; several Cape pigeons have been caught. A vessel is astern.

Friday 11. A steady north-western breeze bears us on east by south-east. Yesterday, and to-day, the sun has been beclouded, so that no observation as to our whereabout could be taken. The cold appearance of the sky and sea, forcibly reminds us of a cold December day at home. Our ship is placarded for a play, "Othello," this evening. I must say, I think these sports out of place; surrounded as we are by danger. I am getting stronger, being able to walk, read, and think; I have been pleased and profited by reading the life of the Rev. Henry Moore.

Saturday 12. Fine day, good progress; seven knots per hour. South lat. 31°. 40′; west lon. 18° 38′. Cape pigeons, albatrosses, and stormy petrels, or, as the sailors term them, "Mother Carey's chickens," fly in groups about our stern, or float upon the troubled wave. All well, except one female, who has never recovered from sea-sickness.

Sunday 13. Sixty-third day out. Very wet. This morning at two o'clock, a sudden squall, and all our sails out: a terrible stir! such shouting, rolling, tumbling, and confusion; it was truly frightful. Only prayers below in the evening; a very trying Sabbath.

Monday 14. Still wet and squally, our course in the right direction, and very rapid. We had a sorry night; slipping off the bed feet, and then tumbled backwards neck and heels; shut up to hear the filthy conversation of the wicked. We hope to see better and brighter days.

Wednesday 16. Very wet and squally. We have had two fearful nights; last night, from ten to two, a perfect gale. We are yet about 6000 miles from Adelaide. We have eleven and a half hours of daylight. Thermometer 64°. South lat. 34° 30'; west lon. 6° 20'. Our keel is loaded with small coal; and to-day they are using means to guard against the coal taking fire. Many of the beds are wet. Our Father cares for us!

Thursday 17. Five days almost constant rain. Last night about twelve we were taken aback; the wind suddenly changed, and blew strong in our teeth, flap back went the sails, and the vessel was in imminent peril. Our second mate was on watch: he ran and called up the first mate, who, without his clothes, rushed on deck. The masts were in danger of being carried away; two or three minutes longer, and the masts must have gone, or the ship have been driven stern down into the sea. Thank God, all is well.

Friday 18. What a change; very fine. South lat. 34°; west lon. 3° 26'.

Sunday 20. Seventy days out. Yesterday very fine, but cold: good wind after a stormy night. South lat. 34° 4'; west lon. 20'. In going down the hatchway to dinner, the ladder having been put to the windward side, and the vessel leaning on the lee side, my foot slipped, and with great violence I fell to the bottom. Quite sick! and very much shaken, I was put to bed. Thank God! though very sore, I can stir about. The war of elements, and bad human passions, make our floating dwelling very uncomfortable. During the last week, our clergyman's wife and the family governess have been fighting. Two of our best sailors are laid aside; one with fighting, and the other by a fall. This morning we are all noise and bustle, the small coal in the keel having choked the pumps: and this must be attended to immediately, consequently there can be no service. Mrs. Roskel is very ill; and Mrs. Henry died this forenoon; she was a fine healthy woman when she left Ireland; but never got over her sea-sickness: she has left a husband, and seven children. South lat. 36° 30'; east lon. 2° 28'.

Monday 21. Funeral at sea. About eleven A.M. the tolling bell told that the body of the late Mrs. Henry was to be committed to the deep. The body—stitched in canvass, and heavily weighted at the feet, stretched upon a bier, covered with the national flag—

was borne by four sailors, from her cabin to the leeward gangway; poor Mr. Henry and his two eldest sons following. The silence was only broken, by my reading "I am the resurrection and the life, &c." At her particular request, I conducted the service; and on reading the words, "We therefore commit her body to the deep;" the bier was gently raised, and in a moment, the corpse was plunged into the unfathomable ocean. South lat. 37°; east lon. 6° 10′. The youngest child is likely soon to follow its mother.

Tuesday 22. Very stormy through the night; pumps choked, and passengers alarmed. We have one case of delirium tremens. East lon. 10° 14′. God be merciful to us.

Wednesday 23. Wet, and becalmed several hours.

Friday, July 25. A fine cold day; the two last nights have been very, very trying. Yesterday, at three P.M., two large water spouts rose to windward; the sky looked fearful, and just as our sail was taken in, the storm came upon us with great violence, and continued until midnight. At times the rolling was truly alarming. East lon. 16° 20′.

Saturday 26. The stormy Cape we are now rounding; a fine day and strong breeze: our main decks never dry. Royals, and main, and studding sails all down. Thermometer 54°; east lon. 20° 10′. The scene is awfully grand. God of the waves, preserve us!

Sabbath 27. Seventy-seventh day at sea. Morning prayers between decks; squally afternoon. By the captain's request, I now take the evening instead of the afternoon service, which I much prefer. I improved the death of Mrs. Henry from the words, "The living know that they shall die," Eccles. ix. 5. A solemn service, and a very large attendance. East lon. 24° 34′. A splendid run in twenty-four hours.

Monday 28. Very good night, and fine day. Calm from seven A.M. to one P.M. We are leaving Cape Coast, and entering the Indian Ocean. Hundreds of whale birds, very small, and can fly fast. East lon. 27° 1′.

Tuesday 29. North-east wind very high: sea washing over the decks perpetually. We never saw the sea so rough before. One of our male passengers was very near being washed off the poop. Mrs. T. and I had just left the poop. We are crossing Mozambique Channel; south lat. 39° 38′; east lon. 30° 3′. O Lord, preserve us! A beautiful sunset last night, at ten minutes past five—we are ninety-five minutes before Greenwich time—at which time there was an almost total solar eclipse visible in England.

Wednesday, July 30. Strong north-east breeze: about a quarter before ten A.M. a cross sea broke over the ship, and carried away our weather bulwarks. A condensed body of water rolled as high as our topmast, and the report was as loud as if the ship had struck with fearful violence upon a rock. I was upon the poop holding on and saw the whole affair. The water rushed down the hatchways as if the sea had been let in upon us; and some of the berths were filled, boxes were floated, and broken with the shock. One lady was completely drenched while in bed; Mrs. T. was in her cabin, and sickened at the sight. One young man, unaccustomed to pray, was heard to say, "Lord Jesus, have mercy upon us, the old ship has struck upon a —— rock." Such screaming and terror; our first mate up to the middle in water, crying, "All's right! all's right!" My prayer was, "O Lord, moderate the wind, and save us." Thank God no person is seriously hurt, and the wind somewhat abated; south lat. 40° 48'; east lon. 34° 18'.

Thursday 31. A sudden fearful squall this morning: wind changed to north-west: fine dry sailing, and drying of wet and spoiled clothes. May God bless the sittings of the Annual Assembly: no Townend there; frequently, Thomas, Elisha, and myself, were present. Three years since, this day, Elisha went to heaven. I am sorrowful, but happy.

Friday, August 1, 1851. Beautiful sailing, thermometer 60°; east lon. 39°. The captain's lady very ill. The bad weather has left me very weak. Mrs. Townend is but poorly; most of our passengers are reduced in strength and injured in appearance.

Saturday, August 2. Boisterous and wet; east lon. 43°.

Sunday 3. Eighty-fourth day at sea. Yesterday strong south-west breeze, rough and squally. Prayers in the morning. Mr. Henry's baby, aged eight months, died; just fourteen days after its mother: I read the funeral service; and, in the presence of our ship's company, at five P.M., committed the body to the deep. I preached in the evening from Luke xvi. 31.; very good attendance, and a deeply solemn time. Our course is rapid; weather very cold and trying; east lon. 51° 30'.

Monday 4. Thank God! the strong south-west wind holds out, and though the weather is cold and the sea rough, yet we get on rapidly. Yesterday Mrs. Townend and I had very heavy falls: Oh how thankful we should be that our limbs are not broken; east lon. 56°.

Wednesday 6. Yesterday, in the afternoon, the wind from the

north-west blew a perfect gale. Oh the majesty and awful grandeur of Old Ocean, when roused to anger by the continued lashings of the furious winds. For the last three months we have never seen land—

> " Our pillow has been the ocean wave,
> Our home upon the deep."

I stood with surprise and awe, when, without any hyperbole, the sea rose mountains high: and what a night! I really thought at times that the ship was sinking; such pitching, rolling, and lurching. What thoughts ran through my mind of the land we had left, perhaps never more to see; its Sabbaths, sanctuaries, and friendships: our present condition, and the uncertain future, whether we should see the land of our adoption. All pressed sore upon me: but I did not repent the step I had taken; and casting myself upon the merits of my Saviour, I felt, that "for me to live was Christ, but to die would be gain." Still, when I thought of the number of wicked persons on board, and of the work in which we had embarked, I did most earnestly pray, as I have ever done, that we might be preserved, and blessed in our work. Mrs. Townend and Amelia are as well as could be expected. This morning the wind has died away, but there are heavy swells, and the sea looks surly, as if remembering the lashings of yesterday: east lon. 60° 5'.

Thursday 7. Eight hours calm; a good night; east lon. 62° 19'.

Friday 8. Very good south-west breeze, fine and cold; east lon. 67°.

Saturday 9. Charming sailing, but rather hazy weather; east lon. 70° 14'.

August 10th. Sabbath-day. A gale from the north-west; the wind changed to south-west at four P.M.: prayers in the morning, no sailors present. Our evening service was numerously attended. Text, Heb. ii. 10.

August 11. Ninety-one days out at sea. Just passed the islands of St. Paul, and Amsterdam; we are in a latitude too high to see them. The day is fine, and cold; passengers in health and spirits, all prophesying when we shall see land, or make Adelaide. South lat. 41° 7'; east lon. 80° 19'. The Lord be praised, and may we still be preserved.

Tuesday 12. Last night was about the roughest we have had,

the wind changing to the south-west. We awoke with our heads downwards; the wind roaring, the vivid lightning glaring, and the rain descending in torrents. What a terrible noise of shouting, roaring, and rattling of feet and ropes! The day is squally, with intervals of sunshine. East lon. 84° 20′.

Wednesday 13. Some fearful rolling, and shipping of seas from our stern portholes and the hatchways, still our cooking fires can be kept in. Most of the company are in good health, and we are talking of landing by Sunday or Monday week. Our preachers at home will be in their circuits before me. God bless them! South lat. 41°; east lon. 88° 30′.

Thursday 14. Fine south-west breeze; frequent squalls of rain and hail: thermometer 48. South lat. 41° 10′; east lon. 92° 35′.

Friday, Aug. 15. A good south-western wind; very cold, like a north-east wind in February at home. This morning I had another heavy fall: I am truly thankful that my limbs are not broken. South lat. 39° 44′; east lon. 96° 39′.

Saturday 16. South-west breeze; a very stormy night. One of the midship boys fell from the gaff of the driver upon the hen-roost, but was only shaken. This is the finest day we have had a long time. Lat. 38° 2′; lon. 101° 3′. Hallelujah!

Sabbath, August 17. Ninety-seventh day at sea. We have had twenty-four hours calm. Prayers in the morning: evening very large attendance, and good singing; we forgot we were in the ship. I had great liberty in speaking "On the Nature and Consequences of Infidelity." I am very thankful God is with us.

Monday 18. Fourteen weeks to-day since we left Southampton, or have seen land. A fine steady north-east wind, calm sea, and clear sky. Passengers in good spirits. East lon. 105° 25′. Praise the Lord!

Tuesday 19. Most delightful sailing. South lat. 39°; lon. 110°.

Wednesday, August 20. The one-hundredth day of sailing; and what a day of disappointment! The wind changed early this morning, and by nine o'clock blew a gale from the very quarter to which we wish to sail. The motion of the vessel is very trying, and a sea-sickness has taken hold of many. After two such fine days, and such cheering prospects of landing soon, we were ill-prepared for such a change. Lord, help us not to repine; and in thy own good time bring us safe to land!

Thursday 21. Last night very heavy rain, with a strong east

wind: just now, two P.M., the wind is dying away, and we anticipate a favourable change. We are happy. East lon. 101° 3′.

Saturday, August 23. South wind, so that we go pretty near our course. We are past the *Australian promontory*, Cape Lewin. Our spirits are cheered, but some of us rejoice with trembling. Last night a quarrel took place between our clergyman and Dr. Lewis; the former spitting in the face of the latter. Alas, for our adopted country, if it is to be supplied with such ministers and candidates for holy orders as are on board the 'Asia'!

Sabbath, August 24. One hundred and four days since we left Southampton. A serene and beautiful day. About six persons attended prayers this morning, and for the first time I absented myself. Evening service the largest attendance we have ever had: singing very good, and special unction attended the Word. Gen. xxxii. 9—13. We are expecting to see land to-morrow morning. South lat. 36°; east lon. 117° 4″.

Monday 25. Tossing night; afraid we may run upon the land, it being very dark. About midnight the ship was tacked off from the land. We had to change in our bed, so as not to lie with our heads downwards. What a bustling night! At early dawn, six o'clock this morning, what clapping of hands, and shouting! "Land, land! And a fair wind!" So it was: I saw it distinctly; and by the north-east breeze from off the land, we can make our course. Lat. 37° 2″; lon. 119°. Hallelujah, hallelujah!

Tuesday 26. Yesterday the vessel tossed with a strong wind; and heavy rain, as well, made it very unpleasant. Last night the wind roared terribly, and the old ship lying on one side dashed through the deep. The bows of the ship, with the phosphorus, seemed hung round with silvery lights, whilst the forecastle completely dipped itself in the sea. To-day we are pleasantly sailing before the wind, hoping that the breeze will continue, and heave us quickly to the land we seek. Many of the passengers are getting peevish and irritable: the food is very stale, and the desire to be ashore is so strong. What a mercy! We are all well. Lat. 36° 12′; lon. 121°.

Wednesday 27. We are sailing rapidly under mizen-topsail, main-topsail, main-gallant, fore, and foregallant-sail, direct east, before a strong western breeze. The great question is, "Shall we make Adelaide before Sabbath?" No more land to be seen before we reach Kangaroo Island. Weather warmer, and the atmosphere clearer when free from squalls.

Thursday 28. Last night we had a gale, with sheet-lightning: we got another good tossing. A lovely day: our ship with all her canvas spread sails gallantly before a steady south-wester. Lat. 32° 44'; lon. 128° 15'.

Friday 29. Strong west breeze. The old ship has been cleaned, that we may enter harbour decently. It seems as if we were going to have a holiday. We expect to reach Kangaroo Island to-morrow by noon. East lon. 132°.

Saturday 30. Lovely, like an April day at home; sky and sea appear like English. All is bustle and life, except our friend the Rev. J. Tester, who is very ill indeed. No one was more joyful at the thought of meeting friends and relatives in the new country. He has children and grandchildren in and about Adelaide. I trust his life will be spared. Whilst I write the sailors are hauling upon deck the cable, and from the poop and forecastle land can be seen. South lat. 35° 44'; east lon. 135°.

> "We've looked astern on many a storm,
> Which Christ hath brought us through:
> We're looking now ahead, and Lo!
> The land appears in view."

Sabbath, August 31. One hundred and eleven days out. At three o'clock this morning, we were suddenly awoke with the shout of, "All hands up! All hands up!" It turned out that we were close upon the western point of Kangaroo Island. Most of the male passengers ran up almost undressed; when, lo, the vessel was driving before a strong breeze, and was making right against the frightful rocks, which seemed as if a biscuit might be thrown upon them with ease; the females below were in the greatest fright; the ship, however, was instantly turned in the right direction. During the great alarm, Mrs. Townend was fast asleep, for, being very hard of hearing, she got many a sound sleep when I was wakeful with fear. About seven in the morning, the captain ordered the ship to be turned round, as he thought we had got to the wrong side of the island, but—the view being taken from the mast-head—it was found that we were in the right course; so with great joy the ship was again turned round, and a favourable breeze wafted us towards our adopted land. The day was still and hazy; no morning prayers. In the evening we had the most quiet and impressive service we ever held on board the 'Asia.' I spoke from Heb. ii. 10, and concluded with an address and farewell to those who were leaving us at Adelaide. At half-past eleven that night we dropped anchor in sight of the light-ship in Holdfast Bay, near Port Adelaide. Hallelujah to the Triune God! Oh! with what feelings of gratitude and joy did we lie down that night!

September 3, 1851. Yesterday, in the afternoon, while lying at anchor, the mail-boat came for letters, bringing Messrs. Gellingham, Tester, and Dare, all of Adelaide, to visit their relatives on board who had come out with us. Our ship lay seven miles from the port, and, simply to be brought to the ship, the party paid 3*l* 10*s*. The sea was running high at the time, and just as Messrs. Tester and Dare had got out of the boat, and were climbing up the bulwarks, the boat capsized, and the five watermen and Mr. Gellingham were swimming or sprawling in the water. It was an awful sight. Ropes, and the two life-buoys were thrown to the sufferers; and in a few minutes, all, except one man, were trembling and dripping upon the deck: the mail-boat, the wrong side up, was drifting away from the ship, and the poor fellow was sprawling upon the boat's bottom, and clinging to its sides. His loud cries for help, and look of despair, as the boat drifted further and further, were truly piercing: the waves now and then washing over him, and drowning his cries. At length our whaleboat was lowered and manned by our crew, and soon the man was rescued from his perilous situation. The names were then called, and to our great joy the coxswain cried out, "All hands safe!" Our brave fellows then went in pursuit of the mail-boat, and at considerable risk brought her to the ship: after all, she drifted and was lost, unless picked up elsewhere. The wind continued high, and at seven that evening our captain and several of our number came safe from the port; but well drenched by the sea washing over their boat. Our visitors and the five watermen durst not return that night, but remained with us until the morning. The boiler of the steam-tug having bursted, our Adelaide passengers, with their luggage, have to be landed in an old barge. Mr. Henry has just returned from port, and presented me with two loaves of *new* bread, a bunch of turnips, and a fine leg of mutton; which, under our circumstances, are princely presents. We are having fresh beef and potatoes to dinner. Our ship is all bustle—packing and cording of boxes, &c.

September 9. I am now sitting upon the poop, surrounded with the lovely scenery of Port Adelaide. We were a week in the Bay, until the tide rose sufficiently to allow our heavy ship to pass the *bar*, or sand-bank, near the mouth of the creek that runs up to the port. Yesterday morning, at ten, we weighed anchor, and by twenty minutes past three in the afternoon we safely crossed the bar. O how interesting and exciting it was to come so near the land, and to quaff the sweet fragrance brought by the balmy land-breeze! The creek is sufficiently wide to allow two or three vessels to pass in safety. On each side are cultivated patches of land, with here and there a wooden house, built in the rural English style, with out-houses for cattle, &c.—the larger houses like small chapels, standing out of the sand or water (which surrounds many of them in the rainy season), on large wooden props, formed from the stumps of trees. The basin at the port is about a quarter of a mile wide, and half a mile long. There are about fifty vessels lying at anchor, with numbers of small boats plying in every direction. The 'Blundell' and the 'Thetis' are lying close to us, having brought emigrants from England. On one side of the harbour are some twenty small wooden houses, built by watermen; and on the other side is the small town of Port Adelaide—containing three small places of worship, Church, Wesleyan, and Independent—several large warehouses, shops, and drunkeries. In the wet season, the place is almost one swamp. The bread, animal food, potatoes, butter, &c., are very good; and we are delighted with our change of food. Now the 'Adelaide' passengers are gone, we have more room, and are quiet in the ship; and we are expecting, in a day or two, once more to tread upon terra firma, it being seventeen weeks and a day since we came on board. Last Sabbath I preached on the Transfiguration of Jesus; which was the only service we held on board. We are all in good health, and thankful that we have made this distant port in safety: the weather is very wet and cold; it has been a terrible winter for rain; the last summer was unusually hot and dry. At present, provisions are dear.

Saturday, September 13. I went to Adelaide; Mrs. Townend not being very well, and the weather being unsettled, durst not venture with me. The road from the Port to Adelaide is very flat, and with the heavy rains, the country is almost one vast swamp: and on account of the pits and cart-ruts on the road, it is scarcely safe to ride, except on horseback. I called on Mrs. Dare, who came out with us, and enjoyed a cup of tea with the family, who are Wesleyans, and reside at Bowden, a village a mile and a half from the city.

Mr. Dare, jun., accompanied me to the city that night; we

reached North Adelaide about eight in the evening; it was quite dark, and a heavy storm of thunder and lightning occured just after he went, and left me in the Wellington Hotel for the night. I sat in a private parlour, on a wood-bottomed chair, by a log fire, reading Australian news until nine o'clock, when I rang the bell, and requested the landlord to show me my room; who said, "You must put on your hat, as you will have to go outside." This, like most of the houses here, is only one storey high. We went outside, the wind and rain beat furiously upon us, and in two minutes I was in my bedroom, which was low, damp, and cold, with bare white-washed walls and stone floor: a small table, one wood chair, glass, brush, comb, &c. The bed was small and very hard, but clean; I felt solitary; thoughts of home and bygone friendships rushed into my mind: then I thought of the ship, the stormy Cape, Mozambique Channel, and the dangers we had passed. With mingled tears of sorrow and thankfulness I knelt down, and committed myself, and relatives and friends, to the care of Almighty God; and had a very comfortable night. I had an excellent breakfast in the neat little parlour, and having paid two shillings for bed and breakfast, I wound my way to South Adelaide, which is better than a mile from where I slept. The road is very interesting, but like a neglected gentleman's park. I fell in with a Swiss and a German, both of whom delighted to tell me anything respecting the place. We crossed the wooden flat bridge over the river Torrens, which runs between North and South Adelaide. The late floods have carried away part of the banks, and one of the bridges. About half way between North and South Adelaide, on the banks of the river, there is a community of aborigines; there are from fifty to one hundred wurlies, or native huts; their log fires are near the mouth or entrance to the wigwams, and so arranged as always to have the fire to the lee side, so as to take off part of the smoke; as they creep in, the smoke meets them. The children, and frequently their mothers, are perfectly naked: even in the streets of South Adelaide, I have seen them with nothing upon them but an old piece of skin or cloth, carelessly thrown over one shoulder, and under the other arm, and by no means reaching below the knee: and whilst the men are both better clothed and fed, the females have to fetch the wood and water, and go out to beg. On arriving in South Adelaide, I enquired for the Wesleyan Chapel, and, it not being time for service, I went into the school. There were about one hundred children present; the school was being conducted in much the same way as schools are at home. The superintendent came and shook me by the hand; and on his asking if I belonged to the Society, I told him I had come out with the 'Asia,' and, as a Missionary on behalf of the Association, was going on to Melbourne. He enquired if I knew Mr. Gilchrist, and mentioned several of our Ministers of whom I could speak. I sat with him, and heard the Rev. Mr. Hull, who commenced the service by giving out, "Lo! God is here, &c." After the first prayer, the choir, the people all sitting, sang three verses of "Come Holy Ghost, our hearts, &c.," ending with, "Glory be to the Father, and to the Son, and to the Holy Ghost, &c." No musical instruments. After the lesson we sang, "Come let us who in Christ believe," and as I expected, he read for text, Rev. iii. 20: and preached a very impressive and superior sermon, concluding with, "When shall thy love constrain, and force me to thy breast."

The friend who had taken me by the hand said, "Now, you will do me the honour to make my humble cottage your home; and though I have to preach at the Port this afternoon and evening, I think you will be happy with my family; and we shall be very glad if you will give an address to the children of the Sabbath-school this afternoon." I thankfully accepted his kind offer, and found his name was William Orchard, a Wesleyan Local Preacher, late of Cornwall, Helston Circuit. I spoke to the children, went to see the community of aborigines; attended evening service; heard a good sermon from the superintendent, the Rev. Mr. Draper; remained at the prayer-meeting, and, at the request of Mr. Draper, engaged in prayer; had a sofa-bed in the dining-room of Mr. Orchard, and had the sweetest night's rest I have enjoyed since I left the home of my dear friend, the Rev. R. Eckett. Next morning Mr. Orchard took me round the suburbs of South Adelaide, and pointed out its intended future boundary. It was a serene morning and we had a delightful stroll. The governor's house, the post-office, banks, hotels, churches, and chapels, are beautiful buildings. The streets, crossing at right angles, are very wide, long, and even. The lungs, or park lands, around the city, are beautifully studded with the native gum tree. The public and private gardens are very fine, and emit a most delightful fragrance. The great drawback is the want of sewerage and of good roads. In the wet season the streets and roads are almost impassable; and in the dry season there is abundance of dust. On my way to the Port in the afternoon, I fell in with a fine young man, a ship-mate, and we walked on together. He told me that my dear friend and messmate, the Rev. J. Tester, had died that morning, at an inn in the Port. We came to the wharf by five p.m., but the wind was very high, and no boatman would take us to the ship under double fare, and would not pledge to bring us safely to the ship; so we were glad to take shelter from the wind and rain in a public eating-house; and, the storm increasing, we sorrowfully retired for the night to the chief hotel—the very house where the corpse of my friend Mr. Tester was lying. The landlord kindly showed me the body, and also gave me particulars respecting his death. Poor man! How frequently and fondly did he talk, during our long and trying voyage, of the happiness he anticipated in the bosom of his relatives and friends. Up to within a week of our dropping anchor in the Bay, no one on board enjoyed better health and spirits than he. He was sixty-three years of age, had left a small Baptist interest in the neighbourhood of Windsor; and now, I trust, rests in the peaceful harbour of eternal repose. How little we know of the future.

Monday, September 22. We are still lying in harbour, having to buy our own bread, milk, and other little comforts; and, except, which is rarely the case, we can obtain the ship's boat, it costs a shilling per head to go and return from the shore. We frequently cross the peninsula between the harbour and the sea, which is about a mile and a half wide, thickly wooded, with here and there a wood house. The coast is beautiful, abounding with shells, and offering fine facilities for sea-bathing. Yesterday morning Mrs. Townend accompanied me to church: about forty persons present. After prayers, the minister preached from Heb. xi. 13, gave a rapid sketch of the characters of Noah, Abraham, Jacob, and Job; published the banns of matrimony; and after preaching eighteen minutes, concluded by saying, "I have nothing further to add, but that in order that the Gospel may be preached in this place, a collection will now be made. The building of the new church is stopped for lack of funds; and Government aid being withheld from all denominations, churches must be supported on the voluntary principle, or cease to exist." In the afternoon I attended the Wesleyan service, held in a small wooden building; eighteen persons were present. Their new chapel is of Gothic structure, and will hold from two to three hundred. We cannot have service on board ship whilst in harbour, or I should have felt more pleasure in preaching to our ship's crew and passengers. Oh how I long for these days of imprisonment to be past! Our vessel is nearly cleared of cargo; but we have a superabundance of rats, which scamper over our beds, and over our faces, and disturb our rest. We are lying close to the ship 'Reliance,' from Plymouth. She has 300 passengers, and has had, up to the 22nd of September, twenty deaths.

Friday, September 26. This week my dear wife and niece have been with me to Adelaide; the weather is fine, and we were much pleased with our journey. We visited the wurlies (huts) of the aborigines, but the scene was so revolting, that we turned away with mingled feelings of sorrow, shame, and disgust.

Monday, September 29. Yesterday morning I heard the Rev. Mr. Hodge (Independent), at the Port; and in the evening at Albert Town, a mile on the Adelaide road. The services were edifying, especially in the morning. I had an interview with Mr. Hodge, who requested me to preach for him in the evening; but he not knowing me, and not being urgent, I declined. The weather is now very warm, as much so yesterday morning in the chapel as ever I felt it at home in July. If it be so hot here in September, what may we expect in January and February? We are in good health and spirits, the air is fine and clear.

Monday, October 6, 1851. Still in harbour, but weighing anchor, and expecting to sail for Port Philip to-morrow. It has proved both painful and expensive to remain here so long. Yesterday I attended Divine service connected with the opening of the new Wesleyan chapel in Port Adelaide. There are only eight members in the society. The superintendent, Mr. Draper, preached in the morning from, "He remembered us in our low estate, for his mercy endureth for ever;" and in the afternoon and evening the Rev. Mr. Hull preached: his text in the evening was, "As Moses lifted up the serpent in the wilderness, even so must the Son of man be lifted up," &c. It was a blessed season; the sermon was able, searching, and rousing. I returned to my floating habitation very much encouraged. I am sorry to say that my niece Amelia is laid up of rheumatic fever. Yesterday I was obliged to go on shore in search of leeches to apply to her chest, as the pain was getting very near her heart. This morning the doctor says she is much better. May this affliction be sanctified to us all; and may all the trials endured in leaving our friends and country redound to the glory of Christ, and the salvation of precious souls. During the week the weather has been very warm and fine; on Friday and Saturday we had a little of what is termed the hot winds; and on Saturday evening we had an awful storm of wind, lightning, and rain, but not much thunder; and now the weather is very cold.

Thursday, October 9. On Monday evening last I attended the tea-meeting connected with the opening of the Wesleyan chapel in this Port. The provisions were very good, and tastefully arranged and served. Tickets one shilling each. I was requested by the superintendent of the circuit to speak at the public meeting; with which request I cheerfully complied. The attendance and speeches were good. The ground for this little chapel has cost from 200*l.* to 300*l.*; total cost 800*l.* Yesterday we moved out of the harbour to the north arm of the creek; and we expect this evening, or to-morrow, at high tide, to cross the bar; the Pilot is on board. We have five more passengers on board than when we left Southampton; so that we have, in our ship, a very uncomfortable and bustling scene. I received a letter yesterday by the captain of the 'Rattler,' (a small vessel which sails between Adelaide and Port Philip), of which the following is a copy—

"Collingwood, Melbourne, 25th Sept., 1851.

"Rev. and dear Sir,—Your note of the . . . . . . arrived in due course, and afforded us great pleasure. We are anxiously waiting your arrival, having no doubt that your labours will be rendered successful. We shall look for the return of the 'Rattler,' as we hear that the 'Asia' will be detained for some weeks at Adelaide; and suppose you will probably come with the 'Rattler.' Mr. Taylor" (who left our ship and went forward with the 'Rattler' on its last voyage,) "arrived safely. Many parties are looking for letters by you. Some of us will be on board as soon as possible. We have long been praying for your arrival, and trust that the Head of the Church will in this new and important sphere of labour continue to bless you. With respects to Mrs. Townend and your niece, we are, Rev. and Dear Sir, yours truly,

"J. ANKERS MARSDEN.
JAMES STEVENS.
G. R. COX.

"P. S.—It has been arranged that you spend a month with us: we shall do all that Yorkshire folks can do to make you comfortable. Should any unforeseen circumstance prevent my being on board when you arrive, come at once to Brunswick-street, Collingwood.

"J. A. MARSDEN."

By the reception of this letter we are very much cheered, and as it is probable the 'Asia' will be at Port Philip as soon as the 'Rattler,' we deem it prudent to remain on board our old ship. I am sorry to say my niece is very ill, still confined to her bed.

Friday, October 10. At a quarter after two this morning I was awoke by the shrill whistle and hoarse voice of the boatswain, calling up all hands; by which we knew that the wind had changed, and the sand bank was about to be crossed. The idea of making a start for Port Philip was so cheering, that I could not sleep: so I arose and shaved, which now I can do in the dark with ease, although the berth is so small, that, besides the space occupied by the bed, it is extremely difficult for two persons to stand. By the time I was upon the poop, the 'Asia' was once more clear of her anchor, and gently moving in the right direction; the deep and stern voice of the Pilot saying to the man at the wheel, "Starboard—port—steady!" We safely crossed the bar, whilst the grinding of the ship against the bank was distinctly felt by those who were in bed. The decks were wet with the heavy dew which had fallen in the night; but whilst the sun rose in splendour, we cheerfully bade adieu to Port Adelaide, after a stay of five weeks and four days. It is a beautiful forenoon, and we are imperceptibly gliding along Spencer's Gulf. Thank God! Amelia is much better, and Mrs. Townend and myself are very well.

Sunday morning, eleven o'clock. After a fruitless struggle, since two o'clock on Friday afternoon, to make the Back Straits Passage, out of Spencer's Gulf, between Cape Jarvis on the main land, and Cape Willoughby on Kangaroo Island, we have been obliged to seek shelter and drop anchor. A fair wind by to-morrow evening, or Tuesday morning, would have brought us to anchor at Port Philip. With struggling against a head wind so long, we have most of us been again laid up with sea-sickness. Mrs Townend and I have been very sick, and most of the time in bed. We have met with many disappointments since we left England, but this has been the greatest. Still we do not murmur, and we have much for which we feel thankful. It is five calendar months this morning since we bade adieu to our native shores. God be gracious to us, and bless us! The weather is very cold; top-coats and cloaks are needful on deck; the wind being southern. O how sweet it was this morning—after a homely breakfast of old, hard, mouldy biscuit, and tea, whilst shut up in our narrow berth—my dear wife read to me the sixth chapter in Mark's Gospel. In this far distant land, whilst surrounded by desolation itself, we are "in the Spirit on the Lord's-day."

Friday, October 17. Still on board the 'Asia,' sailing very slowly abreast Cape Patten, and within twenty miles of the headings, or narrow pass into Port Philip Bay. We weighed anchor at Kangaroo Island last Monday morning at ten o'clock, and could not make Back Straits Passage until midnight, the wind being against us; since then we have had most delightful sailing. The view of the land from our present position is very grand; the mountain ridge stretching from Cape Otway to Cape Patten being thirty miles along the coast. We are living on salt beef and pea-soup: no potatoes allowed, and the flour and biscuits are very bad. Amelia is fast recovering. Mrs. Townend and myself are well, and hoping to spend the Sabbath in our new sphere of labour. May the Lord give us favour in the eyes of the people!

TO THE REV. JOSEPH TOWNEND.

Servant of Christ, thy Master calls thee,
Leave thy friends, thy native land;
Fearless cross the trackless ocean,
Hasten to yon distant strand.

Plant thereon Messiah's standard,
There proclaim the Prince of Peace,
Claim for him supreme dominion,
Bid opposing evils cease.

In thy hands no carnal weapon
Spreading desolation round,
But the Word of Truth, more mighty,
Casting strongholds to the ground.

Go! thy Master will be with thee,
All thy footsteps He will guide;
Go! thy friends will not forget thee,
Severed by the rolling tide.

Nor shalt thou 'midst Pagan darkness
All alone unaided toil—
English voices cry "Come over,
Britons cultivate the soil."

Kindred souls will gather round thee,
In thy feelings sympathise,
Share thy labour and rejoicing,
See Australian churches rise.

These to regions still beyond them
  Holding forth the faithful Word,
Till the last benighted heathen
  Sees the glory of the Lord.

April 28, 1851. REV. WILLIAM PATTERSON.

CHAPTER V.

Arrival at Melbourne—Opening of Mission—Temperance Hall Rented—House Purchased—Discouragements—Attacked and robbed by Highwaymen—Apprehension of the Thieves—Public Sympathy—Trial of the Highwaymen—Wages and Prices at Melbourne.

SATURDAY, October 18, 1851. This morning about nine o'clock, by the aid of a squall, (which has, most likely, driven many a vessel against the rocks) we safely entered the heads, and by two P.M., to our great joy, anchored in Hobson's Bay, and at five o'clock took steamer to proceed to the city of Melbourne.

Mr. Marsden had been at the flag-staff twice that day; but no ship being in sight, he had gone home. No one met us at the ship or wharf, so we made our way up the main street and on to Collingwood; and by eight o'clock we were comfortably seated in Mr. Marsden's house. Mr. Marsden was grieved that he had not met us at the wharf; we met with a hearty reception, and expect to remain here until a house can be provided.

Monday, October 20. Our only preaching-place here is at Collingwood, where I opened my mission yesterday morning at eleven o'clock. There were about forty persons present. We opened the service by singing the 492nd hymn, beginning with—

> "What shall we offer our good Lord,
> Poor nothings, for his boundless grace."

We had a sweet time in prayer: read the sixth chapter in Mark, and I preached from 1 Samuel x. 26. We had a profitable service, and the friends were much cheered. In the evening, at half-past six, I preached from Lamentations iii. 24. About sixty persons were present. We had a gracious influence, and a good prayer-meeting. Several of our leading friends were absent, at the gold-diggings; and the place at Melbourne had been given up on account of the delay in the arriving of the preacher.

The annexed copy of a letter from our friends at Geelong to the brethren here, will give an idea of the state of our Society at Geelong.

"Geelong, April 26, 1851.

"Dear Brethren,—We write to let you know how we are doing in this place. At a meeting of the Society held towards the close of the year, it was decided by a majority of votes, that the Society for the present should be broken up; and that when the preacher should arrive here, he should commence the cause afresh. After this resolution, we agreed to form a class, and met together for Christian fellowship and prayer, and for that purpose we chose brother Booley as leader. Since then, we have continued to meet together, and have had a small increase. Since the breaking up of the Society, there has been no preaching at Geelong; but the preaching at Kildare has continued to the present; and we hope, by the blessing of the Almighty, to have preaching again at the old place at Geelong. We quite agree with you, brethren, that the preacher, when he arrives, should remain in Melbourne for the space of a month, and then come here for the same length of time; after which we hope that arrangements will be made which will be best for both societies. We are quite willing to bear our portion of the expense of the preacher.

"In conclusion, we pray that God would pour out His Holy Spirit upon you, that His cause may extend more and more, and that you may be blessed in your own souls. We, remain yours,

"ROBERT BOOLEY, J. W. MATTHEWS,
G. KNEEBONE, R. HAINE,
G. GREENAWAY, G. R. COX."
WILLIAM JENKINS,

October 29. I received a letter from Ballarat gold-diggings, bearing the signatures of the brethren Jenkins, Kneebone, and Haine, earnestly requesting me to spend a Sabbath there, as several ministers are there attending to the spiritual wants of the diggers of the precious metal. I have given them the reasons why I, with the friends, think it expedient that I should not leave Collingwood and Melbourne at present. After preaching in the evening of the 29th, according to announcement on the previous Sabbath, the members and friends remained to consult as to our future plans. Present, Messrs. Marsden, Stevens, Evans, Maynard, and myself.

Resolved 1st,—That the Temperance Hall, Russel Street, Melbourne, be engaged for Sabbath services, and Sabbath-school, at an annual rent of £20.

Resolved 2nd,—That, if possible, a suitable house be purchased and furnished for the minister; and that Mesdames Marsden, Townend, and Maynard, with Messrs. Marsden, Townend, Little, and Maynard, be appointed collectors to obtain the needful sum.

The Temperance Hall is a very eligible and comfortable room, capable of holding 400 persons. It cannot be expected that our entire expense can be raised here; and we earnestly entreat that a grant of 50*l.* at least, be sent from home, to assist us in the purchase of house and furniture. We adopt this course as a matter of expediency, a five-roomed cottage renting as high as 30*l.* or 40*l.* per year. Mr. Marsden has introduced me to the Mayor, Messrs. Heap and Grice, and several other influential persons; all of whom received us cordially, assuring us that there is plenty of room and work in and about Melbourne. His Excellency the Governor received us very kindly. The day on which we opened the Hall was a very wet day, and, in going to the morning service, Mrs. Townend tumbled in the mud, and had to return and undress. Only ten persons were at the morning service, and in the evening from thirty to forty. Collections, thirty-two shillings; nearly half of which had to be paid for printing. Whilst I preached in the Hall, Mr. M. preached in our little place at Collingwood, and thus our little cause was divided, which weakened us at both places. About this time, I was severely tried, frequently having to set the tunes and lead the singing; and our congregations were very small; while the collections at the door only paid for the rent of the room. By the time that we had collected about 25*l.* towards the house and furniture, just as I began to see, and bitterly to feel, that I was in bad and unworthy hands, a house was offered to be sold for 250*l.* with a mortgage of 150*l.* at 15 per cent. per annum, which I purchased and secured, and, by the good providence of God, just before rents, furniture, and labour rose prodigiously, on account of the diggings, and vast numbers flocking to Melbourne, and its vicinity, on account of its proximity to the gold fields. It was now abundantly clear that, if we valued our own comfort, and the credit of the cause we had espoused, we must quit our lodgings, and discontinue all religious association with those who had chiefly been instrumental, by their application to the officers of our Connexion, in bringing us to this place. We did so, and without furniture, or a bed to lie upon, we entered the purchased house, on the same day that the former tenants removed; we opened our large cases, spread our bed clothes on the bare floor, and committed our case into the hands of the Searcher of hearts. This bold step was taken without a single angry word, and met with the hearty concurrence of the few trembling members, who had for some time dreaded our arrival, on account of the situation they knew we should be placed in; but in two or three weeks, we were living in a most comfortable house; and the little Church was cleared of parties who were anything but her real friends.

December 11. Last Sabbath was a very trying day: only seven persons present in the Hall at the forenoon service, and about twenty in the evening; when we were sadly disturbed by the loud talking of the people in the house behind the hall. After service, I called in the woman, and told her how we had been disturbed; she promised in future to lock the door, and come to service.

Benjamin Heap, Esq., from Rochdale and his lady, have shown us great kindness: they have lost their dear boy, about six months old. I was honoured with an invitation to the funeral, and had the mournful pleasure to conduct the service. This circumstance was balmy and painful, and brought vividly to my mind many such scenes which I have witnessed at home.

December 25. Christmas-day: hot winds and very sultry. Many are down from the diggings, and intoxication and excess abound. We have no service to-day; and our Sabbath services are very poorly attended. It is very trying, but hope buoys up our spirits. It is likely we shall give up the Hall, and return to our own little chapel in Collingwood. Jonathan and Samuel Taylor, with William Brown, kindly finished my book-cases yesterday; and I have the pleasure once more to see my valuable library in a neat and quiet resting-place. O God, I thank thee that I am alive and well this Christmas morning, both in body and soul; and though the thoughts of English homes, and Christmas festivities, give a sorrowful and pensive tone to my feelings, yet, believing that I am in the way of duty, I trust to see better days here. My dear wife is very cheerful and well, and quite proud of my new study. In it may I enjoy many blessed hours. Amen.

January 1, 1852. Another year of this short life is gone. An eventful year! Last year I conducted the watch-night service at Bury, Lancashire, amongst a numerous circle of affectionate friends; last night I attended the watch-night service at the Wesleyan Chapel, Collins Street, Melbourne, Victoria, Australia. Not being in circumstances to hold one amongst ourselves, I found melancholy pleasure and profit in worshipping there. A good chapel, beautifully lighted with candles: some good addresses. This moment I feel resolved to give myself afresh to God, and seek only His glory. Several of our friends have been down from the diggings, and been very kind to me. Two brothers, who were formerly connected with our church in Carlisle, gave me 15*l*. I feel truly thankful.

HIGHWAY ROBBERY.

On Thursday, January 8, 1852, as I was returning from meeting my class, held at Mr. Jonathan Taylor's, Little Lonsdale Street, about nine o'clock in the evening, when about an equal distance between the Supreme Court and Collingwood, off Latrobe Street, upon the open common, I was overtaken by two men, who, coming close to me, commanded me to stand still, and, presenting each a pistol to my head, said, if I made any noise or offered any resistance, they would blow out my brains in a moment. I said, "Offer no violence; do not hurt me; *I will not stir nor offer any resistance;* what is it you want?" They replied, "Your money, and whatever you have about you that is valuable." I said, "I am a poor Methodist preacher returning from an evening meeting, to my home in Collingwood, and I have not been three months in the colony." They replied, "We don't want to know either what you are or where you are going." By this time they had each emptied his side of my trousers' pocket. Again the threat was repeated, that if I stirred they would blow out my brains, holding each his pistol close to my head. I said, "Do not talk in that way; my brains are more valuable to me than all the gold at the diggings." I was told to take off my watch-guard, and give up my watch, which I did. I said, "Now you have got all I have. That money I have begged to buy furniture with: will you give me back the purse? it is a keepsake given me by a friend in Manchester." The purse was returned. "And those spectacles will do you no good, and they are valuable to me." They also were returned; for which I thanked them; and when they had counted their booty (for they did not seem to have confidence in each other), they told me to walk right home; and said, that if they saw me turn out of the way, they would shoot me dead on the spot. I then walked off some forty yards, and on looking behind me, I saw that they had made considerable progress in the opposite direction. I then turned from off the common the nearest way into the city, and gave information, and a description of the thieves at the Police Court; and having called at the principal newspaper office, to have the case inserted in the next morning's paper, I returned home, thankful and pensive, and told my disconsolate wife, who had been thinking that something would happen. Next morning, by six o'clock, I went to the Police Court, to give in the number of the watch, when I found that two men had been apprehended; and on seeing them, I felt convinced that they were the men that robbed me on the previous night. I was at the Court again at half-past nine that morning, and saw them both together in the yard, and was fully prepared to swear to their identity.

CASE IN THE POLICE COURT BEFORE THE MAYOR AND THE MAGISTRATES:

Deposition of the chief constable—

"In consequence of the information lodged by Mr. Townend, I went in search of the thieves, and about a quarter before eleven, I saw two men in Little Lonsdale Street West, answering to the description given by Mr. Townend. I rode past, as if I was afraid of them, not being willing to encounter them without help. I saw Mr. Sturt, and got him to assist me, telling him to seize the lesser man, and I would look after the other. I rode after him, as they separated as soon as they discovered that I was after them. The prisoner Wilson I followed into a right-of-way belonging to Mr. Annands, when he threw several stones, and with a piece of old metal struck my horse in the eye, and fractured the bone. I rode against him, close to the wall, when he presented a pistol, which snapped; I did not see the light. I then galloped against him, and with the horse knocked him down, and seized him. I found the pistol about a yard from the spot. The pistol was loaded with thirteen pieces of duck shot: this is the shot, and this is the pistol. I do not say that this is the pistol presented at me; but I *swear* that it is a similar one. On our way to the Police Court, the prisoner said that it was a good thing that the pistol had not gone off."

I was then called into the box and sworn, and gave the particulars as they occurred. Mr. Belcher, the conductor of the examination, said, "Were you not in great terror, Mr. Townend, when you were alone, and two pistols so near your head?" I replied, "No, sir; I was as calm as I am at this moment: yet I saw that there was but a step between me and death." At this stage of the investigation there was great sympathy manifested. I swore to the identity of the men. My friend, Benjamin Heap, Esq., would have been present in his capacity as magistrate, but being busy with the sale of his furniture (which, by the way, was the reason why I had so much money on my person, as I had been at the sale), he kindly addressed a note to Mr. Belcher, telling him that I was a friend of his, and requesting him to give me every needful direction.

Captain Sturt, who had taken the prisoner Wilson, not being present, the case was remanded until Saturday morning.

POLICE COURT, SATURDAY MORNING.

On entering the Court, Mr. Bloomfield, the chief constable, presented me with my watch, which had been found in a pawnshop, for which the broker had paid fifty shillings, which sum he deservedly lost. I was glad to receive back my old friend, for we had been companions ever since I travelled in the Salford Circuit. I bought the watch of Mr. Thomas Taylor, Mason Street, Manchester, and had the number in a memorandum-book. Inspector Bloomfield was called into the witness-box, and the evidence given by him on the previous morning was read, and he assented to it as being correct. I was then called, and my previous day's evidence read, to which I replied, "Correct, sir." Captain Sturt then deposed to having captured the prisoner Wilson, while Mr. Bloomfield was in pursuit of the prisoner Alexander Gough. Wilson dropped a pistol, which was found by Mr. Sturt on the spot where he seized him. It was loaded to the muzzle, and it matched the one which was snapped at the chief constable, and the shot also was similar. There was also found near the spot a bag of powder and shot, with some percussion caps. Mr. Sturt observed that there was the greatest credit due to the chief constable for the very clever manner in which he had captured Gough, who, he remarked, could certainly run, if he could do nothing else. Both prisoners were fully committed for trial. Counsellor Stevens, who appeared for the prisoner Gough, offered no defence; but kindly sent me, by John Matthew Smith, Esq. (the lawyer who made out my house-deed, and charged only 1*l.* 1*s.*), two sovereigns; Benjamin Heap, Esq., Captain Hepburn, and Lawrence Rosthrone, Esq., sent me 5*l.* each towards my loss; which was only eleven sovereigns, five shillings, and sixpence, besides the watch, which was returned.

His Worship, the Mayor of Melbourne, called to sympathise with me, and begged that I would accept the sum of ten guineas, as he considered "the persons and property of clergymen should be held sacred." Thanks be to Almighty God, who, in the hour of imminent peril, spared my unworthy life, and also opened the hearts of those kind gentlemen to give me such aid in the time of need.

Sabbath Day, January 18. I was much cheered; congregations better, and also the collections at the door. A good feeling in the services. The trustees of our little chapel at Collingwood have agreed to offer me the place, as it was by their influence I had been brought out to this country. Mr. Marsden having left the society, it has been locked up for several weeks, except that it has been open for the week-day school.

February 1, 1852. We have given up the Hall, and this day re-opened the little chapel at Collingwood. I had great liberty in speaking; in the morning, from Psalm cxxvi. 5, 6; and also in the evening, from Matthew xvi. 26. The best congregations we have ever had; collections at the door, sixteen shillings and threepence.

February 16. Last Sabbath we had blessed seasons, good attendance, and several strangers from the neighbourhood, who spoke of the satisfaction they felt under my ministry. Since Friday last, I have been very poorly, not at all fit to be out. The doctor says my liver is in a very bad state, and that without help I should very soon sink under its influence.

The Criminal Sessions opened this morning. At half-past ten the honourable judge, A. Beckett, took his seat. Though very unfit to attend, I went to the court. I was alone, not a single person belonging to our church or congregation being present. Sorrowful and pensive I took a seat, or stood in the crowd, as I felt disposed. I thought of home and its endearing associations and friendships, and checked as much as possible the silent tears as they stole down my cheeks.

At twenty minutes before two P.M., the Court adjourned for half-an-hour; after which the Court resumed its sitting. My case was the first called on. The jury being sworn, the counsel for the Crown clearly stated the case; and then the prisoner Gough pleaded guilty. I was called upon, and deposed as at the police court, and swore to the prisoner Wilson. Captain Sturt and the chief constable did the same; and the jury in one minute returned a verdict against the prisoner Wilson. The case was remanded, as are all the heavy cases, until the last day of the sessions. I do not forget to pray for these two reckless young men. The sentence afterwards pronounced against Gough and Wilson was transportation for ten years; the first three in heavy irons.

March 10. I feel very thankful that my health is restored, and that I am endeavouring to live happily and usefully. Our little cause is looking up, and the Lord still raises us up friends; blessed be His holy name.

Joiners and carpenters are receiving 3*l.* and upwards, weekly. Clothing and rents, with provisions, are very high. A young man must pay for very inferior lodgings and board 1*l.* weekly, and if our house had to be rented we should have to pay at least 35*s.* weekly rent. What a providence that I bought the house just in time. A pair of shoes costs 1*l.*, and a pair of good cloth trousers 38*s.*: butcher's meat 3*d.* per lb.; butter 2*s.* per lb; eggs 3*s.* per dozen; milk 8*d.* per quart, and firewood and water are equally dear.

Thursday, April 22, 1852. Latterly I have been severely tempted; but, by the grace of God, I have stood faithful. I feel the need of stricter watchfulness, and more constant and earnest intercourse between Heaven and my soul. Our cause is gathering strength, and—considering the unfavourable state of the colony for the growth of grace, and especially the unsatisfactory state of the small interest to which I have been sent—we are all astonished at the openings of Providence and favourable aspect of things. Yesterday I saw a man leave this mortal state, without giving a satisfactory evidence that he was going to a better world. I have frequently visited him, and thought him sincere. Though strictly honest, yet he was a miser, not even allowing himself the common necessaries of life; and though very quiet and outwardly moral, he never went to the house of prayer. He has left a son, an extravagant and indolent young man. The autumnal quarter has arrived, the weather is warm, the fields and gardens in charming order, something like spring at home.

CHAPTER VI.

Brief description of Australia*—Extent of the Country—A British Possession —General aspect of Scenery—Varieties of the Soil and its Rocky Basis—Supposed Inland Sea—Character of the Rivers; the Murray and other principal streams—Inundations—Interesting natural process of filling the "water holes"—Conclusion.

AUSTRALIA, situated between the parallels of 11° and 39° of south latitude, measures in length from east to west about 2400 miles, with an average breadth of 1200, and a superficial area equal to three-fourths of that of Europe. The discovery and exploration of this vast country has been gradually effected during the last three centuries by the subjects of various nations; but it has been colonized solely by the Government of our own country; and Britain may now be regarded as possessing the entire extent of Australia. Our enterprising countrymen are already, with extraordinary rapidity, overspreading this ample territory. The square uniformity of the coast outline, and the almost total absence of any arm of the sea, to afford access by water conveyance to the interior of so extensive a region, are features that readily strike the eye of the geographer.

The internal aspects of the country have been found equally remarkable with its external configuration. Extensive naked plains, covered with scanty vegetation, are relieved by wooded hills of a moderate elevation, diversified with undulating pastoral country more thickly carpeted with grass, and lightly timbered with the various species of the gum-tree. The coolness and moisture of winter and spring spread a brilliant green over the surface, creating occasional scenes of surpassing beauty, though often tame and monotonous, from the general similarity and sombre hue of the perennial foliage of the gum-trees. The approach of summer reverses the picture; and scorching winds from the interior dissipate the verdant landscape, and spread on every side a scene of drought

* The following general description of Australia, is taken from W. Westgarth's "Australia Felix," published in 1848. Edinburgh: Oliver and Boyd. London: Simpkin, Marshall, and Co.

and sterility. The pastoral portion of Australia thus depicted comprises a large area of its surface. But a still greater extent is devoted to lands in a great measure destitute of any available vegetation; to thickly timbered ranges of hills, poor and scrubby soils, and large tracts of desolate and uninhabitable desert. Arable land, though abundant in certain localities, is of limited extent when compared with so vast a territory. The extensive distribution of sandstone and granite has yielded a soil of a generally light, dry, and sandy description, which is accordingly the prevailing character of the Australian lands. An improvement of the soil usually indicates a change in the nature of the rocks that constitute its base. Those of a siliceous character have disappeared, and some variety of whinstone or basalt is generally found in their place. A large proportion of Australia Felix, situated chiefly between Geelong and the River Glenelg, exhibits this improvement of soil, and forms a striking contrast to the poorer qualities that characterize the Australian territory. In north-eastern Australia also, the recent explorations of Dr. Leichhardt and Sir Thomas Mitchel have laid open a country which appears to be superior in the extent and fertility of its available surface to any other region hitherto explored. The latter traveller, who proceeded by way of Fort Bourke in a north-westerly direction from Sydney, expatiates in glowing terms on the pastoral qualities of the green and well watered downs on which he entered, after traversing the comparatively arid tract that lay between Sydney and the Darling. The River Victoria stretched its wide and noble stream towards the north, apparently in the direction of the Gulf Carpentaria, sweeping through a beautiful and fertile country, which surpassed in extent and luxuriance anything that had yet been met with, even in the best parts of Australia Felix. The lengthened route of Leichhardt, in his successful journey to Port Essington, intersected a country in general less rich and promising, but of more varied aspect, characterized by the frequent occurence of basaltic rocks, and the productive soils that are usually derived from them. The scrub and rugged scenery of Expedition Range contrasted with the open pastures that skirted the broad stream of the Burdekin. Around Peak Range and Mount Lang the extensive elevated plains furnish a cool and bracing climate, suitable for depasturing sheep; while on the lower levels, and moist and warm regions of York Peninsula, fields of cotton and rice may share the soil with the horse, the bullock, and the buffalo, depasturing in unlimited numbers over the green and varied surface. Still more generally distinctive in its character from the light and siliceous soils of Australia, is that of the adjacent colony of Van Diemen's Land, separated by Bass's Straits from the Australian Continent.

It has been estimated that in New South Wales, the area of country containing granite, quartz, sandstone, and other rocks, having over 60 per cent. of silicia, is to that exhibiting basalt, and similar rocks containing less than 60 per cent., as upwards of 4 to 1; while in Van Diemen's, the proportions are reversed, and in the ratio of three of basalt, eurite, &c., to one of the rocks containing the larger proportions of silicia, and producing lighter soils. Van Diemen's Land thus exhibits, says Strezelecki, the greatest extent of volcanic action; and the adaptions generally of the respective places may be inferred, New South Wales being the pastoral, and Van Diemen's Land the agricultural colony.

Nature has not afforded any adequate compensation to Australia, in navigable rivers or internal seas, for the unindented character of her shores. The limited surface of her internal waters, in connection with the existence of extensive deserts, may account for the dryness of the climate, and the occurrence of hot winds in the summer season, blowing occasionally with great severity from the direction of the central regions. An extensive inland sea had been repeatedly conjectured to exist in Central Australia. When the passage of the Blue Mountains laid open the western interior to the exploring enterprise of the colonist, several rivers were discovered flowing in a north-westerly direction; and the Lachlan and Macquarie, two of the most considerable, were severally ascertained to lose themselves in extensive swamps or lakes, whose surface, as far as the eye could reach in an inland direction, was overspread with reeds. A circumstance so remarkable, occurring in the case of both rivers, excited curiosity; and the swamps, conjectured to be continuous throughout the intermediate space of nearly one hundred and fifty miles, were regarded as the eastern margin of an extensive sea. But the expedition of Sturt, during the favourable opportunity of a severe drought in 1827, was the means of ascertaining the final course of the Macquarie. The swamps had disappeared under the protracted drought, and the track of the river was followed until it united with the larger bed of a new river called the Darling, whose waters were seen to take the direction of the south-west, and afterwards ascertained, by the same indefatigable explorer, to unite, in common with other rivers of that locality, with the noble stream of the Murray. It was also ascertained that the Lachlan, after traversing the extensive swamp to which it had first been traced, fell into the Murrumbidgee, a principal tributary of the Murray, which it joins at the higher part of its course. The late arduous expedition of Captain Sturt, in 1845, appears to have finally removed the lingering fancies of an inland sea. Proceeding in a northerly direction from the town of Adelaide, he attained to $24\frac{1}{2}°$ of south latitude, and exposed in that locality the existence of a vast desert of stony plains, and hills of sand, exhibiting for hundreds of miles a waste of utter sterility and solitude. The creeks and rivers of Australia have in general a transitory existence; now swollen by the casual showers, and again rapidly subsiding under the general dryness and heat of the climate. Vast gullies have been scooped out by rushing torrents through the elevated plains of the country: but most of these romantic vales, during the greater portion of the year, are entirely destitute of running water. The rains of the winter and spring supply the various channels, which in general, though by no means regular, begin to flow about the month of July, and continue for a period varying according to the circumstances of the several localities. The ephemeral existence of a week, or even a day, is not an uncommon occurrence; and in general the greater of the temporary streams has ceased to flow towards the conclusion of the year. Even the Darling, with its lengthened course, and its innumerable tributaries from the western and northern parts of the colony, has repeatedly ceased running during seasons of drought; and throughout the great systems of waters to which it pertains, perhaps only the Hume, proceeding from the Australian Alps, maintains the constancy of its stream against the casualties of the climate. (The Murrumbidgee, as I am informed, has been known to cease running. The Yarra-Yarra, as the name imports —*i. e.*, ever-flowing, ranks among the small number of constant streams.) The river Murray, the general recipient of these waters, is a continuation of the Hume, and the largest river in Australia. About the junction of the Murrumbidgee, it has an average breadth of 300 to 400 feet; but below the junction of the Darling—(which at its juncture, when seen by Sturt in January 1831, was twelve feet deep, and a hundred yards wide: its banks are described as beautifully grassed, and interspersed with large trees: the settlers from Port Philip are already advancing into this region with their live stock)—it expands its dimensions to several hundred yards, and rolls onward to the sea charged with the united waters of the many lengthened tributaries. The scenery of this great river is of a varied character. Now it traverses low and monotonous plains, sweeping through steep cliffs, and over occasional cataracts or rapids; again it winds amidst undulating grassy banks and picturesque hills, beneath which lie rich alluvial flats, covered with reeds, and apparently subject to inundation. The devious courses of the rivers are generally marked by a continuous line of gum trees growing upon either bank, and standing out in clear and well-defined relief from the grassy and treeless plains.

The inundation of the principal rivers is occasionally both sudden and extensive. Roots and branches, rocks and turbid waters, are swept in a promiscuous and impetuous torrent through the winding channels; and the banks, and a large area of adjacent country, are almost instantaneously overflowed. Sheep and cattle are sometimes overtaken, and perish ere they can be driven to the nearest elevated ground.

The Murrumbidgee, the Hume, and the Goulburn, are subject to great floods, and several commencing townships laid out upon the banks of these rivers have already suffered from these visitations. In a country were most of the rivers are periodically, and for lengthened intervals, destitute of running streams, the supply of water is secured by an efficient and interesting process of nature. The courses of all the rivers, with scarcely any exception, exhibit a series of ponds, or water-holes, which are usually of much greater depth than the general level of the bed. The most important business of the settler, in selecting his depasturing station, is to ascertain that he will possess an unfailing supply of water. He accordingly constructs his homestead in the vicinity of some deep and permanent reservoir. Months and even years may elapse, ere his ear is saluted with the pleasing noise of a running stream; but he marks without alarm the progressive decrease in the level of his water-holes, while enough still remains for the use of his flocks; and it is a curious circumstance, that the contents of these natural reservoirs, though sometimes much discoloured when the level is unusually low during seasons of drought, rarely becomes unwholesome or unfit for use. Many of the smaller creeks and river-courses have no running water for several years together. The running of the creek is always an important occasion at each pastoral settlement. Is the station situated at a remote distance from the sources of the creek which traverses it?

Weeks and months of rain may have failed to resuscitate the stream in that locality, for a thousand natural cisterns throughout the upper part of its course must overflow, ere the lower reservoirs be replenished. The rushing noise at length announces the approach of a welcome friend; the various water-holes upon the station are successively filled, and the diminished and unnecessary remnant sweeps on towards the sea. The rains of the entire year are frequently absorbed in this manner by means of these creeks, or chains of ponds, which only during seasons of unusual moisture permit the escape of the surplus waters from a parched and thirsty country.

COPY OF CONVEYANCE OF LAND FROM THE ABORIGINES TO JOHN BATMAN, ESQ., 1835.

There were two tracts of country purchased by Batman. The following is a copy of the Deed of Conveyance for one of these sections (Dr. Lang's "Philip Land," p. 27). "Know all persons, that we, three brothers, Jagajaga, Jagajaga, Jagajaga, being the principal chiefs, and also Cooloolock, Bungarie, Yanyan, Moowhip, Momarmalar, being the chiefs of a certain native tribe called Dutigallee, situated at or near Port Philip, called by us, the above-named chiefs, Irausnoo and Geelong, being possessed of the tract of land herein-mentioned, for and in consideration of 20 pairs of blankets, 30 knives, 12 tomahawks, 10 looking-glasses, 12 pairs of scissors, 50 handkerchiefs, 12 red shirts, 4 flannel jackets, 4 suits of clothes, and 50 pounds of flour, delivered to us by John Batman, Esq., do give, grant, &c., all that tract of country, about 100,000 acres, in consideration of the yearly tribute of 50 pairs of blankets, 50 knives, 50 tomahawks, 50 pairs of scissors, 50 looking-glasses, 20 suits of slop or clothing, and 2 tons of flour."

To this deed were appended the names, or rather marks and seals, of the aborigines enumerated in it. The same extensive proprietors subsequently alienated an additional portion of their territory to the extent of 500,000 acres, more or less, for 20 pairs of blankets, 30 tomahawks, 100 knives, 30 pairs of scissors, 30 looking-glasses, 200 handkerchiefs, 100 pounds of flour, and 6 shirts, with a yearly tribute similar to the preceding. WESTGARTH, p. 392.

I must now close this imperfect sketch of my eventful, but unworthy life. Whatever others may think of me, I feel that I have been very unfaithful, and have need this moment to prostrate myself in confusion of face before the Author of my being. And O, I am sure that even this act of sincere prostration would be the highest presumption, were it not done in the name of Jesus. As to learning I make no pretensions; and although I might in this respect have made better out, yet when I think of the poverty, afflictions, and early factory toil for thirteen and fourteen hours a day; and the anxiety, responsibility, and labour of my more public life, I feel that I should lie against my conscience were I to intimate that I had been an idler. How strange that I should speak of closing this sketch of my life! Why, here I am at the antipodes of my native land, with a handful of kindred spirits in our little church in Collingwood, Melbourne, Australia, so to speak, just beginning the world over again.

JOSEPH TOWNEND.

May 26, 1852.

APPENDIX.

As more than two years have elapsed since the Rev. Joseph Townend transmitted the copy of his Autobiography to this country—various circumstances, which need not be detailed, having deferred its publication—it will be interesting to the reader to be informed that Mr. Townend still continues to labour in the same locality, and that his ministry has been honoured with considerable success. He has been the means of raising a very excellent chapel at Collingwood, and the number of the church members, though not large, steadily increases. He has requested that more ministers may be sent out, and has expressed a willingness to be employed in visiting other localities, to introduce the Gospel of Jesus Christ. The Rev. M. W. Bradney, in the latter part of September, 1854, left England, to be a colleague with Mr. Townend. We shall now lay before the reader part of a letter which we received some months since, containing important information relative to Mr. Townend's labours:—

LETTER FROM MR. W. H. ALSOP, TO THE REV. R. ECKETT.

Collingwood, Victoria, 24th Nov., 1853.

Reverend Sir,—The gracious dealings of Almighty God with this branch of our beloved Association, call upon us to make our brethren at home partakers in the joy derivable from our present position and future prospects. When we look back and see what the Lord hath wrought for us, we are lost in wonder, love, and praise; and are constrained with the Psalmist to exclaim, "Truly God is good to Israel."

On Lord's-day, the 11th September, we removed from the inconveniently small room, hitherto occupied by us, to our new chapel. It is a substantial stone building, light and elegant in appearance: in the Norman style of architecture, after a design by Brother George Cox. Its dimensions are 70 feet long, by 33 feet wide; 13 feet in height to the spring of the roof, which is open.

It is capable of accommodating, without gallery, from 600 to 700 persons. The weather was exceedingly unpropitious. At seven o'clock in the morning a public prayer-meeting was held. At eleven o'clock our esteemed pastor, the Rev. Joseph Townend, occupied the pulpit, and preached an impressive sermon, from the latter part of 1 Chron. xxix. 5. In the afternoon Brother I. Brown Young preached from the former part of Rev. vii. 15; and in the evening, at six o'clock, the Rev. John Reid, Presbyterian, gave a most delightful paraphrase on the first four verses of Ps. lxxxiv. On the following Wednesday evening, Brother James Copperthwaite, of the Primitives, preached from Matthew xxii. 30. On Lord's-day following, the services were continued. The preachers were,—In the morning, the Rev. W. B. Landells, Independent, from Exodus xxviii. 8; in the afternoon, Brother George Middleton, from Matthew v. 16; and in the evening the Rev. Joseph Townend, from Luke xvi. 31. On the Wednesday evening following, the whole was crowned with a public tea-meeting, when nearly 400 sat down to tea. The trays were gratuitously furnished by the friends. After the removal of the fragments, Henry Langlands, Esq., M.L.C., took the chair. The report having been read, the meeting was addressed by the Revs. — Simmonds, Wesleyan Conference; A. Clowes, Episcopalian; — Simper, Independent; — Hamilton, Presbyterian; and Brs. Copperthwaite, Middleton, and others. It was encouraging to witness the friends from our more powerful sister churches extending the right hand of Christian sympathy, and bidding us good speed in the name of the Lord.

Our financial position calls for our warmest gratitude to Almighty God, and thanks to those friends who have so nobly contributed of their substance to relieve our necessities. We also tender our thanks especially to the Rev. Joseph Townend, for his munificent donation, and for his zealous and untiring perseverance in the good work to its successful completion. The total cost of the building, to the present time, is £2,675,—towards which we have received:—Donations, £630; donation from the Rev. Joseph Townend, £250; rent of old room, let off for day-school, and dwelling-house attached, £62; collections at opening services, £700; making a total of £1,642. Borrowed by the Trustees, for three years, on personal security, £900; amount due to the Treasurer, £133. A further outlay of at least £500 will be required to complete the internal arrangements; and it is intended to make another appeal to Christian liberality on the ensuing Christmas.

Our enrolled members number near upon 60 [since increased. —Ed.]; and although we cannot boast of many accessions from the kingdom of Satan, yet we have had the drops, and are earnestly praying for the promised shower. A series of revival services have been held in union with our friends the Reformers, through the instrumentality of which some have been added to the church.

We have a promising cause at Kew about three miles hence; and at Brunswick, about two miles hence. At the former place the friends are contemplating the erection of a chapel.

Our Sabbath-school is progressing satisfactorily. In proportion to our increased accommodation, we are seeking a like increase in its efficiency. We have a band of truly devoted Christian teachers, who have the eternal interests of the children at heart. There are 104 names on the books, and amongst them are many who evidence that the instruction imparted is not altogether in vain. A Band of Hope is organized in connection with the school; and upwards of forty children have pledged abstinence from intoxicating liquors for life.

It is with sincere regret we hear of the disruptions which have occurred in the various branches of the Wesleyan family at home; and earnestly pray that the great Head of the Church will again restore that peace and unity, so essential to their prosperity, and the spread of the Redeemer's kingdom.

We are anxiously looking for more labourers from home, to reap an abundant harvest of perishing souls in this golden land. The friends at Geelong are only waiting the arrival of a pastor, to at once rally round him, and concentrate their energies to the furtherance of the great work.

May the Holy Spirit, in rich abundance, descend on every section of our branch of Christ's Militant Church, that she may become powerful in pulling down the strongholds of Satan, and planting the standard of Emmanuel.

W. H. Alsop,
Assistant-Secretary to the Quarterly Meeting.

To the Rev. Robert Eckett.

PART II.

REMINISCENCES OF MISSIONARY LABOURS IN AUSTRALIA.

CHAPTER I.

Discovery of gold in Australia—Rush to the diggings—Depreciation of property—Influx of convicts—Bushrangers—Increase of population—Want of house accommodation—Emigrants' Home—Canvas tents—Prospect of Mission discouraging—Ministers gone to the gold-fields—New arrivals—English letters—Painful records in diary—Public Cemetery—Struggle for right of interment—New Chapel—Price of labour—Opening services—Painful trial on account of dwelling-house.

THE first part of my Autobiography was written and sent to England in May, 1852, being about seven months after I landed in Australia; and as the publication was delayed more than two years, my much-esteemed friend the Rev. R. Eckett added the letter from the Secretary, Mr. Alsop. I shall now endeavour to supply some account of my labours, and incidents occurring in the interim before the opening of our first chapel, to which the above-named letter refers.

No intimation of the discovery of gold in Australia had reached England when we sailed from thence in May, 1851; we first heard of it during our stay in Adelaide, and, on reaching Melbourne, there was abundant evidence of the excitement prevailing among all classes of society. The discovery of gold was first made in New South Wales in the month of February, 1851, by a gentleman who had visited the Californian gold-fields. At this time the Port Philip district, of which Melbourne was the chief town, formed a part of New South Wales; but in July of the same year it was constituted into a separate colony, under the name of Victoria, with an independent Government, the first Parliament of which commenced its sittings the month after my arrival.

The years 1862 and 1863 were of the most exciting character ever witnessed in the colony before or since. The rich gold-fields of Ballarat, Bendigo, and Mount Alexander were about the first discovered in Victoria, towards the close of 1851; and the marvellous statements constantly reaching Melbourne of the success of those already on the ground, caused a general rush of the inhabitants who were at all able to leave; some of the churches were deserted, and many schools were closed. Property, for a time, greatly depreciated in value, so anxious was everyone to realise sufficient to take them to the diggings. Thousands of the inhabitants of the adjacent colonies were attracted to Victoria; but the worst feature of all was the great influx of the convict class from the different penal settlements; many of these had served their term of transportation, and had settled to various occupations, but a great number were "ticket-of-leave" men, and many more came *without leave*. Numbers of these betook themselves to bushranging and highway robbery as being an easier method to obtain gold than digging for it; frequently the armed escort was waylaid and robbed when bringing the precious metal from the different gold-fields.

When the lucky diggers began to return to town, some tired of the hardships and privations experienced on the gold-fields, and others to get rid of their newly-acquired wealth, Melbourne presented a strange and motley scene; fierce-looking men paraded the streets with long beards, unshaven faces, attired in a cabbage-tree hat, and a loose blouse fastened round the waist with a belt, from which hung conspicuously bowie knives and pistols; scarcely a day passed that did not record some act of violence or robbery. People were robbed in broad daylight within a few yards of their own door, for the police had struck for wages and gone to the diggings. The most outrageous case occurred one Saturday afternoon, on the high road between Melbourne and St. Kilda. A company of five or six bushrangers took up a position about a mile from town, and (to use a colonial phrase) "stuck up" every person that passed, whether on foot or horseback, and, after robbing them of everything valuable under threat of instant death, they were led off into the bush, out of sight of the main road, and there tied to the trees, one of the bushrangers remaining guard; in this way some twenty individuals were waylaid, and then the robbers made off, leaving the captives to release themselves as best they could. By the good providence of God no violence was ever offered me except in the case already narrated, though I was frequently obliged to traverse lonely districts late at night when returning from preaching appointments, but I generally took the precaution to leave my watch at home and carry no money.

The sudden increase in the population, and the consequent demand for all the necessaries of life, caused a speedy increase in price of all articles of consumption; and though gold was rapidly pouring into Melbourne (for in the month of October, 1851, no less than a ton weight was brought into town in a single week), still there were numbers of families who suffered great distress and privation from having to depend on fixed and limited incomes, which, for a time, were not materially altered by the circumstances surrounding.

About the middle of 1852 the tide of emigration had fairly set in from England, and before the close of the year frequently three and four thousand persons landed at the port of Melbourne in a single week. As may be supposed, there was great suffering and distress experienced by multitudes of the new arrivals; hundreds were compelled to sleep in the open air, or sit guarding their boxes all night. There was no adequate house accommodation; rents had risen to such a figure as to place them beyond the reach of ordinary incomes; a four-roomed cottage would command £4, £5, and even £6 per week. On several occasions we permitted families to sleep in our little chapel; wrapping themselves in their blankets, they lay on the forms or floor, and, kindling a fire in the yard, would there cook their victuals. On one occasion this was the means of saving the chapel from being burnt down; we had been having service, and suppose that, in putting out the pulpit candles, the snuff had dropped on the cushion; when the friends went in to sleep, the Bible, hymn-book, and cushion were on fire, the pulpit slightly injured, but no further damage done. A party of five or six young men from Clitheroe, Lancashire, landed at Melbourne, on their way to Queensland; I put them in the chapel to sleep for several nights; they were not tempted by the gold-diggings to stay in Victoria, but went on to Brisbane to join their friends who had gone out some years before under Dr. Lang; and on my going to Brisbane about ten years after, these young men, with a few others, formed the nucleus of our little church there.

The Government endeavoured to make some provision to meet the emergency by erecting canvas barracks, which afterwards gave place to more substantial buildings of brick, now called the "Emigrants' Home." This has been a great boon in affording temporary shelter when anything like a roof overhead was such a privilege that people were glad to pay a shilling a night to sleep on the floor like herrings in a barrel; and I have heard that those who slept on the table paid a shilling extra for that luxury. Very soon a number of canvas tents were erected, and there was one large settlement entirely of such, which acquired the name of "Canvas Town;" it was formed into streets bearing names, and at the doors of the tents might be seen placards and boards to tell the trade or profession of the occupant, or the merchandise that might be purchased within. These tents might be rendered very comfortable in a country where the atmosphere is so very pure and buoyant, and the sky the most part of the year clear and brilliant; but during the season of heavy rains—and after a long drought it literally comes down in torrents—then living in a tent was no pleasant matter, especially as, the fires being principally outside, the cooking must all be done in the open air. I have known delicate women who, soon after confinement, have had to sit up in bed holding an umbrella to protect themselves and infant. Frequently when I have walked out and looked around on the tents studding the landscape in every direction, and glistening in the strong sunlight, I have felt I could more clearly understand the force and beauty of many of the allusions and illustrations of Scripture; but when I came to look beneath the surface and witnessed the profanity, the drunkenness, the Sabbath desecration, and licentiousness almost everywhere prevailing, my spirit has been weighed down and oppressed, to think how this otherwise fair scene was blighted and cursed by sin.

Amid such stirring and exciting scenes as these I commenced my mission, and, as may be supposed, the prospect at first was very gloomy and discouraging. I have already mentioned in the previous edition, that the small interest to which I had been sent I found in a most unsatisfactory state. For some time they had been quarrelling among themselves, and about twelve months before, owing to some arbitrary proceedings on the part of one or two individuals, the cause had been divided, and the society nearly broken up, only fourteen members remaining, and some of these were away at the diggings. The small chapel, on which was a debt of £100, would seat about sixty persons. For some time we rented the Temperance Hall, Melbourne, but we found this weakened us at both places; so we decided to give it up, and when I was able to concentrate my labours on the one place in Collingwood, our congregations steadily increased and things began to wear a brighter aspect. Several ministers were gone to the diggings;

their congregations having gone before, the shepherds followed the sheep to preach to them on the gold-fields. I was strongly urged to go also, but, after mature thought, I decided it was my duty to remain at my post, and after-experience convinced me of the wisdom of this course. Very soon my hands were full of work, and my time chiefly occupied in looking after new arrivals, and aiding them in every possible way I could. Hundreds on landing made their way to our house, I being the only person they knew, even by name; numbers were quite unfit to bear the privations and toil of gold-seeking, and having very little pecuniary means at their disposal, they knew not where to look or what employment to turn their hands to. Day after day I spent endeavouring to find them work and places to live in, and be reference for them; and frequently, when they had tided over their first difficulties, they would move off, and I should never see them again. For some time my house was like a post-office, great numbers on leaving England having directed their friends to send their letters to my care, and even after landing, such was the migratory course of most, that they could give no other address. The postman would bring me a bag of letters, and tumble them out on the floor saying, "Mr. Townend, you must sort them yourself." Some of these I was requested to open and send a reply according to circumstances; others I had to forward to various parts of the colony, and others keep until called for.

As I had travelled in several circuits at home, and being the first missionary of our body, I was well known; but this work of assisting new arrivals was very laborious and trying. The jottings in my diary of this period contain many painful cases; though I had not time to keep anything like a continuous record, still they serve as landmarks to bring many things to my remembrance. Under date November 16, 1852, I find:—"To-day I have had two painfully interesting cases—a mother putting her infant into the coffin, and a sweet girl, four years of age, dying in the cradle; her husband recently ran off, leaving her comparatively destitute. James Sutcliffe just arrived by the ship 'Hope;' he has buried his two children in the great deep, one the day before landing, and has left his wife sitting on their boxes upon the wharf until he found me out. I have given him a note for ten days' reception at the Benevolent Asylum."

Some families arrived from Cornwall about this time, and the weather being very hot and trying, several died, two young men,

Cuttance and Oppy, and Miss Freeman died in a few weeks after landing; these cases I visited almost daily and committed them to the silent grave. A ship chartered from Sunderland brought several connected with our society there. Mr. John Eggers, local preacher, died within a few days' sail of Melbourne, and was buried in the great ocean; his widow with four children I assisted, and put her in the way of earning a good living by keeping young men boarders; by this she saved a considerable sum of money, and then returned to Sunderland.

There had been a large tract of land set apart at Melbourne as a public cemetery, sections of it being apportioned to various denominations. After I had interred several bodies in the portion set apart for "Wesleyan Methodists," I began to find out that by the cemetery regulations a fee was allowed to the minister officiating—viz., eight shillings for an adult, four shillings for a child, this fee being paid into the office with the charges for the grave. I inquired of the Primitive Methodist minister, and he had buried for some time in the Wesleyan department, but knew nothing of the fees. I then applied at the office, when I ascertained that all our fees had gone into the exchequer of the Wesleyan Methodists. I now drew up a petition to the Governor, signed by the official members of the church, soliciting, as a section of the great Methodist family, the right of interment in the public cemetery. I received the following reply.

Colonial Secretary's Office,
Melbourne, 8th June, 1852.

Sir,—I have the honour to acknowledge the receipt of your letter of the 2nd of March last, soliciting, on behalf of the members of the Wesleyan Methodist Association, the privilege of interment in the public burying-ground, either in a portion allotted to themselves or in connection with some other branch of the Wesleyan Church. In reply I am directed by his Excellency the Lieutenant-Governor to state, that he has reason to believe that the members of your association have hitherto interred their dead in the portion of the Cemetery allotted to the Wesleyan denomination, and that his Excellency does not apprehend that there would be any objection, legal or otherwise, to a continuance of that course.

Should this, however, be objected to by the Wesleyan Association, His Excellency does not consider the association entitled to have a distinct portion of the cemetery allotted to their body, other than the right of interment in the portion of ground set apart for "other Protestant Denominations."

I have the honour to be, Sir,
Your most obedient servant,
Rev. J. Townend. (signed by the Secretary.)

After this, for several funerals I went into the office and received the fee; until one day Mr. B., the Wesleyan Minister, who was chairman of the district, ascertained by the books in the office that the money had been paid to me; he grew very angry and told the clerk never to give me the fee again. On the next occasion of my going, the clerk said, "I dare not pay you the fee, sir; Mr. B. has been here and forbid me ever to do so again." I now wrote to Mr. B. complaining of what I considered an injustice—that as the different sections of Presbyterians buried in one department, the same with the Baptists, that as the land had been given by Government,—never costing them a penny—though I was willing to regard it a privilege to bury our dead in the Wesleyan Methodist department, I considered by right I was entitled to the fees. Mr. B. replied that, "no obstacle would be thrown in the way of our interring, and that if I would regard the fees simply in a financial point of view, they were willing, in consideration of our circumstances, to return the fees, as a privilege, at the end of each quarter, by my applying to them for it." I replied, "*I will never consent to receive as a privilege that which I deem mine by right.*" After several letters had passed between Mr. B. and myself on this subject, I presented a second memorial to the Governor, detailing my grievance. I afterwards had a personal interview with his Excellency; but he was a man of irresolute character, almost afraid to do right lest he should be doing wrong. He now said, that the Wesleyans were such a large and influential body he did not wish to oppose them. And he thought we had better inter our dead in that part of the Cemetery set apart for "other denominations;" which to me really amounted to this;—"the place to bury strangers in," for nearly every religious persuasion had been specified, even to the Chinese.

I next went to Judge Pohlman, who, I ascertained, was chairman to the Cemetery Board of Trustees. He was a pious good man, an Episcopalian. I saw him in his private office. After hearing the details of my case he paused awhile, when he said, "Mr. Townend, you have been robbed by a brother Minister. No one has a right to your fees, no more than they have a right to go to your private drawer. My advice is, go to Mr. Purchas, the secretary, and follow the course he points out." I went to Mr. Purchas; he was very indignant. "Cannot members of the same religious family," he said, "be allowed to sleep quiet in their graves together? Mr. Townend, every time you have a funeral, go into the office; *demand* the fee, don't leave until you get it; then let the Wesleyans throw it into a court of justice, and we will stand by you."

I did so, and we were never interfered with afterwards. I felt this to be an important battle to fight, as it secured to our Churches the right of interment in perpetuity, without let or hindrance. I afterwards purchased a piece of ground as a burying-place, in which repose my beloved wife and niece, to whose memory I erected a substantial monument, and just before leaving the colony I planted two cypress trees on their grave. The Melbourne Cemetry is a very beautiful place, many parts of it like a well-kept gentleman's garden, planted with semi-tropical shrubs and flowers, interspersed with handsome marble monuments.

The Primitive Methodists, not willing to go through the same struggle as I did, ultimately obtained a small portion of the cemetery to themselves, in a corner next the Jews.

September 27th, 1852. We held a meeting to consider the ways and means for the erection of a new chapel. Our little preaching-room had become quite inadequate to our requirements, and though the price of labour at this time was exorbitant, there was no immediate prospect of its becoming more reasonable. We received promises at this meeting of about 200*l.*; and there was sufficient land attached to the chapel in Collingwood on which to erect a large building. I may here mention that Collingwood was a suburb of Melbourne, though it may now almost be considered a part of Melbourne, as both places grew until they met and united.

Nearly all the work of collecting devolved on me. We had no one who could spare the time required, and this was a very laborious and anxious time. I experienced the truth of an expression a good Baptist minister used at a public meeting: "If you want to have sleepless nights, begin to build a chapel."

I, however, met with a large amount of sympathy from other denominations, and many liberal donations were given by members of the various Churches. I had, from the first of my landing in the colony, taken an active part in the temperance cause, and attended all public meetings in Melbourne convened for any benevolent or philanthropic object, so that I was well known; even my robbery had been overruled by God for good, in bringing me so prominently before the public.

After I had got a good number of subscribers, I waited on the Governor to ask for a donation, but he would not subscribe. "Our Church was not known to him. He had already given to some things, and found out afterwards that he ought not." But I replied, "Your Excellency will see by my subscription list that several members of parliament, magistrates, and merchants have contributed, and that is some guarantee of its being a genuine case." Still he would give nothing except this promise, that if we were going to have a Sabbath-school and would let him know when the chapel was opened, he would send us bibles and testaments for the school. Of course I took care at the proper time to remind him of this promise, and obtained the books.

Week by week I begged the money to pay the workmen. The treasurer would sometimes say, "Mr. Townend, if you have not money to pay the workmen on Saturday, the work will have to stand still!" Some idea of the difficulties may be formed when I mention that we paid stonemasons and carpenters 1*l.* 12*s.* per day each man; that every load of stones cost 2*l.*—at the quarry 1*l.*, and 1*l.* for carting, and the wretched horses employed in those days did not bring us very large loads, and however often the men might drop work to smoke their pipes, it was no use to complain about it. Such was the demand for house-building that workmen were quite independent: and numbers, tempted by the high price of labour, engaged themselves for house-building who had never touched such work before, perhaps had been drapers, tailors, or shoemakers. A schoolmaster carried stones for the workmen during the building of this chapel.

On the Saturday at noon, the day preceding the opening services, there was not a single seat made, except a few from the old preaching-room. A number of men came with hammers and saws and set to work; several were our own members. We had a quantity of New Zealand pine on hand; with this they soon constructed rough benches, and by twelve o'clock at night we had got them all in their places, and the chapel swept out, when we sang—

Praise God from whom all blessings flow;

The chapel had cost up to the time of opening in September 1853, the sum of £2675. But it was then in a most unfinished state, the walls on the inside were neither plastered nor whitewashed, just the rough unhewn stone. The roof was covered with broad boards, and as the chapel was open to the roof, when the wood began to shrink—for it had been put on in a green state—we could look up and see the stars through. On the night of the opening tea-meeting it rained very heavily, and, the water coming through the roof, people had to put up their umbrellas. We realised by the Sabbath services, and the tea-meeting, the handsome sum of £700.

It will now be necessary to go back a little, in order to make plain some very painful circumstances, through which about this time I had to pass. When I landed in the Colony, no arrangement had been made for my reception, so far as a house was concerned, and the home authorities had guaranteed nothing for furniture. It had been agreed before my arrival that for a time I should stay at the house of one of the members. I soon found this very uncongenial and unsatisfactory in every respect, and that even if I valued my own credit I must quit my lodgings. Just at this time many people were anxious to sell their property in order to go to the diggings. A good Scotchman, of the name of Mackenzie, came to me one day and said, "Mr. Townend, I hear you are seeking a house; there is one to sell in King William Street, for £250, I recommend you to buy it, the owner only wants £40 cash to go to the gold-fields, the rest can remain as mortage." I replied, "That settles the question at once, for I have only £20; it is true I am expecting some money from England, but don't know when it may arrive." He said, "Buy the house, and I will lend you £20."—"Will you really lend the money to me, a perfect stranger?" "Yes! you are come to this country to preach the gospel, and do us good, I shall be pleased to let you have it." I bought the house. A Wesleyan minister had previously looked at it, and thought it too dear. Very thankful was I to quit my lodgings and enter the purchased house, without any furniture. This was only a few weeks after landing.

I made an offer to the Society to convey the property to them if they were able to raise the purchase money. I also wrote to the committee in England, making the same offer, and urging them to make a grant towards it of £50. But the Missionary Committee passed a resolution, that they could have nothing to do with house property in Australia. The Society also, after canvassing for some time, found at the December quarterly meeting, 1851, that the sum actually collected only amounted to £23 18s. 9d. They therefore decided, having with this exception nearly an empty exchequer, to appropriate this amount to Society purposes, and abandon their original project of purchasing the house as incapable of attainment. On the 17th of March 1852, the Society assembled for reorganisation. The fifth resolution recorded on the books, reads thus.—"That the Preacher's salary be £130 per annum, the preacher to provide himself with house and furniture of every description." For some time I was greatly straitened in circumstances. Having to pay the mortage on the house, I was obliged to borrow some money, and until I had paid it back and got some furniture, and began to see the way clearing before me, I lived in the most economical way. For more than twelve months I could not afford the luxury of butter, milk, or eggs. Butter rose to 4s. 6d. per pound, milk to 2s. per quart, eggs sixpence each, and all very scarce at that price. Wood and water, and everything involving labour, equally high. A good woman made me a present of a hen; I took the eggs to a grocer who lived close by, and he would give me six pounds of good crystalised sugar for six eggs; I did this until I got a famous stock of sugar in the house; fortunately animal food such as mutton and beef continued very cheap.

No further effort was made by the Society, or any wish expressed to purchase the house. In June, 1853, our new chapel was in course of erection, and for want of funds the work was standing. I now resolved (having had an offer) to sell the house, in order that I might be able to assist the trustees. The reader will be surprised to learn that after having lived in the house one year and seven months, I sold it for £1700. But I had then to rent two small rooms in which to reside, for which I paid, for a considerable time £2 per week. I received £700 cash, the rest remained on mortgage. From this, I gave a donation to the chapel of £250 and fifty more at the opening, £300 in all. I also lent the trustees £450 on note of hand.

While I was negociating the sale of the house, to the great astonishment of the Society, in steps Mr. G. R. C., a local preacher, and claims the property as belonging to the Society, on the ground that my original proffer gave them a claim to it. He called a Society meeting, and with great assiduity canvassed the members to secure a good attendance; but they, attaching no importance to his arguments, passed the following resolution:—"This meeting is of opinion that the house occupied by the Rev.

J. Townend is his own individual property, and that this Society have neither legal or moral claim thereto." Everyone present voted for the resolution, except two and one neutral; the former G. R. C. and brother, the latter Mr. T. B. Y.

Notwithstanding this decision, G. R. C. continued to agitate the Society up to the beginning of 1854, and had also been joined in this crusade against me by another individual, Mr. T. B. Y., who had arrived from England towards the close of 1852. This latter individual had held an official position in our Churches in England, was of an overbearing and haughty disposition, and of a somewhat commanding appearance. I felt an instinctive dread of his coming, and from the first he was much disappointed that the Society did not pay him that amount of homage he would like. But we had been warned by several who had come from the same town never to let the reins of government fall into his hands; besides people in the colonies are apt to take persons for what they are worth there, and not for what they have been in England. After giving us a great deal of trouble, by trying to destroy mutual confidence among the members, Mr. T. B. Y. published three hundred circulars, headed, "House Case," in which he accused me of selling a house belonging to the Society. A number of these he forwarded to England, and also sent them to ministers and members of various Churches in Melbourne.

The Society now entreated me to bring an action against him for libel, at the Supreme Court. This I felt I could not do. It would give me no pleasure to see his poor wife and children thrown into greater trouble and distress. I was lying awake one night, thinking over the matter, when the thought struck me, "Call in four of the neighbouring ministers to examine into, and report on, the whole case." This met with the concurrence of the Society, and we requested the Episcopalian, Presbyterian, Independent and Wesleyan ministers, whose churches were nearest to us, to adjudicate. The following is the decision to which they arrived:—

"The undersigned having been requested by the Rev. Joseph Townend, and the Society over which he presides, to examine into certain charges contained in a printed letter, signed by 'T. B. Y.,' seriously affecting the character of Mr. Townend, in reference to the purchase and sale of a house in King William Street, met in the Wesleyan chapel, Albert Street, Collingwood, on Monday, 15th May, 1854.

"The charges contained in the aforesaid letter were carefully investigated. The official books and papers belonging to the Society were inspected, and witnesses were examined in reference to the official documents, and to all the matters affecting the case.

"The whole having been most carefully considered, they unanimously agreed to state, that in their judgment the Rev. Mr. Townend had both a legal and moral right to the property in dispute—a decision to which they find the Society had previously come.

"They would also add, that throughout the whole of Mr. Townend's connection with the Society, he had manifested a spirit of enlarged generosity.

"(Signed)

"WILLIAM BURNS LANDELLS, Independent Minister.

"JOHN C. SYMONS, Wesleyan Minister.

"ROBERT HAMILTON, United Presbyterian Minister.

"JAMES A. CLOWES, Minister of St. Mark's, Collingwood."

The Society also drew up the following resolutions:—

"We, the undersigned members of the Wesleyan Methodist Association, Collingwood, Victoria, do hereby declare that the printed letter headed 'Case of the Preacher's House belonging to the Wesleyan Association, Collingwood,' and signed 'T. B. Y.', is, from first to last, a tissue of garbled fact, misrepresentation, and falsehood, and evidently intended to mislead the public, to the prejudice of the Rev. Joseph Townend, and ourselves as a Society.

"We unhesitatingly bear our testimony to the righteousness of the decision come to by the Revs. W. B. Landells, John C. Symons, Robert Hamilton, and James A. Clowes, as confirmatory to that arrived at by this Society on two special occasions.

"We take this opportunity of testifying our unqualified confidence in Mr. Townend, and pray he may long be spared to minister the word of eternal life to us.

"We tender our hearty thanks to the rev. gentlemen who so promptly responded, with true Christian liberality, to our solicited adjudication.

"Collingwood, May 24th, 1854."

Signed by 66 Members; at the diggings and elsewhere out of the neighbourhood, 13; not yet seen, 1; total on books, 80 members.

A few days after the decision arrived at by the above-named gentlemen, "T. B. Y." published another letter in one of the Melbourne papers, to the effect "that four clerical rogues had met and thrown the shelter of their sacerdotal garments over an erring brother." On the morning this was published, I was coming up the principal street, Melbourne, when a leading journalist tapped me on the shoulder and said, "Mr. Townend, who is this 'T. B. Y.' that is writing about you? The letter in to-day's paper renders him *morally* a dead man in the eyes of a discerning public. A man who can write as he has concerning four such well-known and respected ministers is unworthy of credit, and his malignity is so apparent that he will never be able to obtain a position in respectable society." During all this struggle we only lost two members besides "G. R. C." and "T. B. Y.," and these had been requested some time previous to this to withdraw from the Society.

A copy of the resolutions arrived at, both by the ministers and Society, together with a plain statement of the whole case, was published in three Melbourne papers, the *Argus*, *Banner*, and *Express*. Also circulars were printed addressed to the "Christian Public," dated 30th May, 1854.

These events were to me very painful; but my consciousness of rectitude, and the harmonious decision of the Church, supported me under the severe trial. Mrs. Townend, however, though possessed of great fortitude and endurance, quailed beneath the blast as it swept over us, and for several days was quite out of her mind. Just before reason lost its balance she said, "*Joseph, we have done nothing wrong, have we?*" By judicious medical treatment and the blessing of God she was restored.

The great Searcher of hearts knows best the motives that actuated "T. B. Y." in this cruel attack; but this I have reason to believe, that I gave offence by not assisting him with pecuniary aid, or finding him some one who could lend him three or four hundred pounds. I may say I have been in perils on the sea, in perils on land, in perils by robbers, and in perils among false brethren; but I have found the last the hardest to bear of all.

CHAPTER II.

Congregation increases—Deaths of Henry Dent and C. Stocks—Visits Geelong—Commences a Mission at Kew and Nunnawadding—Aspect of the Bush—Yarra Bend Lunatic Asylum—Desertion of Wives—Missing Friends—Arrival of Rev. M. Bradney—Commercial Distress—Benevolent Asylum—Roman Catholic Influence—Death of Amelia—Removal of Chapel for Street Improvements—Erection of George Street Chapel—Messrs. Falkner and Batman First Colonists in Victoria—No Dominant Church in Australia—State Aid to Religion—Dissipated Life on board Ship.

After the opening of our new chapel, the congregations continued to increase rapidly, and though the "gold fever" still caused a great migration of the people, keeping society ever fluctuating, we nevertheless were constantly adding to the number of church members and also of stated hearers. At this time we had some good voices and splendid singing; our wooden roof was a good sounding-board, and as we generally had the windows open, in that pure, rare atmosphere the sound went a long way. We were not far from St. Mark's Church, and the clergyman said to me one day, "Mr. Townend, we are very much disturbed by the singing in your chapel; frequently, while reading the prayers, my voice is so drowned, the congregation cannot hear me." I replied, "I am very sorry, but don't see how we are to help it; besides, we are greatly disturbed by the jingling of your bells; for as we begin service at half-past six, and you at seven o'clock, all the time I am reading and at prayer there is a constant tolling and chiming of bells."

Henry Dent, a most amiable young man, called on me several times, gave a subscription to the chapel, but did not stay long in Victoria; he went to Tasmania, where, overtaken by bushfire on the 7th January, 1853, he, with seven of his companions, perished.

Charles Stocks, medical student, with his mother and sisters, arrived after a very trying voyage. I introduced the young man to Dr. Singleton, who at once engaged him as an assistant. Charles, however, was seized with fever and died. It being very hot weather, the body was interred late in the evening of the same day. The good doctor accompanied us to the cemetery, where, with reading, singing, prayers, and tears, we committed the body to the silent tomb until the great rising morn.

Soon after my arrival in the colony I began to visit Geelong, a town 45 miles south-west of Melbourne. Until the railway was opened the passage was by steamer. Geelong is beautifully situated, and commands a fine view of the bay and surrounding country. To the north of the bay are three considerable elevations, called by the natives Yow Yangs, which in our language is "The Three Sisters;" travellers say, reminding you of the Bay of Naples and Mount Vesuvius. Being a sickly voyager, and the passage proverbially rough, it was often very trying to my health and feelings. The success attendant on these visits, however, amply compensated for all the toil. Here I met with Miss McKeand, so well known in the town of Rochdale. On my first visit the Presbyterian and Independent chapels were kindly lent for me to preach in. On my second visit I held two services on the Village-green, Kildare, where land was afterwards purchased, on which stands Kildare Chapel. Many blessed seasons I had with those people in these early days of colonization, chiefly Cornish families.

On returning by steamer, one fine Monday morning, the town-crier, who was quite an oddity, came down to the pier to exhibit himself in a smart suit of clothes of bright colours, which the Geelong gentry had given him. The captain, John Maclean (a jovial dashing fellow, vulgarly called "Hell-fire Jack," on account of his recklessness) invited the crier into his cabin and treated him with something to drink; during which time the vessel was ordered quietly to loose from her moorings and sail. When the crier found the steamer was off, up he rushed, ran about the deck, mounted the paddle-box, and shouted at the pitch of his stentorian voice—"stop her! stop her!" to the great amusement of the passengers and crowd on the pier. Three cheers were given for the bell-man, who took it in good part, saying "he would take care to live well at the captain's expense;" and on reaching the wharf, Melbourne, the crier mounted the paddle-box, rang his bell, and cried—"Lost, stolen, or strayed, a beautiful terrier dog; whoever will bring the same to Captain Maclean, shall be handsomely rewarded." The captain and his jovial passenger returned together next day.

On the 9th January, 1853, I opened our mission in the Bush,

three miles east of Melbourne, now the village of Kew, in the parish of Boroondara. Having ferried across the "Yarra-Yarra," we passed through Studley Park, with here and there a slab house or tent, among which was the beautiful tent of John Hodgson, Esq., afterwards the "honourable," being returned as a member of the Upper House of Parliament. In the dense forest a piece of ground was cleared, and three wood houses, containing two rooms each, were erected; three families, Morgan, Quick, and Derrick, occupied these rude buildings, in one of which I preached, the congregation coming from the neighbouring huts and tents. Mr. James Nuttall, of Rochdale, accompanied me on my first visit.

Subsequently I opened our mission at Nunnawadding, five miles further east. Here were two rude slab houses occupied by the senior and junior Illingworths, wives and children; these had been useful members of our church, and had removed from Melbourne.

The whole country had the appearance of a wild neglected park. The croaking of frogs, the perpetual song of unnumbered locusts—who appear to sing by note, beginning in the minor and ascending to the major key, then coming gradually down to the minor again, then a pause, repeating the same in unvarying succession—the jingling of bells round the necks of oxen that their owners might know their whereabouts, the cooey of the blackfellow, and the sound of the woodman's axe, with the crash of falling trees, constituted the music of those desolate districts. A chapel was afterwards erected in each of those places, belonging to the Methodist Free Churches, where songs of praise and the offering of prayer, Sabbath-schools, and the preaching of the Word have been continuous as revolving Sabbaths.

Some parts of the road from Melbourne to Nunnawadding were very uneven and dangerous, especially to carts and carriages. One part of the road, if road it could be called, went by the name of the "Bay of Biscay!" Here many a vehicle has been capsized, and the contents, inert or active, rolled in the mud or dust. The veritable stormy bay, however, is a terrible reality, where many a noble vessel has foundered, and its living freight found a watery grave. I thank God that I have been preserved mid all these aqueous and terrene dangers.

The village of Kew is now one of the most picturesque and beautiful suburban districts of the city of Melbourne, abounding with churches, shops, schools, and gentlemen's villas. At the opening of the Independent chapel, April, 1861, at the public meeting after tea, the Baptist minister at Kew said, "All honour to Mr. Townend; he was the first man who published the Gospel of Christ in this district of Boroondara."

Across the river Yarra-Yarra, north of Studley Park, on a narrow strip of lowland, stood the Yarra Bend Lunatic Asylum. It was a gloomy dismal place, and untold miseries were suffered and cruelties inflicted there; terrible revelations were made public when government inspection was instituted in that lonely asylum of insanity. Frequently on returning from Kew late at night through the lonely park, have I stood on the high ground and listened with horror to the yells and screams of the inmates of that dismal place. Occasionally I had to apply to the authorities for admission for patients, and often visited the same.

One man, quiet and decent, a member of our congregation, became insane, occasionally violent, and was sent to this asylum. After a while he refused to take any food, and, as the doctor said, had made up his mind to die of starvation; he also refused to speak to anyone. He used to be bound down on his back, and milk or broth poured down his throat. His wife was a very quiet, prudent woman. On one occasion, in company with her, I visited this case. I said to him, "Do you know this woman?" he smiled, and nodded assent. "Would you like to come home to see your friends?" Again he bowed assent. "If the doctor will promise that you shall visit your home, will you now take some food?" He then spoke, and said, "I will." I then went and told the doctor, who ordered a basin of milk and bread, and the doctor promised in our presence that if he would then take that food he should be allowed to go home the following day. He then sat up, took the milk and bread, kissed his wife, and we left the place. The day following was extremely wet, so that the visit was delayed. He seemed to sink with weakness and disappointment, and in two or three days died. Insanity for a time was fearfully prevalent.

Great numbers came to the colony who by birth and education were totally unfit for rough and hard work, and for whom there appeared no opening. When their little means were exhausted they began to sink lower and lower in the social scale, until worn out with disappointment and privation, losing hope and self-respect, they never again were able to regain their proper station in society. Then the hardships endured on the gold-fields, exposed by day to the burning rays of the sun, frequently causing sunstroke, and by night lying on the damp ground with very little shelter in all weathers; the want of proper food, and the excessive use of ardent spirits; all this combined to furnish inmates for the lunatic asylum. Added to this was the frequent desertion of wives and children, by the men who ought to have been their support and protector. Many cases occurred of poor women arriving from England to join their husbands, and finding them married to another. One man that I knew well, who made a profession of religion—for he was a local preacher, but not of our church—advertised in the Melbourne *Argus* the death of his wife in England, and then got married again; the second wife, however, finding out some months after that she had been deceived, and that his former wife was still alive, left him. It was painful to read in the newspapers day after day the advertisements for missing friends, by relatives who had arrived from England and had no clue to their whereabouts.

In the ups and downs of colonial life, people changed their residence a dozen times while communication could be effected with England. Since my return home, many people have come to me inquiring if I knew anything of their relatives in Australia. Some of these had received no letters for ten or twelve years. A few of these I had known for a time and then lost sight of them, others I had never come in contact with; the probability is, they are among the "unrecorded dead;" hundreds have been buried on the gold-fields and elsewhere of whose antecedents nothing was known, perhaps not even their name.

The work now was widely extending, for, besides the stations already referred to, we had regular preaching in several other suburban districts. Application for more ministerial aid to the home authorities had been responded to, and the arrival of the Rev. M. W. Bradney, and his excellent wife, was hailed with joy by myself and all our friends. In a letter to Rev. R. Eckett, and published in magazine, Mr. Bradney wrote as follows:—

"I safely arrived on the shores of Australia on Saturday, December 30th, 1854, being the ninety-fourth day of our sailing from Liverpool. Our excellent friend Mr. Alsop, hearing of the arrival of the ship 'Marion Moore,' hastened to meet us, and his gentlemanly behaviour and Christian kindness very much affected us.

"Upon reaching Collingwood we received a hearty welcome from Mr. and Mrs. Townend, and their niece, who are all well.

"We have a fine chapel and good congregation in Collingwood. The Society is peaceable and prosperous; in fact everything connected with the cause wears an encouraging aspect. Brother Townend is held in high esteem.

"Trade is in a very depressed condition; many persons newly arrived cannot find employment. In Melbourne and Collingwood there are many vacant houses.

"In a few days I am to leave here for Geelong. I intend shortly to forward extracts of my journal kept during the voyage."

Commercial tidal influences are, in newly colonised countries, very variable; and about this time bankruptcy and distress was on every hand. The gentleman who had purchased my house, afterwards built two more cottages on the land attached, expending £1700 on their erection. He had to sell the three houses, which had cost him above £3000, for £1400. He had also speculated largely in various ways, and now passed through the insolvent court, not paying sixpence in the pound. Sums of money were voted by the legislative assembly, to be distributed in food, tickets for which were supplied to ministers of religion, and other influential persons, to give to cases of distress.

I was a member of the Committee of the Benevolent Asylum, and our weekly meetings were long and painful. Cases of wife desertion were frequent and distressing; and the asylum built for the aged and infirm had to receive persons of all descriptions, until the Melbourne hospital was enlarged, and other charitable institutions had been set on foot. When the beds were all filled, the rest had to lie on the floors of the house, and it was no uncommon thing for patients to be brought within the gates and there left.

In the management of this excellent institution we had severe struggles with the Romish party. All ministers of religion at that time were *ex officio* members, and the priests took care to muster in strong force; several had come from the other colonies in order to swell their number in applying for the State grant to religion. I have seen these self-denying men, whose eyes stood out with fatness, flushed with wine and rage, rise to their feet, clench their fists and threaten. On one occasion we had a long contest as to whether a young girl should be brought up a Catholic or Protestant. The mother had recently died, and the priest affirmed that he had administered extreme unction to her within half an hour of her death. It was also proved that she had been a Presbyterian, then an Episcopalian within a very short period; however, the child had to be removed from the Protestant family where she had been placed, and taken into the asylum until Catholic guardians could be found.

This asylum had very nearly fallen under the control of the Catholics. The matron and several of the attendants were Catholics. A commission of inquiry had to be instituted, and three gentlemen were appointed to investigate into the affairs of the institution. When they gave in their report, among other things it was stated that young women in perfect health were inmates who never ought to have been admitted, and that the amount of wine and cordials consumed was something enormous. After this the names of these three gentlemen were read out from the altar of St. Patrick's Church, and for some time it was not safe for them to venture out after dark. It was ultimately decided that ministers should not be *ex-officio* members of committee.

June, 1855. We were now called upon to sustain a severe trial, in the death of our beloved niece Amelia, who had resided with us many years. She was in early life left an orphan, and by a kind Providence directed to make her home at our house, Mrs. Townend being sister to Amelia's mother. When we were stationed at Clitheroe, Amelia was dreadfully burned, so much so that her life was despaired of; but by the blessing of God upon the means used, after very much suffering, she was restored. This painful event left indelible marks upon her otherwise handsome and engaging countenance. This, as she often said, had a salutary effect in humbling her spirit.

When we were stationed in Rochdale, and after the death of my excellent brother, the Rev. Thomas Townend, his second son (Samuel) lingered and died, under the kind care of his bereaved mother, at our house. On one occasion, Amelia having given to Samuel a drink of water, he, in a most solemn and affecting manner, exacted a promise from her that she would meet him in heaven. Amelia was then about fourteen years of age, and this circumstance, in connection with the conduct and happy death of that noble youth, exercised a most salutary influence upon her youthful spirit. On its being finally settled that we should leave our native land on a mission of mercy to Australia, our beloved niece earnestly desired to accompany us, and we cheerfully consented.

On our making the coast of Australia, Amelia was seized with rheumatic fever, which very painful dispensation was borne with surprising fortitude. We had scarcely got well settled in Collingwood ere she was the subject of a long and severe attack of colonial fever, which sickness laid the foundation of the complaint under which she long but patiently suffered.

She now became connected with the church as a member; and under the leadership of the talented and pious Mrs. Thomas, made clear progress in spirituality. As a Sabbath-school teacher, she was affectionate, regular, and earnest. Her death, somewhat sudden and unexpected, was occasioned by a severe cold, which settled upon her wasted and diseased lungs; and despite medical skill, soon laid her in the cold embrace of death. On Saturday, June 9th, she took to her bed, from which she was to rise no more. In the night she was very ill, and spoke most tenderly of the goodness of God; and of our kindness to her in her afflictions. During the Sabbath forenoon, she affectionately embraced her aunt, and touchingly spoke of her probable dissolution. As the day advanced, she seemed to put on strength; as if *preparing* for some great work. It proved her last earthly Sabbath—her last day on earth. Oh, it was a day of suffering, of power, and of conquest! "Uncle," said she, "I never forget the dying admonition of Cousin Samuel. Oh, do let me see all the teachers, one by one; and all, *every-one* of the dear, dear girls of my class: who can tell,—but that they may never forget."

Her request being granted, she set herself to the work, and from three to five that afternoon she must have personally addressed some fifty children and youths. In those bursts of dying eloquence, there was unutterable sweetness, surprising tact and judgment, and overwhelming power. To an old associate she said, "O Alice! I am glad to see you: our states now are widely different; I am dying, and going to heaven—you are a wife and a mother. O Alice! *do*, do be in earnest about your soul; get happy in Jesus, and then you can bring up your dear child in the right way. Now, my dear, you will think of what I have said; will you not?" In the course of the afternoon, she desired us to sing "Rock of Ages," in which she joined; and, clapping her hands, said, "Oh uncle, I am happy! my dearest, dearest aunt, I am happy! glory, glory be to God." In the evening she was much exhausted, and did not talk much. About twenty minutes before twelve, she said, playfully, "Oh, I feel as if I had somewhere to go—and yet where can I go in this weak state? I should like something to eat." Several things being named, she replied, "No—no—no— !" Our neighbour, Mrs. Wood (late of Lever Street), said "I have some nice coffee, Amelia." "Oh yes;" said she, "that is it; coffee, coffee!" After taking it, with a little bread and butter, she said, "Now, let me have a little of my own way, and then I'm off to sleep." She then, with her own hands, adjusted the pillows and bed-clothes, and having reposed as if in sleep, sunk into the arms of Jesus. Aged 22 years, June 10th, 1855.

Her countenance after death was radiant with serenity and joy, which struck every beholder. An intelligent observer, after silently gazing, remarked, "Mr. Wesley is right:—

> "'Ah! lovely appearance of death!
> What sight upon earth is so fair?'"

While looking on that face I was strongly reminded of the expressive lines of Young, in his "Narcissa"—

> "Like blossom'd trees o'erturned by vernal storm,
> Lovely in death the beauteous ruin lay."

The funeral was very numerously attended. The service was conducted by the Rev. Michael Clark, Primitive Methodist, partly in the chapel, and partly in the cemetery. After tea, which had been provided in the chapel, our esteemed brother, Mr. Joseph Mowbray, from London, conducted a short service and delivered the address.

He commenced by referring to the peculiarly solemn and sorrowful circumstances under which they were placed. "On the same evening one short week ago, our friend and fellow-labourer, now no more, sat down to tea with us, at our monthly teachers' meeting. How sudden and painful the changes which have taken place since that time. One week has rolled by and her presence is no longer seen; that cheerful voice which then conversed with us is now silent in the grave. He need not endeavour to excite their sympathy; the garments of mourning, and the fallen tears, bore witness to the sorrow which moved them. But we sorrow not as others which have no hope. In her experience, while the hand of death was upon her, there were unmistakable evidences that all was well. Now she has exchanged time for eternity. 'That land of pure delight,' of which she so often sang, she is now an inhabitant of—the New Jerusalem—the mere thought of which sends a thrill of joy through our spirits. She has gazed upon the face of her Saviour; she has joined in those anthems of praise which ever burst from angels and the redeemed, in the presence of God and the Lamb. We would not call her back again, but rather remember her dying injunction, and prepare to meet her there. From this solemn event, we each hear a warning voice. To the young—her fellow-teachers, it speaks loudly. It tells us that youth is not an impenetrable shield against the shafts of death. From this event, which has taken from you a dear friend, and an untiring fellow-labourer, learn the imperative necessity of a preparation for death. Listen to the warning voice; it calls you to the Saviour. To those who are not young, and who are still unprepared to die, it speaks in a voice of thunder,—'Awake, thou that sleepest, and arise from the dead!' it calls upon you to beware, lest in an hour which ye think not of the Son of Man come. But all present ought to be reminded of this great truth—'Ye are not your own.' Neither our time or talents, nor body or soul, belong to us. We have been bought—the price paid for our redemption was the blood of the everlasting covenant. Let this cause us to labour, while the day still continues with us; to lay ourselves a willing sacrifice upon the altar of Divine love—to live as in sight of eternity, so that when the Bridegroom comes, we may be found of Him in peace."

Whilst our churches were in peace and prosperity, an unexpected trial overtook the church in Collingwood. We received notice from the City Corporation that our new chapel, then filled with attentive worshippers, stood in the centre of an intended new street, and must be removed. In the early days of the colony, people had bought large allotments, which, when land became more valuable, they divided and subdivided, selling it again without much regard for good streets; but when wealth began to pour into Melbourne, and it was seen that it would become a large and influential city, it became necessary for the corporation to see to the proper laying out of broad and regular streets, and great numbers of houses had to be taken down.

A long and tiresome struggle with the council ended in their giving us compensation to the amount of £1,900 and the old materials. At once we set to the great work, and purchased a good site of land for the sum of £616, on which stands our George Street Chapel; and the old preaching-room, which had been converted into two dwellings, three rooms for myself, and two very small ones for chapel-keeper, together with the chapel, were taken down and removed.

The Municipal Council Chamber, Fitzroy, in the same neighbourhood, was rented for Sabbath services, which room was much too small and badly ventilated, but nothing better could be obtained. On this account we suffered severe unavoidable loss of our congregation.

The foundation-stone of our new house of prayer was laid by the Honorable John Pascoe Falkner, M.L.C., and an address on our principles and polity was given by myself. Mr. Falkner, being a Nonconformist, showed much kindness to Liberal Methodism. Many a time I have ridden in the good old gentleman's carriage, for if he passed me, and I was going in the same direction, he would stop and invite me to sit with him and have a chat.

John Pascoe Falkner and John Batman were unquestionably the first colonisers of the Port Philip district, which district now bears the name of our noble Queen—Victoria; but to Mr. Falkner belongs the honour of founding the city of Melbourne. He was a lad in Colonel Collins's fleet in 1803, when that gentleman was ordered by Government to establish a penal settlement in the Port Philip district. The convicts, to the number of 307, with 50 marines, were landed near the Heads; but the settlement was abandoned in January, 1804, for want of fresh water, and a very unfavourable report of the land obtained currency, as being unfit for cultivation, or for the abode of civilised man.

Mr. Falkner afterwards settled in Van Diemen's Land, now called Tasmania, and when that island became overstocked with cattle, the settlers became anxious to find pasture-land at a convenient distance to which they could remove their flocks. John Batman formed an association, with a number of gentlemen, to establish sheep stations at Port Philip, and he and his party landed at Indented Heads in 1835. Having some Sydney blacks with him, he managed to arrange with the natives for the purchase of land, and by the payment of blankets, knives, tomahawks, looking-glasses, &c., he bought from them 100,000 acres, and afterwards by the same means purchased 500,000 acres more. The Government, however, afterwards cancelled this bargain, but gave Mr. Batman compensation, as a reward for his enterprise as the first coloniser.

John Pascoe Falkner also formed a party to colonise. He landed the same year at Port Philip, and pitched his tent where the city of Melbourne now stands—at that time an unbroken solitude, save for the presence of the kangaroo and the black fellow, with innumerable birds and insects. The same year Mr. Falkner had nine acres in crop near the site of the present wharf, and he was the first to commence a weekly manuscript newspaper. Melbourne was proclaimed in May, 1837, and the first land sale took place on June 1st. One allotment, purchased by Mr. Falkner for £70, was sold, two years after, for £1,000. According to the census of 1865, just thirty years after the first settlement, the population of Victoria amounted to 616,663; Melbourne alone, with suburbs, containing a population of about 140,000.

Our new chapel was opened for public worship on Sabbaths, 6th and 13th April, 1856. I was honoured with the first service; the Rev. John Reid, Presbyterian, in the evening. In the morning of the 13th, the Rev. J. L. Poore, late of Manchester; and in the evening, the Rev. James Ballantyne, late of Edinburgh, preached; and on the Monday a grand social tea festival was held. The weather was very fine, and all the services were well attended, and gracious influences vouchsafed. The chapel is of the Italian style of architecture, and as labour had become much cheaper, we were enabled to build a far superior chapel to the one first erected. From the laying of the foundation-stone to the closing tea-meeting about £300 was raised. We afterwards erected very excellent and commodious school-rooms at the rear of the chapel, for day and Sabbath schools.

There is no dominant church established by law in the colonies. All churches and ministers enjoy the same status, and though the Episcopalians would like to claim precedence, from having so long enjoyed it in England, they are obliged to be content to stand on the same level with their brethren of other denominations. The Anglican bishop, Dr. Perry, is a pious good man, and he stated in public that he did not wish the titles to be accorded to him customary in England, as he thought in a free country like Australia it must be very offensive to his brethren of other communions. Nevertheless, the Episcopal clergy and laity were determined to assume as much dignity as possible. On one occasion I was present at a large public meeting, convened in aid of the Melbourne City Mission. The bishop was in the chair, and a resolution was put into my hands to move a vote of thanks to the chairman, "The Right Reverend Father in God the Lord Bishop of Melbourne." I thought, as I read it over, "I shall never put it in that form," so I moved "that the thanks of the meeting be presented to 'Dr. Perry, bishop of the Episcopal Church in Victoria.'" A good Baptist had to second it, and he got over the difficulty by simply seconding the resolution, as moved by Mr. Townend. An Episcopalian put it to the meeting, giving full emphasis to all the titles, and saying it had been moved by "*Mr.* Townend; seconded by Henry Langlands, Esq." Some one in the body of the hall, I never knew who, shouted out, "Why do you not say the *Rev.* Mr. Townend, for that is his proper title?" Since then I have been in many prayer-meetings with the good bishop, in connection with the Evangelical Alliance, when he has gone down on his knees, and offered as beautiful and simple a prayer as any Methodist need desire.

The great bone of contention among the different denominations is the State aid to religion. When Victoria was separated from New South Wales, the amount appropriated to religious purposes was 6000*l.* per year. This sum was very soon increased to 30,000*l.* When the New Constitution was formed, in 1854, a clause was inserted, called the 53rd Clause, by which it was proposed to set apart the sum of 50,000*l.* per annum as a grant in aid of ministers' stipends, and for the erection of places of worship. This clause, so far from receiving the public sanction, was all but universally condemned; public meetings were convened to protest against it—the first, held in Collingwood, was in our chapel; and on every occasion, when the question was submitted to a free public assembly, the proposed endowment was strongly condemned. The insertion of this clause took the public by surprise, and though the interval allowed for opposition was very brief, no less than 19 petitions, from all parts of the colony, were presented against it, and only one in its favour, and that was from the Roman Catholics.

It was remarked by Mr. O'Shanassy, a Catholic, then at the head of the Government, as an argument in favour of State aid, that the Wesleyans, a large and influential body, had presented no petition against the endowment. The clause was passed and inserted in the Constitution Act; but the Legislative Council at this time was no fair exponent of the views of the colonists, in proof of which the *Melbourne Argus*, the leading daily paper, for a considerable time headed all reports of the proceedings of the Legislative Council by the following standing advertisement:

"It is necessary to guard those who read the reports of the proceedings of the Legislative Council against looking upon the decisions of that body as expressing the opinions of the colonists of Victoria. While our Legisla-

ture is so constructed that it is simply a mockery of representation, this fact should never be forgotten when estimating the value of its decisions. In an assembly of thirty members, ten are nominees of the Crown; and the right of returning the twenty elected members is so artfully distributed through the colony as very materially to check the free expression of popular opinion." . . . .

According to the framing of the original clause, it provided simply for the maintenance of religion. It was soon seen that according to this wording, the Mahomedan or Hindoo* might lay claim to a share. The word "Christian" was then inserted before "religion;" by this the Jews were dissatisfied, as it excluded them. During the debate on this question in the Council, much angry and bitter feeling was excited, and, from a long article which appeared in the *Melbourne Herald*, the following quotation may suffice:—"The discussion on the clause of the New Constitution Bill, affording State aid to religion, created yesterday a great deal of very excited debating—honourable members frequently approaching, in their personal recriminations, the extreme verge of parliamentary decency. It is a strange and lamentable fact, that whenever religious topics are introduced into a political assembly—whenever what ought to be a standard of general peace is unfurled, some contradictory principle of human nature prompts men to give full swing to all their bitter and acrimonious passions, to be more violent, arrogant, splenetic, and generally un-Christian in their speech and conduct than on any other occasion. Everyone in Council yesterday seemed to be of one accord in their anxiety for the spread of religion and morality; there was the most perfect unanimity as to the ultimate purpose to be attained; and yet, according to the strange perverted principle we have just stated, the Council could not proceed to discuss the means by which the commonly desired end—the worship of God, and the spread of peace and goodwill amongst men—could be promoted without manifesting the bitterest and most angry feelings we ever saw exhibited within the Council walls. The very

---

* I took this cutting from a newspaper just before returning to England.

"The following peculiar application was handed to the Ararat Borough Council on Wednesday, signed by fifteen Celestial ratepayers:—

"Gentlemen,—Hearing that the Market Reserve is to be divided among religious bodies and public bodies, as an old and civilised nation, and great worshippers, we beg for space for a Joss house among the others, wherein to show barbarians what to do good is best, and to lighten darkness, and to remove the cloud of ignorance from the people."

turn the debate took might have afforded a salutary lesson as to the impolicy of mixing politics and religion together, and as to the certainty that while £50,000 a year is paid to maintain churches and ministers of religion, more angry feeling will be excited thereby, than the fifty thousand pounds' worth of parsons will ever be able to allay."

The indiscriminate endowment of religion was felt to be most anomalous, even by the recipients themselves. Bishop Perry on several occasions expressed himself as willing to consent to the immediate withdrawal of the grant, rather than error and truth should be endowed alike. At the Episcopal conference held in Melbourne in 1851, the Bishop in his opening remarks said, "He could not bring himself to regard the State as a collector appointed to save them the difficulty of making a collection; besides, he would point out to them another distinction—viz., that the State, while it collected from all parties, collected from all according to their means; but the amount is not apportioned according to the means of the sects, but according to their numbers. . . . . With regard to whether, on the ground of expediency, or as an absolute moral right, the Government should recognise and support a particular Church, he had no hesitation in expressing a most decided opinion that it would be most inexpedient to do so; and if the government of the colony were at that moment vested in him, he should feel it to be his duty not to do so. He believed that by recognising an established Church, they would be doing that which would prove most injurious to the progress of true religion and piety. . . . Then came the question—it was a difficult one, and he would not blink it—were they to reject the State support and depend entirely upon voluntary assistance. With a full sense of all the difficulty in his way he answered, yes."

When it was proposed to increase the original grant, a deputation waited on the Bishop, to ask him to sign a petition praying for a removal of all State aid. In his reply, which was published in the newspapers at the time, he stated, "that though willing himself to encounter any difficulties that the immediate withdrawal of all assistance from the State might involve; still there were so many of the clergy and laity of his Church who regarded such aid as absolutely necessary for the maintainance of an efficient ministry, that on this ground he must decline to sign the petition."

The grant of £50,000 was first distributed in 1855, and it was soon seen that the manner in which it was distributed was most unfair and unjust. The act provided that the money should be apportioned to the different sects, according to their numbers at the previous census; and as several sections of the Christian Church, the Baptists, Independents, United Presbyterians, Methodist Free Church, and the Primitives, conscientiously refuse to accept State aid, most certainly their proportion of the grant ought to have gone back into the general exchequer, to be employed in the construction of roads and other improvements for the good of the colony at large. Instead of this, it went to swell the amount given to those sects who had no scruples about taking all they could get.* In 1856 the Episcopalians, with less than a third of the population, received £26,614, the Roman Catholics with only 45,011 of the population received £10,837, the Wesleyans received £3,723 (afterwards increased to between £4000 and £5000), the remainder of the grant was given to the Presbyterians, the Lutheran Church, and the Unitarians. Thus one class is paid to teach that Jesus Christ is divine, and died as a mediator to atone for human guilt; and another class is paid to teach that he was a mere man, and died as a martyr to his principles. One class is paid to teach that the Church of Rome is the only true Church, and that all are damned who leave her communion; while other classes are paid from the same fund to denounce her as Antichrist, the mother of harlots, and abomination of the earth. In addition to the £50,000, voted by the Victorian Government, very liberal grants of land are given, as sites for places of worship, schools, and ministers residences. Whenever land is being surveyed for a new township, a section is set apart for religious purposes; those denominations who take State aid then apply for a portion, as much as they require, which is frequently rather a large allotment; and it is sometimes years before they build on it; not until the place becomes sufficiently populous to make it worth their while to enter the field; when, with land costing them nothing, and Government money at their disposal, they are able to erect large and handsome places of worship; while the purely voluntary Churches, having by this time to pay high price for land, and depending on the freewill offerings of their adherents, find it often a painful struggle to maintain their ground. When land in Melbourne became so very

* For many of the above particulars, I am indebted to a pamphlet, published in Melbourne 1856, by my esteemed friend, the Rev. A. M. Ramsay, United Presbyterian Minister, Collins Street.

valuable that good central sites commanded an almost fabulous price; the Wesleyans pulled a chapel down in Collins Street West, and sold the land for a bank, for the immense sum of £38,000. This act, as may readily be supposed, caused great excitement and dissension in the colony, as all land given by Government for religious purposes is on the condition that it shall not be alienated for secular purposes. It so happened, however, that the Episcopalians, about the same time, also wanted to sell some land; and the two communities combined got a special bill passed through Parliament to legalise the transfer. If they had not succeeded in this they would have had to refund the money to Government. With this sum, the Wesleyans were enabled to erect, in another part of Melbourne, on land also given by Government, a splendid edifice, with minister's residence and schools. This building is an outrage on the simplicity of Methodism, and is generally termed the Wesleyan Cathedral, the Episcopalians at that time having nothing equal to it.

Several attempts have been made to get the State Aid Act repealed; and on one occasion a bill for its abolition passed the Lower House of Parliament, but was rejected by the Upper House. The agitation will be continued, however, until this apple of discord is removed, for as long as it continues there will be constant bitterness and heartburnings among the colonists. Let all Churches be put on a level, and allowed to grow by the faith, self-denial, and contributions of their members. State aid has been abolished in South Australia, Queensland, and New South Wales.

As I had from the first taken an active part in opposing State aid to religion, I was much grieved that at our Australian Assembly in 1861, a motion was introduced by Mr. Middleton, that we should apply for our proportion of the grant. The Home Committee had been previously communicated with to ascertain their views on the subject. The Missionary Secretary, in his reply, said "That the Australian churches were best able to judge in the matter, and though the committee expressed different opinions on the subject yet they gave no definite instructions." Had the committee not have left it thus an open question, Mr. Middleton would never have carried the motion. We, however, called a meeting the following week at George Street Chapel, and, as far as our circuit was concerned, repudiated the grant; some of the other Churches did the same, and no one ever applied for it except Mr. Middleton, and that only for one year, as he soon after left our communion.

Much, however, may be said in extenuation of this decision to take State aid; our preachers were placed in a very trying and painful position. The very meagre grants which the committee in England were enabled to make to the mission were totally inadequate to our requirements, aad made it impossible for us either to extend our borders as we had opportunity, or even to maintain our ground. The total amount granted to the Australian mission during the first ten years did not average 150*l.* per annum, including the passage of three missionaries, while the Wesleyans, in addition to their large Government grant, were receiving several thousand pounds per year from England. As far as I was personally concerned I was better able to maintain my position than some of my brethren, Providence having placed a little pecuniary means at my disposal, which enabled me on several occasions to relieve our chapels when in difficulty; and during more than fourteen years' residence, with the exception of about 18 months, I paid my own house-rent and provided myself with furniture.

In a new country like Australia, where every section of religious life is represented, and in the towns competition is even more keen than in England, our liberal church polity is not sufficient of itself to attract either a congregation or adherents if we cannot in some measure keep pace with other Churches, in providing good buildings in which to worship. Nor must it be supposed that all the members of our churches who leave England seek to be identified with us when they land in Australia. Only a very few will settle and reside near enough to join us; and it is deeply to be lamented that a long sea voyage is most detrimental to religious life. The idle dissipated life on board ship, the companionships and friendships formed there have ruined hundreds who were useful and laborious workers in the Church of Christ at home. Again and again I have been bitterly disappointed, after having received letters from England, telling me of certain individuals who were coming, and what a great help I should find them. Some I never saw at all; others sought to do us harm instead of good. There are many people who are kept in the right path by their surroundings; family and social ties have a restraining influence; but just loose them from their moorings, set them adrift among new and strange scenes, removed from the watchful eyes of friends, and their character appears to totally change. A number of others on coming went straight to the Wesleyans; some I knew had been expelled during the agitation in England, which arose on account of the arbitrary proceedings of that body, and when I remonstrated with them for want of fidelity to their principles, they have sought to excuse themselves because of the smallness of our chapels, compared with the accommodation offered by the Wesleyans. This was not the way to help us to provide for the future needs of the colony; to suit such people chapels should spring up spontaneously like mushrooms. As far as they are concerned we might still continue to labour under the same disadvantages.

CHAPTER III.

Temperance Society—Sad Results of Drunkenness—Sunday Closing Act—Houses of Parliament—Vote by Ballot—Removes to Geelong—Marriage Law—Midnight Wedding—Arrival of Messrs. Sayer and Middleton—Opening of Windsor Chapel—Death of Mr. Samuel Heape—Returns to Melbourne—Unholy Men obtain Membership in the Church—Law Cases—Costs of Trials—Untrue Statements published in the *Wesleyan Times*—Career of Mr. J. B.: £1000 Loan to Chapels.

BEING from the commencement of the temperance reformation a staunch teetotaller, I at once identified myself with the movement in Australia, and by labour and contribution assisted in carrying on the good work. At once this introduced me to the public meetings, and fellowship with some choice and kindred spirits, chief of whom at that time were Charles Reed, Henry Langlands, Thomas Fulton, and Richard Heales: three of these gentlemen were afterwards members of parliament.

During the early stages of the diggings the work was very laborious, and for a time I acted as secretary to the Melbourne Society.

The signatures of several public men indicate the dreadful ravages of alcohol. Some were rescued from the terrible vortex, and others went to a drunkard's grave. One day I was called upon to bury the child of a brewer, his wife, whilst intoxicated, having crushed it to death. I often visited this family, but the wife ultimately drank herself to death. Mr. R. A. was a member of our Church, a local preacher, and a good player on the harmonium. He was a fast, demonstrative fellow, and, as a farrier, was rapidly making a fortune. He fell through drink and company, then had a severe illness, during which I frequently visited him: he seemed very penitent, and was restored to health and church fellowship. Again he fell, and was the life of his boon companions. After a long debauch, and with a view to prepare himself for his daily work, he went down to the river Yarra fishing, took with him a boy and a bottle of wine. His boat was tied to a tree in the middle of the stream: the rope broke, and the boat dashed down the current, ran against the stump of a fallen tree, and was upset; the boy seized some overhanging branches and was saved, but the wretched man was drowned. This was on the Wednesday, and the body could not be found. On the Sabbath evening following, I, to a large congregation, improved the melancholy event from Proverbs xxix. 1—"He that, being often reproved, hardeneth his neck, shall suddenly be destroyed, and that without remedy." On the Wednesday following the body was grappled from the sludge of the river, and carried to an outhouse of the nearest drunkery to await a coroner's inquest, at which inquest several of the jury got intoxicated.

Prior to his untimely death he had sent to England for his wife and daughters, who, shortly after the dire event, landed at Melbourne; but instead of receiving the anticipated welcome of a husband and father, we had to meet them with the intelligence of his sad end.

Another case.—Mr. D. L. was a regular attendant at our chapel from the first day of my ministry in Collingwood: he was a good workman, and liberal supporter of our cause. His wife was a truly pious and excellent woman. D. L., however, became a drunkard. On one occasion, when in liquor, his wife tried to keep him from the cash-box, when grasping her round the throat, he so injured her that she died of throat inflammation, of which this was the cause. That dear woman's long and painful illness was intensified by the conduct of her wretched husband. I have often seen him drunk at her bedside. He was drunk at the funeral. He sold three or four cottages and some other property, and drank the money. After breaking his thigh, and lying in bed several months, the first time he went out on crutches he got drunk; and when he had no longer any money to spend, he would loiter at the public-house doors, hoping some of his old companions would treat him. The last time I saw him he came to my house, in an emaciated and diseased state of body, for a note of recommendation to the hospital. This man who, had it not been for drink, would have been a good husband, a successful tradesman, and exemplary Christian, died in the Melbourne hospital, and was buried in a pauper's grave.

Mr. G. H. I persuaded to take the pledge. He kept his vow three years, built a good house, and prospered. Under very exciting circumstances he broke loose and became a reckless man, cruelly treating his pious and delicate wife. On returning late one night from a preaching appointment, on passing a corner drink-shop I heard from the inside the voice of this man. "Landlord," said he, "I am in a fix!" "What is the matter, Hughes?" "I am not quite drunk," he said, "and I am afraid my wife will give me a good talking to." "Oh," said the incarnate demon behind the counter, "you can easily manage that." "How?" asked the staggering man. "Go home, and, as you enter the house, curse your wife, and swear, as if in a rage, that *she has been drinking all the time you have been out*, and she will be glad to let you go quietly to bed." "That will do, landlord; give me another 'nobbler' to strengthen me." (A "nobbler" is sixpennyworth of brandy). Oh cursed, cursed drink! traitor to God, and ruiner of man! mother of woe and death and hell! Some we rescued, pulling them out of the fire, and hating the very garments spotted with the drink. It is of no use telling us that education, or refinement, or social position is a safeguard against intemperance—not even among the female sex is it so.

One Saturday morning a gentleman came to my house. I felt some surprise as I only knew him from being a neighbour, but he had come to tell me his troubles. His wife had become a drunkard; he was almost heartbroken, and had tried every means to wean her from the debasing habit; but he was now feeling he could bear it no longer, nor suffer his children to grow up under such influences. He was in a good Government situation, and I had often thought, as I passed their house and heard her singing and playing on the piano, or saw them walking out with their two beautiful little girls, what a happy couple they were. But here was the skeleton in the house. He wanted me to go to his home, for she was at that time intoxicated, and though he had informed her parents, they would not believe it, and would scarcely speak to him on that account; he, therefore, wished me to corroborate his statement. When I went in he fetched his wife into the parlour, but she was sufficiently sober to feel ashamed on seeing a stranger there, and again staggered out of the room. In about an hour, at his request, I went in again, that I might append a postscript to a letter he had just written her father; she was now lying on the kitchen floor sound asleep, her head resting on her arm, and a blazing fire on the hearth. I stated in my postscript just the state in which she was. I felt reluctant to do this. Her father was a clergyman in the Episcopal Church, and I thought what a bitter humiliation it would be to him On the following day every blind in the house was down, and if death had reigned there, it could not have been more silent. On the Monday forenoon I went in to see them; I prayed with them, and persuaded her to take the pledge. She signed her name, weeping bitterly; and, when she had done so, her husband said, "Now, my dear, you feel better; don't you?" "Oh," she replied, calling him by name, "you must give me time." I hope she kept her pledge. I saw them several times afterwards, but did not like to inquire, unless they introduced the subject.

Mr. Lewis Thomas with his amiable and talented wife were great acquisitions to the temperance cause. This lady, though a very excellent preacher and laborious class-leader in our church at Collingwood, was, if possible, still more popular and successful in the temperance cause. This couple lived at the corner of Gore and Gertrude Streets, Fitzroy, just opposite two much-frequented public houses, and the scenes and sounds of drunkenness and revelry they were compelled to witness day and night were terrific. Oh the cruel mercies of the traffickers in strong drinks, tempting their victims to spend their last penny, and then, in a state of reeling intoxication, turning them out of doors, to be found a few minutes after on all-fours, studying the sublime science of gutterology. In the early days of the diggings, it was a very frequent practice for the diggers to come down to Melbourne with their pockets full of cash, which they would deposit in the hands of the landlord of the inn where they stayed, telling him to let them know when it was done, when they would again return to the goldfields. Such a course as this led to violence, debauchery, and robbery. Oh,

Gold, gold, gold;
Bright and yellow, hard and cold;
Molten, graven, hammered and rolled;
Heavy to get, but light to hold;
Hoarded, bartered, bought and sold;
Stolen, borrowed, squandered and doled;
Spurned by the young, but hugged by the old
To the very verge of the churchyard mould;
Price of many a crime untold;
Gold, gold, gold!

One very beneficial act passed by the Victorian Parliament was that forbidding the opening of public-houses on the Sabbath, so that the streets of Melbourne were comparatively quiet on the Lord's-day. I was much struck on returning to England with the contrast presented by our large towns in this respect. The licensing laws of this country are a reproach to our legislators, especially the iniquitous beer-house system, night licences and Sabbath trading. We first open the flood-gates to vice and crime, and then spend the wealth of the nation to punish it.

There are some other laws in Australia we should do well to copy, such as the "vote by ballot." I have gone and recorded my vote as quietly as paying a private visit to a friend; especially when the polling-place has been at some school-house or rooms, at a distance from any public-house. On entering, each elector is presented with a red pencil and a paper, on which is printed the names of the candidates; you then retire to another room, where there is only a policeman standing. Having crossed out the names of the candidates you do not wish to vote for, you fold the paper, drop it into the ballot-box and retire, no one the wiser as to whom you have voted for. There is no inducement to bribery, for though the cars are running with placards, Vote for such a candidate, you get in, ride to the polling booth, and then vote for whom you like.

In the Australian colonies there are two Houses of Parliament; the upper is the Legislative Council, and the lower the Legislative Assembly. In Victoria, according to the new Electoral Act, passed in 1865, the Upper House is composed of thirty members, who are elected for ten years, one for each province retiring every two years. The qualification of electors for the Legislative Council is—they must be natural born British subjects, and possess a freehold in the colony of the value of £5,000, or an annual rental value of £500; but professional men, such as ministers of religion, barristers, solicitors, legally qualified medical men, and schoolmasters may also vote for a member of the Council for the electoral province in which they reside. The Legislative Assembly is composed of seventy-eight members, and every male person of twenty-one years of age can vote who has been in the colony twelve months, and residing in the locality in which he claims to vote for three months prior to his applying for his elector's right. It is the duty of everyone desirous of voting, and whose name does not appear upon any rate-payers' roll, to call upon the Registrar of the district in which he resides, and request to be enrolled as an elector. It is the duty of the Registrar, in accordance with the Act, to issue to such applicant an "Elector's Right" at a cost of one shilling.

The first time I recorded my vote it was all open voting; the ballot was not then established. The Mayor (J. M. Smith, Esq.) was one of the candidates. This gentleman had been very kind to me—at the time I was robbed he came to my house and generously presented me with ten guineas towards my loss; and though I had a good deal of respect for him, still he was holding political views that I could not agree with. The all-absorbing question of this election was the State aid to religion. Of course we, as voluntaries, were anxious to return a member pledged to disendowment. When I entered the room to vote, Mr. Smith was present, and it was exceedingly painful to my feelings when asked, "Whom are you going to vote for, Mr. Townend?" to reply in favour of the other candidate. And when we see the bribery, corruption, and intimidation practised in England at elections, it does appear quite time to establish a different system, so that a poor man may vote according to his conscience, without being immediately turned off from his employment, or receive notice from his landlord to quit his dwelling.

At our annual meeting, held in George Street Chapel, Collingwood, December, 1856, it was agreed that I should go to Geelong, and Brother Bradney be removed from Geelong to Melbourne. This change would have been very painful to me had I not felt its Connexional propriety, and also had a strong regard for the Geelong friends. Mr. Bradney and his excellent wife were much beloved, and had successfully laboured in that district. January 27th, 1857, we removed to Geelong; here were kindred loving spirits with whom I took sweet counsel—Charles Reed, M.L.A., and his excellent wife, Mr. J. M. Garratt, secretary of the Temperance Society, and Mr. J. D. Mowbray, our indefatigable day-school master and local preacher, with other dear friends.

We had three small chapels—Kildare, Preston Street, and Bellarene Street, with a neat preaching-room on Hearne Hill. Soon after my arrival at Geelong, Miss Pollard, from London, came safely to our shores, with the view of becoming the wife of Mr. Mowbray. The wedding was celebrated in our little sanctuary Hearne Hill, which was comfortably filled with select friends. The festivities were kept up during the day at the residence of Mr. Reed; it was one of the brightest, happiest days of my Australian life. Mr. Reed, though half Methodist and half Quaker, was the jolliest little fellow I ever knew when in the bosom of confiding friends.

When Mrs. Thomas came to visit us in her preaching and temperance labours, we generally arranged to spend an evening together, and, in the absence of the fire-water, our enjoyments were joyful and Christian. May we who mingled in those social scenes below, be again reunited to enjoy the festivities of heaven, where sorrow and parting will be known no more!

Our societies here prospered, Kildare and Preston Street chapels were enlarged, and a good temperance hall was built, where we held weekly meetings, and much good was done.

Geelong is beautifully situated overlooking the blue waters of Corio Bay, and for a time it was thought that the town would be only second in importance to Melbourne; and being conveniently situated for supplying the interior, the hope was entertained that merchant ships would come to Geelong instead of Melbourne. Unfortunately, there was a sand bar which compelled vessels of heavy tonnage to anchor a considerable distance from the town, and by the time the Geelong people were able to remove the bar, at immense cost, the enterprising Melbournites had built splendid piers, with railway and every facility for vessels of the largest size to discharge cargo, and had also opened up railways to Ballarat, Castlemaine, and other parts of the interior; so that capitalists who had invested largely in Geelong were great losers. House and other property depreciated immensely in value, and great commercial distress ensued. The country around Geelong is very fertile, and well adapted for farms and vineyards, especially the Barrabool Hills.

The marriage law in Australia is liberal and unfettered; printed certificates, schedules, and registers are provided by Government, and entrusted to all accredited ministers of all denominations, and the time and place of celebration is left to the choice of the parties concerned. A quarterly return of all marriages must be sent to the Registrar, and are then duly entered at the Supreme Court of the colony. A minister is liable to a heavy penalty for marrying a minor without the consent of parents or guardians, or a certificate from a magistrate appointed for that district. Commonly, weddings were performed at the residence of the minister, or of the bride, and most frequently in the evening. The fee was a gratuity from the parties to the minister, and the amount was according to circumstances. It was a common thing for the diggers, in the first years of the gold-fields, to come into Melbourne when an emigrant ship was expected, in order to select a wife from the new arrivals; and, having made his choice, he would go to a draper's shop, fit her out with more expensive finery than people with even good incomes were able to purchase, and then off to the nearest minister to get married.

In a new country, where persons have not opportunities of knowing each other, a discreet friend may be of essential service in directing and assisting in matrimonial engagements.

One day, when taking tea with a few friends in Geelong, the conversation turned on the slight offered to one of the company by a young woman known to all present. I said "Cheer up, Joseph; I know a young woman that will suit you better." After tea, the young man followed me to the door and said, "Mr. Townend, were you in earnest in what you said at the table?" I replied that I was. I then described to him the kind of person—about his own age, a member of the Church, active, clean, frugal, &c., but that she had removed from Collingwood to Tasmania. He then very earnestly requested that I would write to the young woman and say what I knew of him. I wrote to Miss Hanger, and explained the circumstances—that Joseph Smith was from Oldham, Lancashire, was about her age, a Methodist and teetotaller, had saved a little money, was possessed of some land, had built himself a comfortable house, and that if she was my own sister I could recommend him to her. Her answer was, thanks for my letter, and a request that I would say to Mr. Smith that she would be glad to receive a letter from him.

The correspondence was opened, and ended in my receiving a note from Mr. Smith, asking that Miss H. and himself might be allowed to meet at my residence, at Collingwood, on the Saturday night, giving the date, as she would then arrive by steamer. At the time appointed these two persons, who had never seen each other before, took tea with Mrs. Townend and myself. After tea they went for a walk, on the Sabbath worshipped twice at our chapel, and on the Tuesday morning following I united them in solemn wedlock, and the same day they left by steamer for Geelong. The resemblance was so great that the friends said they were like brother and sister. Within six months I received a letter of thanks from each, unknown to the other, for the part I had taken in the affair. An elderly gentleman, Mr. Parkin, met in my class in Collingwood he had buried his wife in England, and his daughter was now keeping his house. After meeting, one night, he lingered behind; said he wished a little private conversation. He then told me his daughter was going to be married, that he should be left very lonely, and it struck him that I might be able to direct him to a suitable partner. I said "Yes; I think I can," and gave him the address of a good woman, a widow, in Oxford Street. He wished me to introduce him, and the time was fixed when he would call upon me. In the interim, however, he had introduced himself and *succeeded* to the entire satisfaction of each other. This couple were my fast friends as long as I remained in Collingwood.

Mr. Baker, schoolmaster, widower, whose wife I visited in her last sickness, and conducted the funeral service, afterwards removed to a government school at the Werribee, close by the half-way station between Melbourne and Geelong. Subsequently I received an invitation to the Werribee, to unite him in wedlock. He was anxious that the matter should be kept a profound secret from the neighbours until after the ceremony. Four couples and myself as minister found ourselves quietly sitting at tea. Mr. Baker said, "I wish my wedding had been a day later, for to-morrow I shall have been a teetotaller 20 years, and then I could have celebrated both events on the same day." I said, "We can easily arrange that, Mr. Baker." "How?" he eagerly inquired. I replied, "The evening is far advanced, and I suppose we shall none of us return until morning, and we can eat fruit, sing, and enjoy ourselves until past twelve o'clock." All agreed to the proposal. The wedding was to be solemnised in the Episcopal Church which was half a mile distant; the bridegroom had the key of the church, and at half past twelve, like a party of body-stealers, we walked noiselessly through the village, passed under the railway arch, entered the church, which stood by itself in the middle of a paddock, lighted two candles brought with us, went orderly through the service, and quietly returned, no one being the wiser but ourselves. When the reader travels by rail between Melbourne and Geelong, if he looks, he may see the place where at midnight this happy couple were united in marriage.

On one occasion four well-dressed, well-behaved young persons called at my house in Collingwood. It was a wedding; during the service they all wept; and on making the entries it came to my knowledge that these four, two young women and two young men, had been born in the same village and brought up in the same Sunday-school in happy old England. During my residence in Geelong, we were cheered by the arrival from England of the Revs. James Sayer and William Middleton. We had sent a list of names, eight in number; all declined but the above named. This appointment did not turn out well, and ultimately both these brethren left our Connexion and joined the Independents.

October 17th, 1858. I preached the opening sermon at our new Chapel, Windsor, near Melbourne, and was hospitably entertained at the house of Samuel Heape, Esq., South Yarra, formerly of Rochdale. Mr. Heape wept during the service, and spoke of the blessed influence as we walked together to dinner; and although unwell he accompanied me to the city, where I preached in the evening, in the Presbyterian Church, Collins Street, (Rev. A. M. Ramsay's). At the public meeting on the Monday night at Windsor, Mr. Heape presided; and on the Tuesday morning I returned to Geelong, little suspecting that I should see his face no more in this world. So, however, it was; for on the 9th December following I received a telegram from Walter Powell, Esq., requesting me to come over to Melbourne, to conduct the funeral service the following day. I had not heard of his sickness and was unprepared for the stroke. He had died of bilious fever after a very short illness. Half blinded with tears I made my way to the telegraph office and answered the message. Next morning Mr. Powell met me at the Melbourne wharf, and conveyed me to the mournful scene, and introduced me to the stricken, wounded, distracted widow. It has been my lot during life to conduct hundreds of funerals, but never before or since one so numerously attended and deeply solemn as this. The esteem in which Mr. Heape was held by the citizens of Melbourne will be seen by a perusal of the following, taken from the *Age* newspaper:—

"The funeral of the late Samuel Heape, Esq., yesterday, was attended by a lengthy train of the friends of the deceased, including a large number of the merchants and business men of the city. Though not an old colonist, Mr. Heape, by his personal character and the unvariable integrity of his business transactions, had gained a high place in the esteem of his brother merchants. Unobtrusive in his deportment, and occupying no prominent position in public movements, his departure may leave no vacancy among our public men, but it is no less deeply and sincerely felt throughout the circle to which he immediately belonged, and where his estimable qualities seem to have been well appreciated. The demonstration of yesterday was a graceful expression of regard for the memory of a private citizen. It betokens the survival of sentiments of the existence of which, amid the whirl of political conflict, and the engrossing pursuits of selfish interests, we are too prone to become sceptical. It is a grateful proof that the merit of personal virtues unconsciously impresses even a community devoted to politics, commerce, and pleasure, and only awaits a fitting occasion to be publicly honoured. The funeral *cortege* left the residence at twenty minutes past eleven o'clock, and ere it proceeded far was joined by a numerous train of carriages, which extended to almost a mile in length. Since the funeral of the late Sir Charles Hotham, the procession was certainly the largest we have witnessed in Victoria. All the shops were shut along the route. When the bell of St. Paul's Church tolled (which was the signal for the appearance of the funeral at Princess Bridge), Swanston Street was lined with spectators, who seemed to be deeply impressed with the solemnity of the spectacle.

"The body of the deceased gentleman was enclosed in three coffins, the inner one wood, trimmed with satin, the next lead, and the outside wood, covered with black cloth. The inscription, engraved on a brass breast-plate fixed on the lid, was simply—

"SAMUEL HEAPE,
"Died December 8th, 1858.
"Aged 43 years."

The Melbourne *Journal of Commerce*, of December 11th, also bears testimony by the following:—"Recording only the pulsations and throes of the life of commerce, in most cases it would be considered affectation were we to step out of our usual track in order to express our sympathy with the bereavements of human nature; yet in doing so to-day, and in chronicling in our pages the decease, on the 8th instant, of our late fellow-townsman, Mr. Samuel Heape, we are but paying a slight mark of respect to the memory of a man who was so greatly esteemed and loved whilst in life, that his death is not only considered a loss by all, but has caused such general sorrow and regret as are usually felt only on the decease of the dearest and nearest friend. His kindliness of disposition, and his benevolent, unassuming character, had endeared him to everyone who had been at any time brought into acquaintance and contact with him, and has caused such a feeling of intense grief over his early grave amongst all mercantile men, that were this journal to-day not to depart from its usual course, in offering a few words of condolence to his family and friends, it would but ill interpret the feelings uppermost in the minds of the whole of our community.

"Suddenly called away in the prime of life, in the midst of a highly successful and honourable career—if Samuel Heape's life has been short, it has been long enough to establish the fairest fame, and to render his name, first so distinguishedly borne in the earliest commercial annals of Melbourne by his brother, a time-honoured household word with the people of Victoria. Peace be with his ashes! May his sons, as they grow to manhood's estate, be as generally esteemed and loved by the community as their father is universally deplored!"

Mrs. Heape, with her two boys, returned to England soon after the death of her husband; and since my re-appointment to the Rochdale circuit, it has afforded me intense pleasure to renew my friendship with them, and to find her sons, now grown to young men, both useful Sabbath-school teachers and members of our congregation, promising fair to fulfil the hope expressed—that they might follow in the footsteps of their beloved father.

When I had been two years in Geelong, at the urgent request of the Melbourne friends I again returned to my old sphere of labour. Mr. Bradney, after labouring one year in the Melbourne circuit, was removed to Ballarat to open a mission in that district; and the brethren Sayer and Middleton were appointed to the circuit. I had great respect for Mr. Sayer, but he lacked the energy and spirit necessary for colonial work, and at the close of the first year was not invited to remain a second; he was, therefore, appointed to Geelong, and I returned to Melbourne.

During my residence in Geelong, two or three very dangerous characters had obtained membership and official position in the Melbourne district. These had chiefly been introduced by an individual who had been for some time connected with our Church, and of whose sincerity and piety I had not had any occasion to doubt. This man, by name Mr. J. B., was very wealthy, the owner of a fine terrace of houses, in one of which he himself resided. He had worshipped at our chapel in Collingwood for some time before I knew who he was, but on going round with the Rev. Mr. Scott, collecting for the City Mission, we called at his house, when he gave us five pounds, and thanked us for asking him. I soon after took an opportunity of seeing him to ask if he would like to unite with us. He then explained that he had been connected with the Primitives, but owing to some disagreement he had resigned his membership, that the matter in dispute had been referred to the English authorities, and by them decided in his favour. He shewed me a plan of the previous quarter, where his name had been reinstated as local preacher. He became a class leader and local preacher among us, and for a time everything went on smoothly. Mr. B. was a laborious worker and liberal giver, and, being a builder, was entrusted with a good deal of work connected with the erection of several chapels, and also in the purchase of land. It afterwards transpired that all the while he was laying deep schemes to get a hold on the property, and also secure to himself as much power as possible. One man, J. P. O., that Mr. B. introduced into our Church, had been a local preacher among the Wesleyans, at a place eighty miles from Melbourne; he brought his credentials with him, and, as we were greatly in need of a preacher to send to Adelaide, he was engaged for that mission. After a time, it was discovered that he was unworthy a place among us, and was charged by the Adelaide friends with gross sin, and at the end of six months expelled. At the close of the year he returned to Melbourne, and sued the President, the Rev. Mr. Bradney, for six months' salary. He had been paid up to the time of expulsion. He afterwards wrote a damaging untruthful letter in the *Melbourne Argus*. This was answered in the same paper by the Rev. W. Middleton, and on some of its statements was founded a second trial, which, by a jury of twelve, went against J. P. O., but as he had nothing to pay with the costs fell on us. In this trial it was proved that he had left the Wesleyans in disgrace, charged with gross sin, for we had to summon a Wesleyan minister to give evidence; it was also proved that his credentials were all forged in Melbourne.

In another trial which ensued between Mr. Middleton and one J. F., a member of the church at Windsor, relating to some money transactions between them, Mr. B. took sides with J. F., and made statements which we all knew to be false. Our leading friends in Collingwood then determined to bring him before the Church Courts as being unworthy to continue a member among us. I had to prefer the charge, and he was expelled; but he still held possession of some legal documents relating to chapel property, which he refused to give up. One day Mr. Middleton came to my house in high spirits, saying that Mr. B. had consented to sign and give up some papers that we required; and that if we would meet that forenoon at the shop of a Mr. Fisk, things might be amicably settled. On entering the shop Mr. Fisk was alone, with the exception of a young woman behind the counter. He drew us out in conversation, and addressing me said, "Mr. Townend, I have heard you say that Mr. B. is a perjurer." I replied, "If the utterance of falsehood upon oath be not perjury, what else can it be?" Just then out rushed from an inner room J. F., who had been there concealed with Mr. B. to overhear all that was said, addressing me, "I heard you, sir; you may expect a Supreme Court trial." I was fairly entrapped, for up to this time we had regarded Mr. Fisk as a friend, but he had no doubt been bribed to act the part he did.* On this Mr. B. brought an action for libel, and laid damages at £2000; he employed three of the ablest counsellors in the colony. I employed two; the Attorney-General and another. From Thursday at noon until Saturday P.M. it took to examine witnesses; then the foreman of the jury said, "Your Honour, it is the request of the jury that the counsel on each side should forego pleading, as the jury are agreed on the verdict, and think no further light can be thrown on the matter." The Judge then said, "Gentlemen of the jury, this is a serious case; if you give a verdict for defendant you commit plaintiff for perjury." The foreman then asked what verdict would leave each party to pay their own costs. His Honour said, "Anything under forty shillings." In one minute the jury returned a verdict, damages one farthing; and addressing Mr. B. said, "It is a great shame for you to bring such a case here." The Court was much moved, and a gentleman who was unknown to me threw a farthing on the table, saying, "Mr. Townend, pay him that farthing, it is more than he is worth." My costs were £125, and Mr. B.'s considerably over £200. An open verdict would have cleared me from costs, but it would have involved a Crown prosecution against Mr. B., which the Judge appeared anxious to avoid.

After this I was summoned to the county court by Mr. B. to show cause why I did not give up to him the bill of sale of one of our chapels. In this case I obtained a verdict with costs. The reader may be ready to censure us as ministers and Christian men for these law proceedings, but it must be observed there was no alternative, we were compelled to defend ourselves.

---

* Mr. Fisk afterwards came to my house, and confessed he had done wrong, in the part he had acted; he was in great distress of mind, and could not rest until he had begged me to forgive him; he asked me to kneel in prayer with him for pardon from God as well as man.

We appealed to our friends in England for help towards our law expenses, and by private subscription, per Rev. R. Eckett, we received the sum of £86, I also collected £8 in Collingwood, £94 in all. Previous to this I had paid £125 in my own case, and also £85 on behalf of Mr. Bradney, in his suit with J. P. O. This I did at the urgent request of Mr. Bradney, as he wrote me it was inconvenient for him to raise the money just then; and that it would save him coming from Ballarat; and though I had to borrow the money myself, I complied with his request. Towards this £210 that I had individually paid, I received from the above-named £94, the sum of £44; the other £50 was paid to J. M. Smith, Esq., our solicitor, towards the bill still owing him in the cases of Middleton; our instructions from Mr. Eckett being that the money should be divided according to our losses.

I have felt it necessary to enter into these details, because of the garbled, untruthful, and damaging statements which were sent to the *Wesleyan Times* in England, and published in that paper. The editor, without inquiring into the truthfulness of the statements contained in those letters, or as to the trustworthiness of the writers whose names were attached, not only inserted the letters, but founded leading articles on the supposition that they were all true. It was impossible for us to vindicate ourselves; several months elapsed before we even knew of their publication, then three or four months must pass before a reply could appear; under such circumstances it was of no use to attempt it. A number of the signatures attached to the letters were forgeries; they were nearly all written at the instigation of one individual, to whom money was no object in the way of bribery when he wanted to gain his ends. One man insisted upon my going with him to a magistrate, that he might make affidavit that he never wrote a letter, bearing his signature, which appeared in the *Wesleyan Times.* I think newspaper editors should be very careful in inserting articles reflecting on the character of Christian ministers, mentioned by name, who are at so remote a distance that irreparable damage is done them before they even know of such publication. I have seen many letters in religious newspapers since my return, under the heading "From Our own Correspondent," which, from the knowledge I have of colonial matters, I am sure present a very one-sided and unfair view of things. It is possible for even "Our own Correspondent" to write with animus of certain individuals and Churches.

Some persons may feel surprised that men of so bad a character as we had to deal with should ever gain access to Christian Churches; but in a new country like Australia, where society at that time was of such a migratory character, it was quite impossible to ascertain the antecedents of individuals. Nearly all who gave us so much trouble had previously caused the Wesleyans sore trial at different times and in different colonies; but unfortunately with us they met as to time and place; and in our small Churches their power for evil was all the greater. A Wesleyan minister afterwards told me, that, in conversation with several of his brethren, they had come to the conclusion that they had not dealt fairly by us, as by giving us a note of warning we might have been saved most of our troubles.

In the early days of the convict system, many individuals were transported for comparatively minor offences, and only for a certain term of years, and others on account of good conduct had been released. Many of the most wealthy and successful colonists had originally been convicts; they filled important positions in civil life, even sitting on the magistrates' bench; they had married into respectable families and were admitted into good society; and in the constant moving from one colony to another, the fact of their ever having been convicts was lost sight of; nor was it prudent in a very mixed company to talk much of the convict class. Some that I have known were useful and honourable members of Christian Churches, but a great many put on the cloak of religion to give them a position in society; of these we had a share.

I had better anticipate a little and record here some of the subsequent history of Mr. J. B. After doing us all the damage he could, he again sought membership with the Wesleyans; this was refused, but he became a seatholder in one of their chapels. After some time he got elected a member of the Fitzroy Municipal Council; being a wealthy man and an employer of labour, he commanded some influence. Then there arose a contest as to who should fill the office of Mayor. A Mr. C. was the most likely to be elected; but Mr. B., thinking he had some claims to the office, wrote a letter to Mr. C., recommending him to resign in favour of himself, that by so doing he would stand a better chance in the following year. This letter he signed "T. Smith." Mr. C., on receiving it, felt sure that it was the handwriting of Mr. B. (for he both writes and spells badly), and compared it with some of his notices of motion in the Council books. At the next meeting he was accused of being the writer of the letter in question. This he indignantly denied, saying he would lay down 500*l.* if Mr. C. would do the same, and each should nominate three individuals to investigate the matter. (He had also written a letter to one of the newspapers, also signed "T. Smith," of the same purport as the other letter.) Mr. C. instantly wrote a cheque for the same amount, and six gentlemen, after careful investigation, unanimously decided that Mr. B. was the writer of the letter to Mr. C. They expended above 400*l.* of his money, and he retired from the Council in ignominy. The *Melbourne Age* newspaper, of Dec., 1863, after giving full details of the above case, thus concludes:—"Mr. B. has been found guilty of a heinous offence, by judges of his own choosing; for, in addition to the contemptible trick of writing a letter under a pseudonym, he has uttered atrocious falsehoods. In the Council he proposed to court inquiry, and alleged that 'substantial evidence would be found to saddle the letter on Mr. C.'" If there was nothing more in this matter than a mere squabble between councillors of a suburban municipality, it would not be worth notice; but Mr. B. is a man of pretensions. He is a grain of the salt of the earth, a shining light amongst a denomination noted for the demonstrativeness of its Christianity. Moreover, he is one of the pillars of the State, a large holder of property, and one of the few eligible for a seat in the Upper House. There are considerations even beyond this. He narrowly missed being made mayor, and the mayor is a magistrate charged with the duty of protecting the liberties and property of the inhabitants of his borough. In order to obtain the position, Mr. B., in the opinion of his own nominees, was guilty of a disreputable trick, and to screen himself he lied roundly.

What a catalogue of offences will this man have to answer for if he does not sincerely repent of his misdeeds. His ruling passion is love of power, whether in Church or civil matters; he keeps no company, lives in a plain and frugal manner, but will lavish any amount of money to secure power and position, or to ruin those who oppose his projects.

It was in order to redeem some chapels from the hands of Mr. J. B. (who was threatening to sell them) that we obtained from the Home Committee the loan of 1000*l.* We had now fifteen chapels in Victoria, and this was the first help in any form that we had received from England towards chapel property. The money was loaned chiefly on the East St. Kilda, Brunswick, and Pentridge chapels. And though, perhaps, the buildings would not realise more than is lent on them, it should be borne in mind that places of worship have to suffer the same depreciation in value as house and other property; and though the debt left on them at the time they were erected was not more, in proportion to the entire cost, than is usually left, yet in a few years, owing to commercial changes, building materials and labour being so vastly cheaper, the same buildings might be put up at a far less cost.

CHAPTER IV.

Division of Melbourne Circuit—Death of Mrs. Townend—Arrival of Rev. R. Miller—J. Bulmer, Missionary to Aborigines—Character of the Natives—White Man found among the Blacks—Ceremony of making the lads young Men—Cruelty to Natives—Climate of Australia—Hot Winds—Dust Storms—Consents to go to Queensland—Arrival of Rev. T. A. Bayley—Valedictory tea-meeting—Letter from Hon. Richard Heales—Death of Mr. Heales.

SOON after the events recorded in the last chapter, the Melbourne Circuit was divided into three; 1st, 2nd and 3rd Melbourne, Mr. Middleton at his own request having Windsor, East Saint Kilda, Brunswick, and Richmond, while the third circuit comprised Hoddle Street, Kew and Nunnawadding, for which we engaged a young man who had been a local preacher; and I became sole Pastor of the George Street Church. Shortly after this I was deprived of my beloved wife by death; the following memoir I wrote at the time, which was published in the large magazine, June, 1860:—

To the Editor.

Dear Sir:—Scarcely have the billows of sore trial ceased to roll over our Churches, in this distant land, ere I am called upon to sustain one of the keenest domestic bereavements to which I have been ever subjected. I will endeavour in the shortest, simplest, and most candid manner, to sketch the life and death of my late beloved wife. Of her early history I know but little. She was born at Enfield, Lancashire, June 1807, and was early brought to the Sabbath-school, and under the preaching of the glorious Gospel. Her father served in the army, and having received a wound disabling him for service retired with a liberal pension. He was a clever artisan; and had it not been for fits of intemperance would have been in very easy circumstances. He often resolved to conquer this dire besetment and serve his God in sincerity, but when the time came to draw his quarterly pension, he almost invariably fell back through intemperance. The great teetotal reformation was only just being heard of, when my poor father-in-law died. My mother-in-law was a clever, industrious, and ingenious woman; and through years of toil she brought up her children during her husband's military servitude. For her I always entertained the sincerest respect. Shortly after my acquaintance with the family she became decidedly pious; and I have reason to believe that I was personally useful in her conversion to God. The good old lady resided with us when we were requested to leave our native land and open a mission in this distant field of Christian toil. When the matter was mentioned to her she magnanimously said, "Oh, never mind me, I shall soon be in heaven; I thought since first the mission was mentioned that Joseph would have to go. I only wish you were safe over the water." We sailed on May 12, 1851, and on the 3rd June following she landed safe on the shores of eternal deliverance.

My late wife was converted in the same religious awakening in which I was brought to a *saving* knowledge of the truth. Under God we owe our deciding for Christ to the fervent ministry of the Rev. W. Ellingworth, then stationed in the Bacup circuit. We had for years been connected with the Sabbath-school and choir at the Rawtenstall and Longholme Wesleyan Chapel. On the 31st July, 1830, we were united in wedlock in the parish Church, Bury, Lancashire. We were in humble circumstances, and this journey of 16 miles had to be made on foot. It was very cloudy, and portended rain when we left in the morning, but the clouds dispersed and the day was very fine—illustrative, I have often said, of our future course through life. Thank God, through the untiring efforts of the Nonconformists of that time, Dissenters generally now enjoy all their rights and privileges within the circle of their own ministers and Churches.

On our entering the great work of the ministry, Mrs. Townend set herself with all her powers to act as became the wife of a minister of the Cross, humble and sincere, neat in her person, and frugal in her habits, and until by extreme deafness she was rendered incapable of active service, she was ever ready for every good word and work. During the last twenty-five years of my public life I do not remember a single instance when I was called upon to apologise or even offer explanation for the *words* or *works* of my dear wife. Mrs. T. possessed a confiding, heroic spirit, bearing up with cheerful mind amid all the changes and trials through which we have passed, especially when called upon to leave her dear mother and friends, and during our long and painful voyage to this land. It is to be thought of, that we were the first in connection with our denomination to visit Australia ere the discovery of gold or the settlement of a Church. One feature of her conduct is worthy of special record. Though she was unable to hear a sermon, or the giving out of a hymn in a class or prayer-meeting, yet she attended with the utmost regularity, and evidently enjoyed in a high degree the means of grace. During the last four years she had been the subject of considerable bodily weakness, taking exercise in the open air as much as possible. Latterly she had expressed a wish to return to England, in the hope that the voyage and her native air might be serviceable. On Thursday evening, February 16th, 1860, she was at class, and in a most unusually earnest and powerful manner engaged in prayer. The burden of her request was, that God would again visit our Church, and pour out His Spirit. Every member of the class remarked the fervour of her petitions, and the unction attendant thereon. Personally, I turned round to observe the energy of her soul and the attitude of her body.

It was her last visit to the house of prayer. On the Sabbath morning following, when, a little before eight o'clock, we were cheerfully seated at the breakfast-table, Mrs. Townend began to cough; the irritation continued, so much so that she took to her room. Tuesday following, I called in a skilful medical practitioner, who, on applying the stethescope, said, "Oh, Mr. Townend, there is immense damage here. I will do my utmost to relieve, and leave you to open the matter to Mrs. Townend as best you know." I said, "Dr. Tracey, you don't mean that it is consumption? Why, sir, she never coughed until Sabbath morning last." Said he, "I don't care for that at all, it is nothing else; why, see, it has consumed her flesh!"

Early on Thursday morning, I ventured to communicate what the doctor had said. After a short pause, she said with great emphasis, "I am very glad to hear it, Joseph;" and after resting a little, she said, "Oh, it gives me great joy." Sabbath morning following, whilst Brother Sayer occupied the George Street pulpit, I remained in the chamber of my sick wife. By seven that morning she was in her chair in her usual Sabbath attire, Bible and hymn-book conveniently near. It was a sweet forenoon. I felt the chamber of the pious to be privileged. To converse was impossible, her deafness and weakness being extreme. "Joseph," said she, "I am thinking of the great Sabbath that will never end." And then after a while she said, "Joseph, I can't get it out of my mind about the great Sabbath. Indeed, I don't want to drive it away. Oh, I like to think of it." A day or two after, she said, "Joseph, you remember the last watch-night held in George Street?" On moving assent, she said, "Well, just as we arose from the last prayer, that passage was applied with such power to my mind—'This year thou shalt die.' I did not tell *you*, but I never forgot it." To a dear friend she said, "I am not cast down, Mrs. Briggs; never since I knew what was the matter have I had a single doubt." To Mrs. Nuttall she said, "I am told that I am consumptive; *well*, when I think of the world of eternal glory, and that I shall be permitted to join the blessed company there, it fills my soul with great joy. The only drawback is, that I fear it will not come yet. You may think that being deaf, I could not enjoy the means of grace, but you are mistaken, I always enjoyed them; for although I could not hear what was given out, I gave out a verse to myself, and thus had a meeting to myself." In the company, and from the visits of good Mrs. Thomas, she experienced great pleasure and profit.

Friday morning, March 9th, I rose and dressed ere it was day. I pensively thought of the many times I had risen to be in time for coach, steamer, or rail; rarely on such occasions disturbing my wife. I felt as if I had a great work or trial before me; I was oppressively sorrowful, and stole fifteen minutes in the Carlton Gardens, just as the sun mounted above the horizon. It was a clear, cloudless, Australian morn, and the breeze from our noble bay soothingly kissed my fervid brow. I hastened back to the chamber were sat my patient, sinking wife. "Boy," said she, playfully, "I'll have hasty-pudding, with more treacle than yesterday morning." Breakfast being ready she hastily despatched a plate of this said pottage, and adjusting her pillows she spoke of sleep. The cold sweat issued from every pore as she slept and breathed heavily. I went for the doctor, and, on returning, I found her sitting on the side of the bed, borne up by my niece.* We removed her to her chair, and whilst Ann ran for a friend, I bore her sinking head. "Mr. Townend," said our mutual friend, "she is dying." I have

* After the death of Amelia I sent to England for one of my nieces to reside with us.

often spoken of the cold damps of dissolution, and have seen scores of persons die, but never before did I witness such a boiling out of heavy, clammy, cold death-dew. I *gazed*, she was *gone*, GONE!

Mrs. Townend's death was improved in a very excellent and impressive discourse by Rev. J. Sayer, his subject being—"The great Sabbath, or the believer's argument for the observance of the Lord's-day." The George Street Society showed much sympathy in my bereavement, and forwarded me the following consolatory address:—

"TO THE REV. JOSEPH TOWNEND.

"Dear Pastor,—Inscrutable are the ways of Providence, and uncontrollable are the acts of Omnipotence; and equally is it beyond the wisdom and the power of man, either to comprehend the one or to resist the other, and every attempt to do so displays the folly and the weakness of man, while it exalts the sovereign glories of the Supreme Disposer of all events.

"Deeply impressed with the truth of these sentiments, and earnestly desirous of evincing the most perfect resignation to the Divine will, we nevertheless offer to you, dear sir, our most affectionate condolence on the mournful dispensation of God's providence, which has deprived you of the longer sympathy and assistance of your late amiable and beloved wife. Her memory will be cherished, by all who had the privilege of her acquaintance, with the tenderest regard. Still we would not repine, being assured that you are prepared to kiss the hand that has deprived you of the object of your earthly affection. Your loss is her gain. Whilst here she let her light shine in the sphere in which she was permitted to move, but now she has gone to radiate in the celestial hemisphere, and though you can no longer behold her with the eye of flesh, and share with her the joys and sorrows of domestic life, you yet are privileged to contemplate her, by the exercise of faith, amongst the blood-washed throng around the throne of the eternal God. She has 'fought the good fight and finished her course;'

she has 'kept the faith,' and gained the victory, and entered glory.

"'O may we triumph so, when all our warfare's past,
And dying, find our latest foe under our feet at last.'

"With sincere respect and affection,
"We remain, dear Sir,
"THE MEMBERS OF GEORGE STREET U. M. F. CHURCH.
"*March* 26*th*, 1860."

Jan. 4, 1861. The Rev. R. Miller and his excellent wife arrived from England, on their way to Tasmania. They remained at our house nearly a fortnight, waiting for steamer, and during this time Mr. Miller preached at George Street and Windsor chapels, and also visited Geelong. In his communication to the Missionary Secretary, which appeared in June magazine, Mr. Miller records: "During my stay in Melbourne I visited several of our Societies, and of the leading friends in the different circuits; and I am thankful to have to state that I found the congregations good, the Societies in peace, and their numbers increasing."

John Bulmer, a pious intelligent young man, from Sunderland, was connected with our Church in Collingwood for some time. One evening he attended a public meeting on behalf of the Mission to the Aborigines, connected with the Episcopalians. He was deeply impressed, and felt strongly that it was his duty to offer himself as a missionary to the natives. He came next day and told me his convictions. It was a great trial to me to part with him, as he was valuable and useful in our Church; still I told him if these were his views I would introduce him to the Rev. Mr. Chase, and the Dean, who both took great interest in the mission. I felt sure Mr. Bulmer was well adapted for the work, being of a very cheerful and hopeful temperament, with robust health and a constant flow of animal spirits. He was immediately engaged, for the mission to the blacks was so uninviting that it was very difficult to obtain suitable agents. He was sent to the tribes of the Murray district, where he remained six or seven years, and was then removed to Gipp's-land to establish a mission among the tribes of that district. Their language is very meagre, the different tribes speaking quite a different dialect. On one occasion, when Mr. Bulmer came to visit us, he brought a young native whom he had taught in his school. The youth read to us a chapter in English in the New Testament very correctly, with the exception of a little difficulty in the pronunciation of a few words; he took dinner with us, and conducted himself with great propriety. Mr. Bulmer was also supplied by the Government with rations to distribute to the blacks; this enabled him to retain them longer in one locality than he otherwise could have done; but even then they would wander off for months at a time during the fishing season.

Many attempts have been made by societies and individuals to establish missions among the natives. The great difficulty is their migratory, roving habits: their wants are few and simple—they will live on fish, roots, seeds, grub, the kangaroo and opossum, the emu and other birds, but will not take the trouble to cultivate the ground. Many of the tribes go entirely naked, and others will make rugs of the skin of the opossum. If they build huts at all, they are chiefly the bark of trees, put up in the slightest manner. In going through the bush at night I have seen them lying round a large fire, with nothing to shelter them. The restraints of civilised life are to them a perfect burden; and it is generally thought by those conversant with their habits, that they have no form of worship or religious belief, and, until the introduction of whites, no notion of a future state; now they are very fond of saying, that when they die they shall "jump up whitefellow." There have been some very hopeful cases and happy deaths among them, which have encouraged the friends of missions to persevere in their arduous labours. They are fast dying away: the introduction of the vices of the whites have had a disastrous influence on them, such as the use of spirits and tobacco; for though it is forbidden by law to sell them intoxicating drinks, they manage to obtain it from unprincipled persons.

In Queensland the aborigines are much more numerous than in Victoria. I have frequently there met them in parties of from ten to twenty out in the bush, and often seen them with one or two bottles, evidently containing spirits, which they passed from one to another, and by their noisy shouts I could tell they were the worse for liquor. They would frequently come up to me saying: "Blackfellow, white money; blackfellow, white money!" which meant that I was to give them silver coin—they soon learnt it was more valuable than copper, because of the amount of tobacco or spirit which it would procure them; these were the only articles they cared to purchase. When going to my preaching appointments at Eagle Farm, I should frequently see them catching fish in the River Brisbane, they would stand up to their chins in the water, as immovable as the stumps of trees, which I sometimes mistook them to be, until I watched for some movement. They hold in one or each hand a small net, which they make from flax or fibres of trees, and when a fish is caught they come to the bank and lay it on the grass; these can be readily disposed of in the town, and I have seen a black-fellow come into a grocer's shop and lay down three or four shillings for tobacco. The natives are not allowed to come into towns in a state of perfect nudity, but will put on any old article of European clothing which is given them. A man having a pair of trousers would consider that quite enough; and his Lubra (wife), having an old skirt of a gown, her head ornamented with feathers, and a pipe in her mouth, would march by his side, quite independent of the change of fashions. The women, when a gown is given them, always tear the body off, and fastening the band together, pass it under one arm, leaving the shoulder bare, then across the other shoulder, bringing the arm through the opening, the garment then scarcely reaching the knees. Many of the men ornament their bodies with scars; this is done by making incisions in the flesh and laying in small rolls of clay, then close the flesh over and allow it to heal. I have seen some with a well arranged raised pattern, extending from the shoulders to the loins. They manifest mourning for their dead by loud wailing and daubing the head with pipe-clay. Some of the tribes burn their dead, and carry the ashes about wrapped in a sheet of bark, until they get tired, when they will throw it away. Other tribes bury their dead, and some tribes wrap the bodies in sheets of bark, and deposit them in hollow trees, or high up in the branches. Large sheets of bark for this purpose are easily obtained, because the Australian trees do not shed their leaves in autumn, but retain the same foliage year after year; instead of changing leaves they throw off the bark, so that an Australian forest never presents that beautiful verdant green that our English trees have in spring.

During my residence in Queensland, a white man of the name of James Morrill was discovered, who had been living among the blacks for seventeen years. He had been shipwrecked on the coast, in a vessel which sailed from Sydney. The captain and his wife, with some of the passengers and crew, got safe to land, but all soon died from the hardships they endured, except this man. The blacks

treated them kindly, finding them roots and other food to eat when too weak to get it themselves. After the death of all the others, one of the tribes adopted Morrill as their special property. After he had been with them a number of years some of the distant tribes brought him word that in their hunting excursions they had come across marks of strange cattle, from which he concluded he must be near some settled district. After a time he persuaded the tribe with whom he was living to go hunting in the same direction; they were very unwilling for him to leave them, but after great difficulty he succeeded in reaching a cattle station, and was forwarded on to Brisbane, where I saw and conversed with him; and, from a small pamphlet which he published, relating his sojourn among the blacks, I give his description of their method of making the lads into young men:—

"The ceremony of making the lads young men takes place about once every five or six years. For eight or nine months immediately previous they have to go into the bush to provide for themselves, during which time they are never allowed to see a female; this is to test their fitness to take a wife; if they do see a female they think they will waste away. After the nine months are over they are brought into the camp, cane rings are put on their arms and tightened very much, so as to stop the circulation of the blood. Their arms swell very much, which often puts them in great agony. They are then left in that torture all night; their cries are terrible to hear. To keep their fingers from contracting and thus deforming them, they sit with their hands and fingers spread out on the ground, with the heels of their feet tightly pressed on them. In the morning they are brought out, in the presence of their mothers, sisters, and relatives, and, just above and below the mark of the cane ring on their arms, they make small incisions to let the blood flow and prevent inflammation. While this is being done, their mothers and relatives are crying and cutting themselves from head to foot with sharp stones in token of joy at seeing them. When this is somewhat subsided, places are provided for them to sleep under, with boughs to shade them from the sun, as they could get no sleep, of course, during the night. While they are sleeping the old gins (wives) go into the swamps and get roots to make cakes for them by the time they get up in the evening, while the men get all the young men's spears they have been carrying with them during the nine months they have been away, and fix them in the earth on a clear space in a semicircle, fastening from head to head of the spears grass festoons. In the evening, all being ready, they wake up, generally about 80 in number at a time, and they are each seated under a festoon in a reclining position. Then their sisters or female cousins lay with their heads on their swollen arms, to press down the swollen and cut places, and they think nothing harmful will come of it after that. While they are lying there a lot of cakes are thrown up and scrambled for by the lookers-on, who had gone through the ceremony before them; then they go to their several fires. In the morning they are taken a little way in the bush again, and dressed up with shells and the down of birds stuck on their heads, painted and made to look to the best advantage; they are then brought back to choose and take their sweethearts, and the whole ceremony closes with a grand corroboree.

"After this is over, there is a good deal of quarrelling and fighting among them. They steal the wives of the old and weak men and daughters from their parents, which leads to fighting, and often extends between two tribes, and then there is a war, which is not, however, of a very sanguinary nature. They often get some terrible blows, and sometimes one gets killed. But they cannot keep it on many hours, for they are forced to go and get supplies in the shape of food, and they seldom renew the conflict."

The atrocious cruelties practised by the white man towards these poor defenceless natives is a disgrace to our civilization. They have been hunted and shot down like dogs, without having given any provocation; many instances have come to light of this having been done; and if occasionally they do retaliate, and attack a station and murder the settlers, can this be wondered at, or even blamed, from poor untutored savages, when men from a nation civilised and Christianised for centuries can thus treat them. An instance is recorded in the "Life of the Rev. S. Marsden," convict chaplain in New South Wales, of a party of stockmen, about seven in number, employed on a station in the interior, who started with the avowed intention of hunting for blacks. They came across a small, inoffensive tribe of about thirty—men, women, and children—and, after murdering the whole, covered them with the branches of trees, and set fire to the pile. Some shepherds, searching for cattle, discovered their charred remains, the guilt was clearly traced home to these men, and they were brought to punishment. But in too many instances the perpetrators of cruelties on the natives have been screened, instead of being brought to justice. Government has appointed protectors to the aborigines, but, scattered as they are, and always roving from place to place, it is difficult to afford them adequate protection.

I consider the climate of Australia preferable to England—at least, in those parts where I have resided, though, of course, in such an immense country the temperature varies very considerably. Victoria enjoys the coolest climate, being, of all the Australian colonies, the farthest removed from the equator. The pure, buoyant atmosphere, the unclouded, sunny skies, are calculated to impart cheerfulness, and raise the animal spirits. The frequent and long droughts, however, are a great drawback on agricultural operations, and cause much distress in many districts. The hot winds are very unpleasant, though not considered injurious; they rarely extend above two or three days, and it is thought as the country is opened up and cultivated they will be greatly modified. The hot wind is always from the north, and if it prevails in summer, vegetation is burnt up, and everything looks dry and arid; bush-fires, extending for miles, are seen, and frequently the crops and homesteads of the settlers are destroyed. The hot winds are almost invariably succeeded by a cool, refreshing breeze from the ocean, causing the thermometer to fall twenty or thirty degrees in the course of an hour or two.

In the earlier days of Victoria severe dust-storms were frequent, especially before the roads and streets were properly made; the wind would eddy round just like a whirlwind, carrying into the air clouds of fine white dust. On December 4, 1852, I was preaching at the opening of the Independant chapel, Richmond, near Melbourne; the windows were not in, but being the middle of summer that was no great inconvenience. During the afternoon service the wind suddenly chopped round, raising a dust-storm that in a few moments filled the chapel. I could not see the congregation, nor they the preacher, and when it passed we were all like a lot of millers. That same afternoon a house was on fire in Collingwood, and the dust literally choked and put out the fire. At that time people had to buy their water at so much per barrel, and it was too expensive to water the streets. Now Melbourne has a splendid supply of water brought from the Yan-Yean reservoirs; it comes with such force that, in case of fire, the firemen have only to take up the plugs in the street, and fasten on a hose, which will carry the water over the highest house. The towns suffered severely by fires, the houses being chiefly of wood, and during the summer months so dry that there was very little chance of extinguishing a fire, except by pulling down houses to stay its progress. A bill was afterwards passed by Parliament, forbidding wooden houses to be put up within the city boundaries.

In the year 1844 I travelled in the Clitheroe circuit, Lancashire, and had under my care a Bible-class of young men. Several of these afterwards emigrated to Queensland, at that time called the Moreton Bay District; and these, for several years, corresponded with me at Melbourne, with a view to induce me to come to Brisbane, the capital of Queensland, and open a mission in that colony: they also wrote to the Home Committee, requesting them to appoint me. The missionary secretary then wrote to me, asking if I was willing to leave Melbourne for Brisbane. I replied, I was, if the committee would send a suitable man from England to take my place. This led to the appointment of the Rev. T. A. Bayley. Considerable delay occurred in the arrival of Mr. Bayley; Mr. Eckett at first writing that he would sail from England the latter end of 1861. I therefore made all necessary arrangements for my departure—sold off the greater part of my furniture, and communicated to the Brisbane friends that I might be expected in the early part of 1862. It was not, however, until the April following that Mr. Bayley was able to arrange for sailing. The friends in Queensland were becoming impatient, and almost inclined to give up the mission, as so many other denominations had by this time entered the field. Still I knew well that to leave Melbourne before his arrival would be unwise on my part, and disastrous to the Church. It was against the strongest remonstrances of the George Street Society that I consented to go to Brisbane; but I had been with them about eleven years, and I felt it my duty to respond to the call from Queensland. For some months previous to Mr. Bayley's arrival, Mrs. Townend,* in concert with a number of the ladies of the Church, had commenced a sewing meeting, with a view to raising funds for the purchase of furniture for the preacher's house. A few articles we had in use belonged to the Society, and a small grant was afterwards made from England for the same

* I had again formed a matrimonial alliance, having married Miss Bray, formerly a member in Cornwall, and afterwards for many years connected with our Church in London.

purpose. Mr. Bayley landed at Melbourne June 30th, 1862. The friends had previously arranged for a "Valedictory Tea Meeting" for the 14th of July, as I was anxious to have everything ready for starting as soon as he arrived, and knowing the average length of the voyage, we anticipated he would not be far from that date. I was very pleased to see Mr. Bayley, and it gave the friends the opportunity of bidding him welcome and me good-bye at the same time. The following account was published in the *Melbourne Christian Times* of July 26th, 1862:—

"VALEDICTORY TEA MEETING TO THE REV. J. TOWNEND.*

"A meeting of a very interesting character was held on Monday, the 14th instant, at the United Methodist Free Church, George Street, Fitzroy, to afford the Church and congregation an opportunity of taking their farewell of their respected minister, the Rev. Joseph Townend, whose ministerial labours in this colony during eleven years have been greatly blessed, and have secured for him the affections of the people. Mr. Townend preached his farewell sermon to a very large congregation, on the Sunday evening previous, from 1 Cor. xv. 58. Many were deeply affected.

"The tea-meeting took place on Monday, in the schoolroom at the rear of the chapel. Upwards of 170 sat down to tea, which was well furnished by the ladies. Notwithstanding the unfavourable weather, several persons came a long way from the country. After tea the company adjourned to the chapel, where the number was soon largely increased. After singing a hymn, and prayer by the Rev. W. Middleton, the Hon. George Harker was called to the chair, who, in his opening address, expressed the strong regard he entertained for Mr. Townend, whom he had known almost from the time of his arrival in this colony, and his regret that he was about to remove from his sphere of useful labour.

"Letters of apology from the Hon. Richard Heales and the Rev. J. C. McMichael were read.

"Mr. G. W. Bleckly, in moving the first resolution, referred briefly to the various and extensive labours in which Mr. Townend

---

* I have given the above account at full length, because a newspaper was sent to England with a view to its being published in the magazine, the paper miscarried, and as we were unable to procure a copy of that year's magazine, neither the friends in Melbourne or myself were aware, until after my return to England, that it had never appeared, and as this book will be circulated in the colony I now insert it.

had been zealously and usefully employed during his residence in the colony, not only as an evangelist and a pastor, but as an advocate and supporter of the various philanthropic institutions and religious enterprises of the colony, the temperance reformation, the principles of the Peace Society, the scholastic institutions of the colony, the hospital, asylum, &c. To the stranger, the destitute, and the afflicted, his benevolent assistance had been rendered, and he had the sincere and warm affections of the Church and congregation. The resolution was as follows:—'That this meeting records its deep sense of the value and importance of the labours of the Rev. J. Townend, during the eleven years of his ministerial career in connection with the United Methodist Free Churches (formerly Wesleyan Methodist Association) in this colony; its affection and attachment to him as a pastor and a friend; its admiration of the zeal and fidelity with which he has prosecuted his important enterprise, as a minister and missionary; the energy and earnestness with which he has fulfilled his ministry; his readiness to assist in promoting every Christian and philanthropic movement; his kind and benevolent care for the physical and social comforts of the stranger, the afflicted, and the needy, and the spiritual interests of all; it expresses its sympathy and condolence with him under the numerous severe and extraordinary trials through which he has been called to pass, and under which he has been mercifully supported by the strong arm of Jehovah, and up held and encouraged by the prayers and sympathies of his people its thankfulness to God for the benefits and success which have attended his works of faith and love; and its earnest prayer that his future life may be more eminently prosperous and happy; that the enterprise upon which he is about to embark may be one of extensive usefulness; that the protection and blessing of the God of providence and grace may ever rest upon him, and upon his beloved and amiable partner; and that their path may be brilliant and conspicuous as the shining light which shineth more and more unto the perfect day.'

"Mr. J. Woods seconded, and Mr. W. Ellingworth supported the resolution, having known the Rev. J. Townend from the time of his arrival in the colony, and felt great pleasure in bearing their testimony to his worth.

"Mr. J. Nuttall then read the following Address to Mr. Townend:—

"'DEAR SIR,—The occasion on which we meet is not only interesting and grave, but somewhat peculiar; and, therefore, the sentiments and emotions to which it gives rise are complex, if not conflicting. We assemble, so to speak, as reluctant witnesses to observe and take part in the public severance of a relation that has so happily and so long subsisted between us as pastor and people. It is your own decision to which we bow, yet we do so with submission, and not with sullenness; for, on the high and holy ground of Christian liberty, we dare not resist the rights of conscience, even if we do not hear so audibly as yourself the voice of God in this matter; and we trust, therefore, that what you hear in secret will be heard by us as if proclaimed from the house-tops in your happy and successful career in Queensland.

"'Indeed the very reluctance which we feel to part with you, paradoxical as the expression may be, is itself full of consolatory thoughts, both to you and us. To us, who are not unacquainted with the history of many Christian churches and ministers, it suggests how many causes there might have been, but for the grace of God, not only to diminish, or possibly to abolish altogether our reluctance, but even to render us anxious to terminate a connection on which we could look back at the best with pain;—but what intensity does not our reluctance acquire, as we call to mind, not only your unstained honour in social and pastoral life, your incessant labours and serious sacrifices in the cause of Christ, your pure, disinterested, yet frank and truthful demeanour, as a minister and spiritual guide, neither sacrificing your own independence nor "lording it over God's heritage."

"'It is, then, the high esteem and sincere affection in which we hold you which renders us jealous that you should be fully satisfied of your duty before you bid farewell to a people with whom you have laboured with success and honour; and if our partialities have been somewhat rebellious, they have originated in a sense of your worth and our obligations. And were it not repugnant to your own delicacy and our tastes on such an occasion, we should be glad to justify our regrets by details of how instant in season and out of season you have been as a pastor and a friend; how prudent your counsels, and how seasonable your aid, to many even in their temporal affairs; how tender your spirit and self-denying your service to the sick and dying of the neighbourhood—your own flock and others; how regular and faithful have been your visits to the public institutions; how patiently you have endured obloquy and wrong at the hands of wicked men, whose machinations were successful only because you were without guile; how deep the interest and paternal the supervision you have shown in the religious education of the young; how warm and steady your attachment to the principles, and therefore how zealous your exertions for the promotion of temperance, in that definition of it which alone can save the drunkard; and last but not least, your delicate interpretation of the righteous maxim, "The labourer is worthy of his hire," in your ready and graceful acceptance of the willingness of your people when their ability was below their desire, and the generosity with which you used, and, we fear, too much exhausted your own private means, lest you should be burdensome to a people whose piety and not whose property you sought.

"'Our reluctance to bid you farewell is intelligible to everyone, and honourable to yourself and us; and though we cannot hope, and do not pretend to requite your sympathies and labours, what has, no doubt, been the wish of all, has been accomplished by the exertions of a few of your personal friends of the church and congregation—that you should take with you, to Queensland, a visible memorial of our gratitude, affection, and esteem; and we beg your acceptance of this electro-plate tea-service and tray; and, whilst gratifying to yourself, it will serve to remind your friends in Brisbane that you left a people not entirely insensible to your worth and labour, and those of your beloved wife."

"'We do "hold you in high esteem for your work's sake," and are "at peace among ourselves," and this, which was the desire and ambition of the apostle, must, and will be a source of holy satisfaction to your generous mind.

"'Praying that you may be plenteously enriched with all spiritual blessings in Christ Jesus, we bid you farewell.

"'(Signed by the Committee), 'Mrs. L. Thomas,
'Mrs. J. Woods,
'Mrs. W. Sharwell.

"'On behalf of thirty-seven subscribers.'

"Mrs. Thomas, then, with a few appropriate remarks presented the testimonial, which consisted of a very beautiful electro-plate tea-service and tray, richly engraved, of the value of £25; and after singing the 354th hymn, commencing—

'Blest be the dear, uniting love
That will not let us part;
Our bodies may far off remove,
We still are one in heart,'

the Rev. J. Townend rose to address the meeting, evidently under very great emotion. He had come to that meeting expecting to be the subject of powerful feelings at parting with his friends; but he had no previous conception of the degree to which the kindness and warm affection of his friends would be shown. While grateful to them for the kind expression of their regard and affection, he felt incapable of addressing the audience at any length. He briefly referred to the state of the colony, when he came, in a moral and spiritual point of view, and of the changes that had since taken place, and acknowledged the kindness of his friends, which would never be effaced from his memory.

"Mr. R. Fielding next moved a resolution of congratulation to the Rev. T. A. Bayley, who had just arrived from England to succeed Mr. Townend as minister of the first Melbourne circuit:—

"'That this meeting welcomes the arrival of the Rev. T. A. Bayley to this colony, and expresses its thankfulness to the Father of Mercies for the providential care bestowed upon him and his family while exposed to the dangers of the seas, and for bringing them in health and safety to these shores. It hails his coming to labour as minister in the first Melbourne circuit as an auspicious event, and earnestly prays that his career may be one of great and lasting usefulness; that the blessing of heaven may be upon him in all his works of love and mercy; that the churches may flourish under his pastoral care, and maintain "the unity of the spirit in the bond of peace;" and that a large ingathering of souls, turned "from darkness to light, and from the power of Satan unto God," may be the result of his ministry in this place.'

"The resolution was seconded by Mr. C. Fullwood, and carried unanimously.

"After singing two verses of the hymn, beginning—

> 'We bid thee welcome in the name
> Of Jesus, our exalted Head,"

the Rev. T. A. Bayley, in reply, expressed his pleasure at the friendly feeling which actuated the meeting. He was happy in being privileged to labour amongst a people who could thus esteem and love their minister. Whilst it was his lot to be their minister, he would do all in his power, God being his helper, to promote the spiritual welfare of the congregation and neighbourhood.

"Votes of thanks to the ladies for providing tea, and to the chairman for presiding, were passed. The doxology and benediction closed the proceedings of this interesting meeting."

The following is the letter, alluded to in the foregoing report, from the Hon. Richard Heales, M.L.A. :—

"St. Kilda, July 8th, 1862.

"My dear Friend,—I am in receipt of yours of this morning, inviting me to attend your valedictory tea-meeting, to be held on Monday next, the 14th, and I should have availed myself of the opportunity of taking a public farewell of you, but that I have a similar engagement at the same time at Maldon. Being thus deprived of the advantage of uniting with other friends in bidding you a public farewell, allow me now to express my deep regret that either the discipline or arrangements of the Church to which you belong, and of which you have been for so many years in this colony so zealous and faithful a minister, should make your departure necessary.

"It was my pleasure, a few days after your arrival in Melbourne, to make your acquaintance, and in the cause of temperance it was my good fortune to have your hearty co-operation in the public advocacy of that principle, at a time when the services of public speakers were not available. These circumstances brought us closer together, and will justify me in expressing a strong conviction that by you the cause of God and man has been well served, and that you have been blessed, and made a blessing to others, during your sojourn amongst us.

"I trust you may be long spared in the enjoyment of health and strength, and that in your new sphere you may meet with many friends whose warm-hearted co-operation in every good cause will make up for the loss of those you leave behind, whose attachment has been the growth of years, and who in parting with you, I am sure, share with me the feeling that, not only are we, but that the colony is losing one whose devotedness may long be felt, and not soon supplied.

"I shall always be glad to hear from you, and hope you will put me on the list of your correspondents. My dear wife unites with me in best wishes for you and yours.

"Believe me, yours very truly,

"Rev. J. Townend. R. Heales."

At this time Mr. Heales was filling the highest official position in the colony, next the governor, being chief secretary. As he mentions in his letter, it was my privilege to become acquainted with him soon after I landed at Melbourne, and to enjoy his friendship for eleven years. He was one of the most conscientious and honourable, yet modest, men I ever knew. By religious profession he was a Congregationalist; but it was in the temperance cause, of which he was an uncompromising supporter and advocate, that we were thrown so much together. When society at Melbourne was nearly topsy-turvy, on account of the rush to the gold fields, Mr. Heales and myself mainly carried on weekly meetings at the Temperance Hall, with the little floating help we could obtain. He was successful in business, and rose from one important office to another, until he became Premier. At the change of ministry, Mr. Heales became President of the Board of Lands and Survey, and it is thought that the unremitting attention he paid to the duties and cares of office undermined and wore down a naturally robust constitution. He died, universally lamented, June 19th, 1864, at the early age of 42 years.

All classes of the community united to pay respect to his memory. The funeral procession extended about two miles in length, comprising nearly 220 carriages, besides gentlemen on horseback and on foot, among which was a deputation of about 200 teetotallers.

The body of the deceased was first carried to the Congregational Church, St. Kilda, where a preliminary service was held, and an address delivered by the Rev. James Ballantyne, from which I give the following quotation, as it so beautifully expresses the character of the departed:—

"'There is a time to weep.' Grief sits heavily on many a heart this day. Our little community for the time is draped with emblems of woe. A pillar in our State has fallen. A friend and brother, well-beloved, has passed away from our midst. Life's fountain, that for months had been gradually and gently ebbing out, has ceased to flow. The old familiar voice is hushed in a silence not again to be broken; the eye returns the glance of affection no more; 'the right hand has forgotten its cunning.' All that the tenderest solicitude could devise, all that human skill could think of, was powerless to detain the spirit in its tenement of clay. 'The shadow feared of man' fell upon him, and this day 'the mourners go about the streets.' And if Jesus wept at the grave of him of Bethany whom he loved so well, nature may be permitted this day to drop a tear over the mortal remains of one so widely respected, so greatly beloved, so deeply lamented as Richard Heales. But while we mourn we may not murmur. It was no chance stroke by which our brother fell. 'He in whose hand our breath is' has taken him away, and the simple assurance of that must hush every repining thought. 'We would keep silence before thee, O Lord, not opening our mouths, for thou hast done it.' * * * To poor blind sense there is great mystery in the comparatively early departure over which we this day mourn. That old men die we wonder not; that the ever-ailing, ever frail should pass away is what we look for; that men whose names are never breathed beyond the narrowest circles should disappear excites no surprise. But our friend has passed away in his manly prime; his sun has gone down while it was yet high noon. A career of honourable ambition and ever-widening usefulness, moreover, lay before him. That in these circumstances he should have been cut down seems to mere sense a great, deep, a baffling enigma. And yet there is 'a time to die.' That time is God's time, and is, therefore, the best time. That wisdom which balanced the worlds, which comprehends everything that can happen from eternity to eternity, and which is blended with tenderest love, fixed the moment for the heart's last beating. Here, too, then we must say, 'It is well.' And though we speak of early death, equally true is it that 'that life is long that answers life's great end.'

"The life of the departed needs no laboured eulogy. He belonged to Nature's own nobility. Simple in his habits, gentle in manners, kindly and generous in disposition, unfeigned, warm-hearted, and constant in friendship, charitable and forbearing to those who differed from him, tenderly considerate of the unfortunate and fallen, ever ready to lend a helping-hand to the poor and weary struggler in the battle of life, nobly independent in principle, ever open to conviction, prominent in great public movements, oblivious of the interests of self, of incorruptible integrity, courageous enough to be singular, conscientious in duty, assiduous in office, and anxiously alive to all the responsibilities that lay upon him—in a word, in all his private life singularly urbane; in all his public life singularly honourable—he rose from among the people, who may well be proud of him; wrought his way up with sure and steady progress; planted his feet on almost the loftiest position which a subject of a colony can gain, and then, as beseemeth such an earnest toiler for humanity, he fell on the battle-field of progress, and, in the true martyr's spirit, laid down his life on the altar of the public weal. His name will long be fragrant in the memory of thousands. We will not willingly let that name die, and Victoria will never regret the wreath that is this day laid upon his tomb. We can mingle joy with our tears this day. We sorrow not as those who have no hope. Our departed brother, in self-abnegating lowliness, had fixed his eye upon the blessed, glorious Cross. In simple faith he clung to it. Putting other grounds of hope away, he laid down the infinitely momentous concernments of his soul there. With unfaltering voice and placid countenance he could say 'that he trusted all to Jesus.' Oh, sublime thought! the soul is for ever safe in His keeping. And what a balm to lay upon the heart of sorrowing friends, the humble hope that the immortal spirit—blood-washed, white-robed, and sainted—has safely crossed the dark-rolling river, and gained the sunny uplands of the skies, and now, far and for ever away from the drudgery and pain and weariness of earth, is reposing on the bosom of Eternal Love, listening to 'The harpers that on golden harps play,' and gazing with ecstacy on the vision of God. * * * *"

CHAPTER V.

Departure for Brisbane—Curry, the Murderer—Voyage to Sydney—Arrival in Brisbane—House-Rents very High—Opens Mission in Council-Chamber—Removes to the School of Arts—Purchase of Land—Building and Opening of Chapel—Erection of Dwelling-House—Bad Water—Visits to Eagle Farm—Extent of Queensland—Arrival of Emigrants—Death of Mr. and Mrs. Hawken—Disastrous Fires—Climate—Mosquitos—Failure of Health—Desire to Return to England—Arrival of Rev. R. Miller.

ON the 17th of July, 1862, we, on the *City of Sydney* steamer, left Melbourne for Sydney, a distance of five hundred miles, *en route* for Brisbane. I had during the morning been very busy arranging my luggage, and seeing it safe on the pier at Sandbridge (the port of Melbourne). A number of our dear friends had come down by train to bid a final farewell, and see us off; and I was ready with Paul to say, "What mean ye to weep and to break mine heart." While steaming down the bay I relieved my heavy heart by a flood of tears. Just as we were leaving the pier a friend told me that George Curry was standing at some distance watching us off. Poor fellow! he did not like to come near enough to speak. A few months previous to this he had murdered his wife. At that time he was residing in his own cottage, next door to one of our members, and very near my house. He was a member of the volunteer corps, and one evening after returning from exercise, his wife so exasperated him that he turned and shot her dead on the spot. I visited him in prison several times during his confinement, and was locked up with him in his cell. He was evidently very penitent, and after I had talked and prayed with him, he would engage fervently in prayer himself, and while the big tears rolled down his cheek he would say, "O Lord, have mercy upon me, a miserable sinner, and soften this hard heart, and take away the load of guilt, for Jesus Christ's sake." He told me a good deal of his history; that, though a Protestant, he had married a bigoted Roman Catholic, of a violent and irritating temper. She was always teasing him to go with her to the Catholic chapel, and on several occasions to please her he had gone to Mass; she was also constantly wanting him to make over his property to her. He told her he was willing she should share all with him, and he had made his will, leaving all he had to his wife and her boy (by a former husband). He had reason to believe she was influenced in the course she took by the priest, and on the evening when he shot her he had lost all command over himself. He never expected but to suffer the penalty of the law; he told me he intended to plead "Guilty," but his counsel persuaded him not to do so; but when he uttered the words, "Not guilty," he was in such a state of agitation that he could scarcely stand. The jury, to the great surprise of everyone, brought in a verdict of manslaughter. The Judge was amazed and displeased, but said if that was the case then the gun must have gone off by accident, and, of course, Curry must be set at liberty. Much indignation was evinced in Melbourne at such a termination of the case. Curry came to see me once after he was liberated, one evening after dark; but he could not rest or stay in the place; he sold his property, and became, like Cain, "a wanderer," and ultimately he was found dead in the bush, and it was supposed he had committed suicide; though I believe there was no conclusive evidence of it. Poor Curry! I feel sad when I think of his career and end. He was not a drunkard in the ordinary acceptation of that term, and yet had it not been for maddening liquor he had not committed the horrid deed. How immensely important it is that in the closest of all earthly ties, that of marriage, there should be sought not only suitable position in life, but compatibility of temper, and agreement in religious views and aims; there cannot be real happiness where a pious person marries an irreligious one, or where a Protestant is united to a Roman Catholic, and in the bringing-up of a family the discordant influence is sure to be felt. I would even go further, and suggest that where both are professedly pious, yet belonging to churches holding different views, there is not that oneness and unity there ought to exist in the family circle; it always appears to me unseemly for the husband to be worshipping at one place and the wife at another; and the children brought up, some in the religious views of the father, and others in that of the mother.

The voyage I bore pretty well, but Mrs. Townend became very sick directly the steamer was in motion, and had to retire to the ladies' cabin; so that I saw her no more during the passage. On the Saturday evening at sunset we steered through the Heads, and entered the magnificent Sydney harbour, considered one of the finest in the world. As we neared the pier the stewardess brought on deck my sickly wife, whose countenance brightened on seeing me and the City close at hand. We stayed at the Royal Hotel, and were very comfortable, the lady of the house showing us much kindness; and on the Sabbath morning, in our ship attire, as we could get nothing off the steamer, we found our way to a small Wesleyan Chapel, heard a very pretentious but ignorant man preach; about forty persons present. In the evening we attended Pitt Street Independent Chapel. The discourse was on "Moral Heroism," genteelly delivered, founded on 1st Chron. xi. 17 —"O, that one would give me drink of the water of the well of Bethlehem, that is at the gate," I was very hungry, but did not receive much to satisfy my soul; a collection was made for the distress in Lancashire. The chapel is large and handsome, with a fashionable congregation; the pastor at this time was in England; and the Rev Mr. Graham, of London, afterwards became their minister.

On the Monday morning we had a little time to see the city, went to the telegraph office and sent a message to Brisbane, that we were leaving Sydney that evening; then down to the piers and got our luggage off the steamer, and saw it safe on the one bound for Brisbane. What a scene of hurry and confusion attends the unloading and loading of passenger ships! No mercy is shown to one's luggage; it is whipped up in the air, and then bounced down on the wharves, and amid the chaos of bales, boxes, and packages, every one must look sharp after their own. A lady who had come on the same steamer from Melbourne, was proceeding to Queensland to join her husband, and having two little children with her I promised to see her luggage safe as well as my own; I had just got the last package on board, when the bell rang and the steamer was off. We left at 5 P.M., and just as the sun was setting steamed through the "Heads" into the South Pacific Ocean, on our way five hundred miles further north to Brisbane. Mrs. Townend as usual was confined to her berth very ill; nothing stayed on her stomach, but I to keep from sickness stayed on deck the whole time. The sea was calm and the sky clear; though in the depth of winter I sat on deck the whole two nights, and gazed with admiration on the brilliant constellations of the "Chambers of the South."

On the Wednesday evening we arrived at Moreton Bay, entered

the River Brisbane, and, after a serpentine sail of about 16 miles, the vessel was moored close to the city of Brisbane. It was eight o'clock, quite dark when we arrived, but our friends, Messrs. Bulcock and Robinson, were waiting to welcome and conduct us to the lodgings they had secured for us. After a sound night's repose we awoke next morning and found ourselves in a wood-house in "Fortitude Valley." Some years before, a number of people who arrived by the ship "Fortitude" settled in this valley, hence its name. Rents were very high, and houses scarce; two rooms in this wood cottage were offered us for 1*l.* per week, or 3*l.* per week for rooms and board. The friends in Brisbane had guaranteed to raise 70*l.* per annum, and the Home Committee would supplement 50*l.*,* so that 120*l.* was my prospective salary, out of which I had to find house and furniture. Nothing daunted, we set out in search of cheaper accommodation. For a four-room cottage in the town the rent was 1*l.* 5s. per week, but at a distance from town we found a nice new four-room brick cottage, which the owner had built in a poor locality, and by paying six months' rent in advance we obtained it for 15s. per week. We had brought a little furniture from Melbourne, such as could be conveniently packed; and, purchasing all that we required beside, we left our lodgings at the end of the week, and got comfortably settled in our own house.

I opened my mission the first Sabbath after landing, in the Council Chamber, which the Corporation generously lent us for Sabbath service; it would hold about fifty persons. The singing was first-class, and the room became too small. We then rented the hall of the School of Arts until our new chapel was ready. The Queensland Parliament gave neither land nor money for religious purposes, and Nonconformist communities especially were very cordial with each other; and with the Rev. Nathaniel Turner, the oldest Wesleyan missionary then alive in the southern hemisphere, I enjoyed the sincerest mutual fellowship—he was spending the evening of life as a supernumerary at Brisbane. As we could hold no week-night services for want of a suitable place in which to meet, our friends being very scattered, we were anxious to obtain a site of land, and commence to build a chapel as speedily as possible. Brisbane was well supplied with churches and ministers, almost every section of the Church being repre-

* The Home Committee afterwards granted £75 in aid of first year's salary, and also voted £25 towards furniture.

sented. There were a great many Scotch, for whose accommodation there were two or three sections of Presbyterians, the Lutheran Church for the Germans, Episcopalians, Roman Catholics, Wesleyans, General and Particular Baptists, Independents and Primitive Methodists, and, according to the population of Brisbane at that time, there was very nearly one minister for every 500 of the inhabitants. Still our friends, who had some of them been there ten and twelve years, had never felt as if they could make a religious home, except in connection with the Church of their early choice. North Brisbane stands on several hills, with valleys intervening, and on the first rising ground commanding a view of the river and South Brisbane, we purchased a very eligible site of land for the chapel. As the price of the land was £300, the friends felt it was more than they could compass; I therefore offered, if they would secure it, that I would purchase a third part from them for £100, on which to build myself a residence. To this they cheerfully agreed, and we immediately commenced to collect funds for the erection of a chapel. Our few friends in Brisbane were well known and respected, and we soon had the sympathy of the general public.

It was only about twelve individuals who had engaged to give the £70, which was noble, as they were all plain working men, some struggling with large families, and they were none of them in a position to give large sums to the chapel. I began the subscription list myself with £10, a few of our friends gave the like sum, and we raised among our own people about £100, and from the public, and by opening services, £100 more, members of various Churches kindly contributing. The chapel was of wood, very neat, 30ft. by 40ft., which, with land, cost £550, the debt on it being £350 at 10 per cent. per annum. It was opened March 22nd, 1863. The morning sermon was preached by myself, the afternoon by the Rev. J. Fletcher (Wesleyan), and in the evening by the Rev. E. Griffith (Independent): for each of these brethren I had to supply.

After the opening of the chapel we immediately convened a meeting to organise the Church. This was a difficult matter; our friends had been so long unconnected with any society that they had quite got out of the way of class-meetings; the very individuals who had been instrumental in getting me there would not meet in class, though of their piety I had no doubt. We were therefore compelled to draw up a code of rules somewhat different to our usual course; candidates for membership being examined by the minister, and two members of the Church appointed for that purpose, as to their Christian experience and doctrinal views, and if satisfactory were admitted by the vote of the Church meeting, and then a consistent life and a regular attendance at the Lord's Supper, was considered sufficient. A society meeting was held once a quarter, for the members to receive their quarterly tickets, when a special address was given by the minister.

I however commenced a class for those who would attend, and for others who might join—hoping that in time the desire for Christian communion as it is known in that important means of grace might become stronger. A Sabbath-school was commenced and the congregation gradually improved, but as a rule Sabbath-schools were not so well attended there as in England. The exceeding beauty of the weather nearly all the year round is a strong temptation for people to spend a good deal of their time in the open air; and I often used to think the intense heat, having an enervating effect on the body, had also a deadening influence on spiritual life. None of the places of worship in Brisbane, on account of the heat, commenced Sabbath evening service until seven o'clock, so that those who came from a distance could not well stay for a prayer-meeting. I believe that as a rule, in England, we have the greatest accessions to our churches during the winter months.

When we landed in Brisbane there had been a long drought, which continued two or three months more, with only occasional showers, which, falling on the dry and parched ground, frequently made it like one vast vapour bath, but it had no effect in replenishing the water holes, from which we had to purchase water at one shilling per barrel. One day Mrs. Townend and I went to see the water-hole from which we knew the man fetched our water: it was thick with mud, just like a duck-pond in a farm-yard. I have got up in the middle of the night if I heard a shower of rain, and put out every vessel I could to catch a little water,—there were no factory chimneys pouring out volumes of smoke, and the fires were almost entirely of wood, so that the water from the clouds was sweet and delicious, like spring water. At this time nearly all houses were roofed with shingles, generally of iron bark, which had the effect of discolouring and making the water very disagreeable. I therefore resolved, when we built our house, that whatever else we did without we would secure pure water; and though slates were an enormous price (having to be imported from England), I had the roof slated, and an underground cemented tank made to receive all that fell. This was a real luxury; families having sickness have sent to our house daily for a small pitcher of water, some even coming a mile for it. Now Brisbane has a supply of water, brought some distance from a reservoir, which has been formed at considerable expense. I built a good brick residence, with verandah in front and balcony at the back, which commanded a beautiful view of the river and surrounding country; it was ready for us to occupy just before the chapel was opened, which was about eight months after landing. The house was much admired, and gave quite a respectable appearance to the chapel adjoining. Most of the dwellings in the vicinity were of wood, many of them of very rough construction. A few days after I had accepted the tender and signed the contract for the erection of this house, I received a letter from Melbourne, informing me that a friend to whom I had lent 150*l.* was insolvent, and that there would be very little for the creditors. This individual was a local preacher among the Wesleyans. Some years before he had come from the neighbourhood of Bury, which was my last circuit before leaving England; he brought me letters of introduction and recommendation, and I knew him to be very respectably connected. I showed him much kindness, and assisted him several times in pecuniary matters, for I had a very high opinion of him, believing him to be an honourable man. Some eighteen months before leaving Melbourne I lent him this money to buy cattle for his farm, telling him I should require it whenever I left Melbourne. He promised faithfully to repay it when I was leaving for Queensland; but a week or two before I sailed he came with a very plausible tale, that in two or three months cattle would be much increased in value, and it would be much better to sell then; he induced me to take a bill for four months, which I left at the bank for collection. Within three months he became a bankrupt, and, as he owed a year's rent for his farm, the landlord had the first claim, and all I obtained as dividend was 15*l.* He was soon after in business again; but I never saw him afterwards, nor did he ever write to say that if he was in a position at any future time to pay he would do so. The loss greatly inconvenienced me, as I was depending on this money to complete the payments for the house. This is only one instance among many others of ingratitude and deception which I received from persons that I assisted in temporal matters in that distant land.

During the second quarter after the opening of chapel, we had let about fifty sittings, and as none of our friends at that time could attend to the office of letting seats and receiving rents, Mrs. Townend, for above twelve months, acted as chapel steward, and, to save expense, two of the members alternately gratuitously cleaned the chapel and lit it for Sabbath services, but for week evenings we always lighted it ourselves. There was no gas at this time in Brisbane; shops and places of worship were all lit with kerosene lamps. The days in Australia are much more equal than in England—not nearly so long in summer nor so short in winter, and very little twilight; when the sun sets it grows dark almost immediately.

Some of our families resided at Eagle Farm, about four miles from Brisbane; they came regularly twice on the Sabbath, but were unable to come so far for week evening services. Once a fortnight I went to preach there, and for some time held the service in one of their houses. The Wesleyan minister then offered me the use of their chapel, which was in the immediate locality. This we accepted, he preaching one week and I the other. The services were well attended, though the congregation lived very scattered, being chiefly farmers or market gardeners. I went one day and returned the next, and these visits I much enjoyed. Mr. John Fielding, formerly of Clitheroe, resided at Eagle Farm; he had a large and interesting family; father, mother, and the seven children were good singers. Mrs. Bulcock, a widow, also from Clitheroe, with her three daughters lived close by: about seven years previous to this, her husband, when fetching water from a water-hole, fell in and was drowned—as he occasionally was subject to fits, it was thought in stooping down he had been seized with a fit and so fallen in. We generally gathered all the young people together, and often sitting in the open air on logs of wood, we should sing some sweet melodies, such as "Morn among the Mountains," or "Give me a Glass from the Crystal Spring," every member of both families being firm teetotallers.

With the various Nonconformist ministers in Brisbane I enjoyed sincere fellowship. We had an Evangelical Alliance and met once a month at each other's houses to breakfast, after which we held a meeting for prayer and religious converse. In the evening of the same day a united prayer-meeting was held in our chapels in rotation.

There was also a vigorous Total Abstinence Society, in which I took a lively interest. A few weeks after my arrival I delivered a lecture in the School of Arts to a very large audience.

The Governor, Sir George Bowen, laid the foundation-stone of our new Temperance Hall, after which I gave the address to the assembled multitude; and in the evening a temperance soirée was held in the Wesleyan chapel. Many good families in Brisbane and its suburbs were abstainers; and we needed such a breakwater to stem in some measure the tide of intemperance setting in upon the colony. On one occasion, when I was sitting by the bed-side of a sick man whom I had frequently visited, a man of considerable wealth and civic position came into the room, somewhat the worse for liquor, and, frowning on me, said to the sick man, "Cheer up! you are not going to die. God Almighty is too good to send anybody to hell. I will lend you money to build a new shop and increase your business." Previous to this, when collecting for our chapel, in company with a friend I called on this individual. I had been recommended to do so by some of our friends who had business transactions with him, and who thought he would give a donation. With an oath he said that "if it had been for a theatre, or race-course, or a public-house, he would willingly subscribe." This wealthy blaspheming man was suddenly called to stand before the Judge of the whole earth.

The Colony of Queensland was separated from New South Wales at the close of 1859, and the first Parliament commenced its sittings in May, 1860. The colonists had for many years been struggling for separation and self-government; the great grievance being the centralising policy pursued by the Sydney authorities, and the neglect of the outlying districts; the revenue derived from the whole being chiefly expended on the towns, especially in costly improvements for the metropolis, from which the settlers at so remote a distance derived no benefit.

Queensland is the largest of all the Australian Colonies, possessing an area larger than England, Ireland, Scotland, Wales, France and Spain all added together, and has a seaboard of about 2200 miles. Large tracts of land are taken up for pastoral occupation, a sheep station, or run, frequently being from fifty to a hundred miles square. At the census taken in September, 1862, two months after I landed, the population of this immense territory only amounted to 42,000 persons, exclusive of the aborigines, who were supposed to number nearly 15,000. Just about this time commenced a stream of immigration from England. The government had instituted a liberal land order system, and also granted free and assisted passages from the mother country. An Emigration

Agent was sent to England to lecture on the capabilities and resources of Queensland, and very glowing accounts were given as to its being a desirable field for emigration;—but I am afraid sufficient emphasis was not laid on the capital required to develope those resources; and much disappointment, and frequently real distress, was experienced by the newly-arrived immigrant. During the ever-memorable and long-protracted cotton famine in Lancashire, great numbers of factory operatives came to Queensland, and never having been accustomed to out-door labour, they were ill adapted for the work required there. The Government provided food and shelter for ten days after landing; sometimes five or eight hundred persons landed in a single week. Mrs. Townend and I occasionally went down to the Government depôt, when we knew the steamer was bringing the immigrants up from the bay; who when they came in sight of the city would raise a shout of joy, and well they might after the dangers and privations of so long a voyage.

The depôt presented a painful and strange medley: in one part might be seen a group eagerly devouring a loaf of bread, while another group were dividing a large piece of beef as best they could; such luxuries as knives, forks, and plates are not to be mentioned. One division of the depôt was assigned to the young men, another for the single women, and another for the married couples and their children. Small iron bedsteads ranged round the walls were the only things provided in the form of beds, which folded up by day and formed a seat; but the accommodation, such as it was (being merely wooden sheds), was infinitely better than to land and have no shelter at all.

One day, when we were in the depôt, a poor man was brought in who had just been struck down with sun-stroke. He had only landed about an hour before, and had unwisely gone to a public-house and got drink on an empty stomach, and was more susceptible in such a state to the effects of the sun: it was very trying to emigrants who arrived in the middle of summer. Many poor families had found it as much as they could do, on leaving England, to provide sufficient clothing for the voyage; and I have known families of father, mother, and four or five children who had not five shillings when they landed. It was Melbourne experiences over again on a small scale. Several families who belonged to us in England arrived. We sought, as far as possible, to get them work in town; but of course numbers had to go into the country districts, and very few who remained were able to be of much use to the Church in a pecuniary point of view; but rather they needed help, and the kindness of our friends to new arrivals was worthy of all praise.

A great many on landing made their way to our house: I assisted them as far as I was able, and used every effort to find them employment. Some months before I left Melbourne, a local preacher and his wife arrived from the Exeter circuit. He was unable to find employment, there being very little demand for his business. Seeing his wife in trouble about it when I left, I told her to cheer up, and I would try what I could do in Brisbane for them. A week or two after I arrived I went to the Government office, and obtained for him the situation of Government bookbinder. He was telegraphed for to Melbourne to come by next steamer, at a salary of £3 12s. per week, which was increased to £4 weekly within four months, and it will most likely be a situation for life. He was thought to be in consumption on leaving England, but the very warm climate of Queensland restored him to good health. I believe the climate of Queensland is very conducive to the recovery of persons having a tendency to consumption, if they go during the early stages of the complaint; but if the disease has acquired a firm hold on the constitution, there is not much hope of a cure.

A letter, with a *carte de visite*, arrived from a gentleman in Manchester—his only son, an unsettled, but very clever youth, had left his home for Australia. After being on board ship he had written his parents to say where he had gone; his only object in going appeared a strong desire to see the world. His father wrote, enclosing his likeness, requesting me to look after him; and as the mail came quicker than the sailing vessel, I got the letter a few days before he arrived. On the Sabbath following I discerned the person in the congregation clearly portrayed by the photograph. After service I walked up to the youth and said, "You are a new arrival?" he replied, "I am." "Where do you come from?" "Manchester," he answered. I said, "Your name is ———." "Yes," he said, blushing up to the ears. I put my hand on his shoulder, saying, "You are my prisoner;" and taking him with me into our house, I shewed him *himself*. I obtained for him a situation in an architect's office, and he lodged with us some months.

Mr. Henry Hawken, a local preacher from one of our Cornish

circuits, with his wife, came to the colony. They were just married before leaving. I felt sure from the first that they had made a mistake in coming. Mrs. H. had been genteelly and delicately brought up, and was altogether unfit to *rough it*, as we say. Mr. H. had been brought up on a farm, but farming in Australia is a totally different thing to what it is in England. He obtained daily work at whatever offered, and for several months they lived with us, until he built himself a small wood house. He had a long sickness, and died just as we left Brisbane. Subsequently the delicate, pensive widow, after a short illness, succumbed to the King of Terrors, and was laid by the side of her husband. They, however, sleep in Jesus at the antipodes of their native land, and heaven is as near from the southern as the northern hemisphere. Their infant child was kindly cared for by some members of the Church, until an opportunity offered of sending it to England. It weathered the long voyage, and is being caressed in the bosom of the relatives of the departed.

In the same vessel with the Hawkens came Mrs. Greenwood, from Newchurch, Rossendale. On the voyage, while hanging some clothes on a line, her husband was over-balanced, and fell into the sea. There was a shout, "A man overboard!" but all attempts to rescue him were unavailing. Mrs. Greenwood was in her berth unwell; she had one child, and on landing was near confinement of a second. She was safely delivered. I baptized the infant, saw her off by steamer to join the ship then lying in Moreton Bay, the same in which she had come; the captain generously giving her a free passage home. I have seen her since my return; both children alive, and she in good health.

During my residence in Brisbane I witnessed many disastrous scenes, both by flood and fire. Often were we awoke at night by the well-known notes of the fire-bell, sounding clear and loud, for in that buoyant atmosphere sound travels a great deal better than in the thick, murky atmosphere of England. One morning, about three o'clock, we heard the first note of the bell, and hastily going out on the balcony a slight flame was visible ascending from about the middle of Queen-street, which is the principal street. We could see it was very near where one of our members, Mr. R. Bulcock, had recently, at considerable expense, much improved and enlarged his premises, having added a number of offices, which he had let, and, after having been there about fourteen years, was just getting into a position of doing well, and reaping the fruit of his former toils. When we reached the spot the fire was confined to a shop three or four houses removed from that of our friend, and he was busy helping his neighbours to remove their goods—not thinking the fire would reach his own, on account of a high brick building that intervened, and which was thought would stay the progress of the flames. Unfortunately, there was a small end window, and though the party wall stood entire, the flame, rushing through this window, communicated with Mr. Bulcock's premises, which, being of wood, were in a few moments a mass of fire. The roof was of zinc, which had the effect of sending the flames out at the front, instantly communicating with the goods and furniture which had been removed from the houses and placed in the centre of the street, which is a very broad one, so there were two fires raging, and with difficulty the opposite houses were saved by the inmates covering the fronts and roofs with wet blankets. Fourteen shops in a short space of time were a heap of smoking ruins, for though there were fire-engines there was no water, except what was brought in buckets from the tanks of adjoining houses. Mr. B.'s building was partly covered by insurance, but the loss in business was very great. Several of the burnt-out families built temporary shops of wood on a vacant piece of land near, while their buildings were in course of erection. Again, a fire broke out in a small shop adjoining Mr. Bulcock's, and a second time his premises were destroyed, and, being only intended for a few months' occupation, were not insured.

Soon after the Parliament passed an Act not to allow any more wood buildings to be put up within the city boundary.

The climate of Queensland is adapted for the growth of nearly all tropical and semitropical fruits—such as bananas, melons, oranges, lemons, and pomegranates; even pine-apples flourish in the open air, all the year round. Sugar and cotton plantations are also being extensively cultivated. The first summer I was in Brisbane was a very trying one, owing to the long drought and intense heat, the thermometer being sometimes from 120 to 130 degrees. Insect life is very prolific; especially do mosquitos during the summer months prove a great nuisance. They do not trouble one so much by day, but directly it is dusk they commence their onslaughts. There is no reading, writing, or sewing in comfort, unless one keeps up a perpetual warfare, brushing them off with a handkerchief; even then they bite through one's stockings, and on going to bed there is a pitched battle. Turning up the mosquito-net curtains we should take a long towel and vigorously brush them out of the bed, then quickly drop the curtains, tuck them in tight all round, and lay our heads on the pillows, thinking the enemy fairly expelled; but just as one is dropping asleep there comes that peculiar singing noise which a mosquito makes, and the moment it ceases you know it has settled somewhere—you suppose on your face, and give yourself a smart slap, but rarely succeed in hitting the right place. After vainly trying to sleep, with, perhaps, a dozen mosquitos inside the curtains, you jump out in desperation for another attempt to exclude the intruders. Some persons they never touch; but their sting is very irritating, especially to new arrivals. I have known immigrants so stung the first few nights after landing as not to be able to put on their stockings for weeks, having incautiously, by scratching the affected parts, increased the irritation and caused wounds. Mosquitos breed in water, and and at this time people had to keep their supply of water in open barrels, which was a fruitful source for multiplying them.

It is a remarkable feature that in such an immense territory as Australia there are no very large or fierce animals, the largest being the kangaroo and dingo or native dog, which is half like a fox, of a reddish-brown colour, with a large bushy tail. Most of the animals are of the marsupial or pouch-bearing species. Of birds there is a very great variety, the largest being the emu and the native companion or ardea: parrots, cockatoos, parrakeets, and other birds of brilliant plumage are in vast numbers; while the swans are black. Lizards and snakes abound; some of the snakes are very poisonous. Alligators are found in the northern rivers.

My health began to fail soon after reaching Brisbane; the constant and strong sunlight was very trying to my weak sight, frequently causing severe inflammation in the eyes. In addition to this I suffered much from a severe rupture, which I met with a few months before leaving Melbourne, while travelling through the bush from Heathcote to Kyneton. I had gone there to preach anniversary sermons and attend a tea-meeting. Unfortunately on my return I was the only passenger—had the coach been full it would have balanced it a little; for whatever obstacles are in the way, whether a deep gully or a fallen tree, the horses dash on at full gallop, the passengers are bumped one against another in a most unceremonious fashion, and have to keep a firm hold, or they stand a good chance of being pitched out. Many of the coaches were like large omnibuses, and open at the sides. On this journey

I sat down at the bottom of the coach, and held on with both hands, and was as sick as if I was crossing the Bay of Biscay in a hurricane. On all previous occasions when returning from Heathcote, I had travelled through the night, 40 miles through the bush to Kilmore, the remaining 40 miles to Melbourne being a good macadamised road; but to save night travelling this time I returned by way of Kyneton.

When the Church in Brisbane became well established and in good working order, we felt it desirable to extend our borders, but the state of my health forbade much travelling; horse exercise would have imperilled my life. Under these circumstances I wrote to the Home Committee, requesting leave to return to England, which was readily granted, and the Rev. Richard Miller was appointed my successor.

As there was a good piece of land at the rear of the chapel, it was thought desirable to erect a preacher's residence, which could at any time, when required, be taken to enlarge the chapel. The house was in course of erection when I left, and would be ready for Mr. Miller to occupy soon after his arrival.

The second year after my arrival in Brisbane, the small church raised £100 for the support of the ministry, although some of the first subscribers, finding they had promised more than the claims of their families would allow, were obliged to reduce the amount of their subscriptions. Mr. and Mrs. Miller arrived the night before our farewell tea-meeting, having come much sooner than we expected, on account of having fortunately met with a vessel coming straight from Tasmania, instead of going by way of Melbourne or Sydney. The Church now numbered 34 members, with a steady and increasing congregation.

Since that time the colony of Queensland has passed through a season of great commercial depression, spreading poverty and distress on every hand, and materially affecting the prosperity of the Churches.

CHAPTER VI

Voyage to Sydney—Stormy passage to Melbourne—Visits Ballarat—State of the Mission there—Is stationed at Ballarat—Chinese Population—Labours during one Year—Desire to return to England—Attends District Meeting—Death of the three Carnes—Farewell of Friends—Journal of return voyage to England.

On Wednesday, the 9th of November, 1864, surrounded by sympathising friends, we embarked on board the 'Lady Bowen' steamer on our way to Sydney, from thence to Melbourne in order to take ship for England. After a pleasant voyage, although Mrs. Townend again suffered much from sea-sickness, we reached Sydney on Friday evening, and had to wait five days for a steamer, one having sailed just before our arrival. Sabbath morning we worshipped in the leading Wesleyan Chapel, the opening hymn being "Praise ye the Lord, 'tis good to raise," then a portion of the Church of England prayers were read, with a good deal of chanting by the choir, which left very little time for the sermon. In the afternoon we visited some of the schools, among others the Roman Catholic; the priest, seeing we were strangers, very politely came up to us, saying, he would much like us to hear the children sing, and, giving them a sign, they instantly commenced a hymn of praise to the "Blessed Virgin." In the evening I preached in the Bethel Church, to an attentive audience, at the urgent request of my old friend the Rev. John Reid, Presbyterian Minister, formerly of Melbourne, who had preached at the opening of our Albert Street Chapel, and also at the opening of George Street Chapel. Since then Mr. Reid has joined the Church triumphant above.

On the Tuesday afternoon we attended a public meeting in the "Sailors' Home," on the occasion of its being formally opened by the Governor (Sir John Young). At five o'clock p.m., on Wednesday, we embarked on the steamer for Melbourne. It was a very old boat, and heavily laden (persons on the wharves remarking that it was not safe to go to sea with such a cargo), causing the steamer to be a great depth in the water. On passing the Heads and entering the ocean we encountered a heavy swell. Mrs. Townend became very ill, and was confined to her berth the whole way. It was a terrific voyage. On the Thursday we encountered a heavy gale of wind blowing directly in our teeth; and from eleven a.m. until six p.m. the hatches were closed, and the sea incessantly washing over us, the sailors sometimes up to their waists in water. The captain, on reaching Twofold Bay, ran in for shelter. This bay is a deep basin, surrounded with high hills, and has been a "fair haven" for many a distressed vessel; and had we not had such a refuge, I believe our vessel would have foundered. About midnight the storm somewhat abated; and having got round the point of land, we obtained a favourable wind. During this voyage I remained on deck most of the time, and while the sea washed over us, I sat on the grating that screened the engine fires. On the Saturday afternoon we joyfully steamed up Hobson's Bay, and by five p.m. were alongside the pier. Mrs. Townend was so utterly prostrated that with great difficulty I got her off the boat, the captain and passengers remarking that she would never be able to bear the voyage to England. She was kindly treated by the station-master's wife, and, after resting two hours, was so far restored as to go on by train to Melbourne, where we were most affectionately received and hospitably entertained at the residence of our dear friends, Mr. and Mrs. Thomas.

On the following Sabbath I attended George Street Chapel, and met with the dear friends with whom we had been accustomed to worship. It was a "hot wind" day, and I was in a very haggard and prostrate condition. A few days sufficed to restore us to moderate health and spirits. We, however, fully gave up the idea of ever returning to England, so completely were we sickened with the sea, and fully believing that such a voyage would be more than Mrs. Townend could bear. This we felt to be a trial, after having cherished the hope of once again meeting our friends and relatives, and mingling in fellowship with our churches in Old England.

Having preached anniversary sermons at George Street, Richmond, and Geelong, I visited Ballarat with a view of ascertaining the state of the Society, and the probability of resuscitating our cause in that important locality: this was my first visit to this far-famed gold-field. The mission at Ballarat had suffered severely through the retiring from our connection of Messrs. Sayer and Bradney, who had become ministers of the Congregational Union of Victoria. These brethren had had, no doubt, serious difficulties to encounter; but as old servants of our connection, I think they would have acted more nobly in standing by the body which had confided to them these important trusts. Mr. Bradney first visited Ballarat during the latter part of 1857, and commenced preaching in the township. At our yearly meeting, in January, 1858, he was appointed to labour there as stated minister, and during the first two years, the churches in the Melbourne locality raised above £250 to aid in supporting the Ballarat Mission. Two small wood chapels were erected during Mr. Bradney's labours at Ballarat, but at the time he seceded, at the close of 1862, one society and congregation left with him, and the chapel in which they worshipped was also alienated from us. The Peel Street Chapel, which would seat from 150 to 200, and on which was a debt of £120, remained to us, and for a short time was under the pastoral care of Mr. Sayer. After the resignation of these two brethren, the Church suffered much from the want of a stated minister, as there was no one who could be appointed, and the friends, after having been two years with such occasional help as they could obtain, had almost come to the conclusion to sell the chapel and break up the Society. A good brother, in whom I had great confidence, Mr. G. Bleckly, local preacher, who for some years was connected with the George Street Society, had removed to Ballarat, and he and the brethren Odger and Walker, with a few others faithful to our principles, stood firm by the cause, and they now earnestly entreated me to come and labour among them, and try to build up the wreck, that the breaches made in our Zion might be again healed. After spending a week preaching anniversary sermons, visiting and consulting with the members—and deeming the case not hopeless—I consented to the appointment.

I returned to Melbourne to attend the sittings of the District Meeting, and in January, 1865, we removed to our future field of labour, and set to work with a good heart. The Ballarat Society, when urging their case, gave me to understand that they were utterly unable to raise sufficient funds to support a minister, £50 being the utmost they could promise; but this was a large sum for so few to give. I must say that the liberality of our attached members in Australia is worthy of praise; the regular class-money both at Melbourne and Ballarat at that time was a shilling per week, and collections at the door every Sabbath. The District meeting also voted £50 in aid out of the grant from England, and I provided house and what additional furniture I required, there being a little belonging to the Society.

As my health was still rather precarious, making long walks undesirable, and Mrs. Townend being anxious to assist in the Sabbath-school, we felt the necessity of living near to the chapel; and the only house we were able to obtain was one in the same street, which, by always paying a month's rent in advance, we obtained for £50 per year, but by going a considerable distance we might have got one cheaper.

I spent a very happy year at Ballarat; we enjoyed peace in the church, and a measure of prosperity; the members were increased from eighteen to thirty-four, the Sabbath-school doubled its numbers, and the congregation also greatly improved, and the debt on the chapel was, during the year, reduced by twenty pounds. Ballarat contained a population of from thirty to forty thousand, and was well supplied with places of worship of every denomination, and with the various Dissenting ministers I enjoyed a very friendly intercourse. An Evangelical Alliance existed, the ministers meeting for breakfast and discussion, at each other's houses, monthly; and a public meeting on the evening of the same day was held in our different chapels in rotation.

Tea-meetings were held without number. I think the Australian churches carry this institution to greater excess even than it is done in England, but no sort of public meeting appeared to succeed unless a tea or fruit soirée was connected with it. To most of these meetings I was invited, and it was a source of pleasure to me, isolated as I was from any other of our own churches. Ballarat has been one of the richest of the gold-fields, but at the time we were there the alluvial diggings had been long worked out, and it was all deep sinking and underground work similar to coal-mining, the quartz in which the gold is embedded being crushed by machinery, and when reduced to a powder undergoing various washings, until the gold is separated. These operations are carried on day and night without ceasing, three relays of men being engaged, each working eight hours; so there is the constant stamping noise of machinery, all over the township. A good deal of reckless speculation prevails. A company is formed who take up a claim, and then issue their prospectus, with a beautiful map showing veins of gold in various directions, and the certainty of its proving a very rich mine is held out to all intending shareholders, who to their cost often find out, after having erected expensive machinery, and gone down a great depth, there is no gold to repay the outlay.

A great number of Chinese resided at Ballarat, following various occupations. A good many were market gardeners, and were very successful in raising vegetables; they used the method of irrigation by watering with the foot, and being plodding and persevering, and satisfied with smaller earnings than Europeans, they managed on a very small plot of ground to earn a livelihood. When taking their vegetables round for sale they carry them in two large wicker panniers suspended from each end of a pole, which is laid across the shoulders. Among the Chinese are storekeepers, doctors, chemists, tailors, barbers, butchers, &c., but the greater proportion seek employment on the gold-fields. They also make very good labourers, sheep-shearers, and harvest-men, and though they cannot do as much work as a European, they give satisfaction to their employers, as what they do is done carefully and steadily.

In 1859, the Chinese population of Victoria was estimated at 45,000, but since the palmy days of the gold-fields have passed away their number has greatly diminished, until, in 1867, it was supposed they did not number much above 20,000, and were becoming increasingly sunk in poverty and degradation.

The vices of opium-smoking and gambling have a fearfully disastrous influence on them; also the absence of their wives and families has a very demoralising effect. A very few have married European wives; but they are great lovers of their country, and their chief hope and expectation appears to be to realize sufficient that they may return to their native land, and they are content to toil amid many difficulties and privations until they can obtain sufficient to carry out their desire. They, therefore, will not bring their women to the country, having no intention of settling permanently. The more wealthy among them even send the bones of their deceased relatives and friends, packed in small wooden boxes, to be interred in their fatherland, where they are sure the sacrifices to the remains of the departed ones will be performed at the proper seasons.

On one occasion I was waiting in the office at the Melbourne general cemetery, when a number of cars rushed past, at a very unseemly rate for a funeral. I inquired of the clerk what it meant;

he replied, "You had better go and see, as you have sufficient time before your funeral will arrive." I made my way to the Chinese department; by the time I reached the spot they had emptied the cars and laid the contents out on the grave of a deceased relative.

In the centre was a beautiful roasted pig of considerable size; they had just cut it open down the back, from snout to tail, but divided it no further. There was also a variety of confectionary laid out, with a number of small torches stuck in the ground, apparently made of painted paper, which, when they had lighted them sent forth a pleasant perfume. They also poured out libations of what appeared to be wine, and then one and another laid himself flat on the grave with his face downwards, whether to invoke the dead man to arise and partake I could not tell, but if so they appeared in no way disappointed that he did not make his appearance. After waiting awhile, they in great glee gathered up the provisions and drove off to hold a feast at their own home.

On one occasion their torches set fire to the dry grass, and a little child belonging to one of the employés who was playing in the grounds, was burnt to death; after this I believe they were not allowed to light torches. Three Protestant missions have been established among the Chinese in Victoria, but have not met with much success. According to a recent report prepared by the Rev. W. Young, who was missionary to the Chinese at Ballarat, the number of baptized Chinese does not exceed fifty. The Roman Catholics have also a mission established among them. Mr. Young, who was employed by the Minister of Justice to collect information relative to the condition of the Chinese in Victoria, states in his report that "the Chinese who emigrate from China to Australia are chiefly from the province of Canton. They generally belong to the rural agricultural population spread over the country from 70 to 150 miles south of Canton, and perhaps about the same distance westward of Hongkong and Macao. Among these agriculturists there is a goodly number of artisans. They are usually a peaceful and easily governed people. Besides those who come from the province of Canton there are also those who come from the adjoining province of Hokkeen, or Fuhkien. In Australia these commonly go by the name of Amoy Chinese. The Chinese population of the colony is composed of Su-yap, Sam-yap, Heang-San, and Amoy Chinese. Their dialects differ; but, with all their differences, the natives of the three tribes first named manage to understand each other with tolerable ease; but between the dialects of these three tribes, and that spoken by the Amoy Chinese there is as wide a difference as between English and French.

Ballarat is 102 miles distant from Melbourne by rail, and being much higher, is considerably colder than Melbourne. One night, about ten o'clock, there was a very slight fall of snow, and people turned out to an unsuccessful attempt at snow-balling, as it melted almost immediately it fell. This was the only time I saw snow during my fourteen years' residence, though on the high mountain ranges snow prevails. After a few months' residence, Mrs. Townend's health, and also my own, greatly improved. We began to feel that a colder climate would perhaps be conducive to our general health, and with returning strength of body the desire to return to England revived, and we resolved once more to brave the perils of the sea. I therefore informed the friends that at the close of the year we should leave; this intimation was received with much sorrow and regret.

At a farewell breakfast-meeting, which was held on Christmas Day, in Peel Street Chapel, an album, containing the likeness of each member of the Church and some of the congregation, was presented. Also to Mrs. Townend, a full-sized photograph of her husband was given. This was a most interesting meeting: the strong affection of our friends was unmistakably manifested, and we parted with them in mutual sorrow, not expecting ever to meet again until we unite with the great congregation in the upper and better sanctuary, where the pain of parting is for ever unknown.

On the following day, by rail, we arrived at Melbourne. We found the friends of George Street Chapel overwhelmed with trouble. Three families had been overtaken with severe accidents, and Christmas cheer exchanged for deep sorrow.

A fine little boy, son of Mr. and Mrs. Woods, had fallen over the balcony rail, a great height, sustaining severe fractured skull, and was lying in a critical state.

Our friends John and William Carne, brothers, lived next door to each other. After the Christmas dinner, two of William's sons and one of John's went a short distance to spend the afternoon on the banks of the "Merrie Creek." It being very hot weather, the youngest of the three stripped, and plunged into a deep water-hole to bathe, not knowing, or, it would seem, thinking about its depth. His brother, seeing him struggling in the water, jumped in to his assistance, but was unable to rescue him, or get out himself. The cousin, seeing the condition in which they were in, leapt into the pit with a view of rescuing his companions. *All three were drowned.* Some little boys near had seen them sink, and ran to tell the nearest residents what had occurred. With considerable difficulty the bodies were brought up. No one up to this time appeared to have known the depth of the water-hole, but on measuring it was ascertained to be nearly twenty feet.

These places are extremely treacherous; long after a river or creek has ceased to flow, and the bed has become quite dry, these waterholes remain like a chain of pools.

These youths had been trained in our George Street day-school, under a very efficient teacher. They had for several years been connected with the Sabbath-school, the two eldest—one about seventeen, and the other eighteen years of age—had become teachers, were members of the Church, and promising fair for a life of usefulness. All the members of the district-meeting (sitting at the time) attended the funeral, accompanied by a large concourse of sympathising spectators. They were laid in the same grave in the Melbourne general cemetery.

The Honourable John P. Falkner, the oldest colonist in Victoria—to whom I have already referred—took a great interest in the two eldest of these youths, lending them books from his library, and showing them much kindness in various ways. The good old gentleman, verging upon eighty years of age, showed his sympathy by attending the funeral in his private carriage.

The Sabbath-morning following, I preached in George Street Chapel, the bereaved families being present. I selected for my text Job ix. 12, "Behold, he taketh away, who can hinder him? who will say unto him, What doest thou?"

The afflicted father, who had lost two sons, was much comforted, and told me afterwards that he felt constrained to stand up and join in the singing of the last hymn, feeling that he could say, "It is the Lord, let him do what seemeth him right."

A farewell tea-meeting was again given us by our dear friends in George Street Chapel, and on the 5th of January, 1866, we found ourselves on board the 'Result,' having taken our passage for London. The ship was delayed sailing until the following day, so we had plenty of time to put our cabin in comfortable order, which is a very important thing to attend to before the ship is in motion and one is prostrate with sickness.

Every one making a long voyage should take a hammer, with some nails and crooks of various sizes to secure their boxes and for hanging their things on, as nothing can be laid out of the hand a minute in rough weather, without rolling to the opposite side of the cabin. During our first day on board many of the friends came to see us on the ship and say farewell. As the 'Result' lay alongside Sandridge Pier, we went in the evening to the Wesleyan Chapel, service being held in the various churches to pray for rain, as the long drought was causing disease and death among cattle and human beings to a fearful extent. After service we returned pensively to the ship for the first night, being the only passengers who slept on board. The following day there was a fearfully hot wind, and there was the usual confusion of passengers and luggage being brought on board up to the last minute; some even had to follow in small boats, while we "lay to" in order to pick them up.

As we were being towed down Hobson's Bay by the steamer, the wind, being very high, split one of our sails, and, although two miles from the port of Williamstown, the dust swept over our ship in darkening clouds. Hopefully and pensively I mused, as the city receded from our view, "Farewell Melbourne! in thee have I experienced much of the pleasurable, and some of the most painful events of my chequered life. Good-bye, ye hot winds, sunny skies, and Austral scenes. What changes since October, 1851, when first I set foot in Melbourne! It was then a mere outline, with comparatively few inhabitants; it is now the queen of southern cities, comprising within its proper and suburban districts above 140,000 inhabitants. To its ministers, churches, schools, hospitals, and busy population I would say farewell!"

Second day at sea. Last night at anchor inside the "Heads;" this morning passed through the Heads; heavy swell; many are sick; Mrs. T. keeps her bed; I am sick, but vomiting freely relieves my head. We have interest in the prayers of our Victorian friends. God of the seas, our trust is in thee.

Third day. Yesterday was Sabbath on land, but not on board the 'Result.' We had strong conflicting winds and nasty cross-seas; several of our passengers got drenched with sea-water, and others went to their berths sick. I was glad to lie in my clothes all night, being as helpless as a child. The steward showed us much kindness, and spoke soothingly and encouragingly. This morning a fair wind bears us delightfully along Bass's Straits. The rocky scenery is very bold and picturesque—a sad place to navigate on a dark night, or in stormy or foggy weather. I rose at five, shaved and washed, and against inclination sat at breakfast table. Our captain is a clever modest gentleman, our chief officer benevolent, affable, and cheerful; the doctor hardly looks as if he would be able to keep us all in perfect health.

Tuesday, 9th. Yesterday, fine and favourable wind; the rolling of the ship causes many to be sick sailing along the Pacific. I am somewhat better; weather getting cold; looking forward to seventy or eighty days of sea life is cheerless, but our trust is in God; captain and officers very kind. Progress last twenty-four hours, 248 knots; south lat. 46° 52′.

Thursday, 11th. Fine, but slow, only six knots per hour. I am much better; Mrs. Townend is very low, unable to lift her head from the pillow. Seagulls fly and porpoises gamble around our floating house. All around one unbounded waste of water.

Friday, 12th. Very stormy wind, bearing us in our right course; stormy night, with thunder and lightning; early on deck this morning, assisted by Mr. Cooper, our chief officer. The scene was awfully grand! Oh, the power of Him who "holds the winds in his fist, and measures the waters in the hollow of his hand." Progress last twenty-four hours, 262 knots, south lat. 49°. We are south of New Zealand, clear of the "Snares and Traps," thanks to our heavenly Father.

Saturday, 13th. Slow and easy sailing; comfortable night; warm and fine morning. With line and hook our chief mate has caught two fine albatrosses, measuring ten feet from tip to tip of outspread wings; they appear to have no power to raise themselves off the deck; I should like to give them a lift. The passengers must all see them before they are killed to be stuffed. Since yesterday this time, 185 knots, lat. 49° 22′, long. 165° 25′.

Sabbath, 14th. Stormy through the night and this morning; very jerking, disagreeable motion; nearly all sick. Church service by the Rev. Mr. Mackie; few present. The captain thought to have sighted the Antipodes Islands, but stormy wind prevented. Progress, 240 knots. God bless us and help us on our stormy passage.

Monday—ten days out; stormy through the night. Evening service in the saloon. Though sick, I preached with comfort, and received the thanks of the captain and many of the passengers, who requested me to preach every Sabbath evening. This day is fine; Mrs. T. is in her chair on the main deck; she cannot bear to be on the poop, as the motion of the vessel is more felt there than on the main-deck, which is nearer the centre of the ship; she is extremely weak, not able to dress herself or stand without assistance; nothing settles on her stomach. Gentle breeze and pleasant sailing; all in good spirits. South lat. 50° 41', west long. 159° 15', our course due east. Distance from Cape Horn, 4277 miles.

Monday, Jan. 16th. Having passed the meridian, we have two Mondays and eight days this week: we are making west longitude. The Greenwich time is nearly twelve hours in advance of ours, but by the time we reach London we shall be equal. Weather very warm for this latitude; fair wind and pleasant sailing; Mrs. T. is better. Just as the sailors were sitting down to breakfast, orders were given to set stunsails; two refused to do so until after breakfast. They were immediately handcuffed, and stowed away to be fed on bread and water; they have to learn subordination. Progress 228 knots.

Wednesday, 18th. Cloudy and drizzling rain; no observations, the sun not breaking the clouds. The swell makes us sick; we are afraid of a head easterly wind. Our commander does not intend going much further south; he prefers safety and comfort to risk and discomfort. We are truly thankful for past mercies. Our two insubordinates are still in close custody.

Saturday, January 21st. A fortnight this morning since leaving Queenscliffe, and bidding good-bye to the pilot; steady, quiet sailing; bright and sunny day. We have only seven saloon passengers—five ladies and two gentlemen—who, with the captain and his little boy, the two chief officers, and the doctor, make our party twelve. For intelligence and eloquence I think the ladies will bear away the palm. Miss Roberts, an Irish lady, who has travelled a great deal, is an embodiment of general and particular knowledge, in converse changing from theology to navigation, or discoveries in the Arctic regions, from that to politics, and at any time equal to any two of us on history or geography. Mrs. Renshaw (sister to the Rev. Mr. MacLaren, Manchester), who, with her husband, is returning from a tour in Australia, is a very intelligent lady, and truly pious; indeed, when, in smooth water and in our best mood, we find ourselves in the full tide of social converse, the hours glide pleasantly and profitably away. The captain is half a Methodist; he is the son of a clergyman, but has married a Methodist. Mr. and Mrs. Renshaw are decided Nonconformists; Miss Roberts is Anglican, the doctor goes with the winning party, and Mrs. Townend and myself are fairly committed to Methodism. Steady sailing; bright and sunny day. Piebald porpoises and whales are seen round our ship. Mrs. Townend is keeping her bed, hoping to obtain a settlement of food on her stomach. Progress since yesterday, 230 miles.

Monday, January 22nd. Yesterday bright and clear. Morning service by our clergyman, who, with his amiable wife, are second-cabin passengers. He appears with surplice, bands, and book, has a somewhat defective utterance, and lacks the qualification for public speaking; he is in half holy orders, has been several years in America, but was obliged to leave on account of the war in that country; has been a short time employed by the Bishop of Melbourne, and is now on his way to England to try and get in under the Bishop of London. He has imbibed some High Church notions, and tries to instruct his audience in matters of faith and practice, backed up with, not what the Bible says, but what the Church in her *unerring wisdom* teaches. He is, however, no bigot, for he cordially joins in our service, and often leads the singing. In the evening I preached with considerable liberty from Acts xii. 17. It is quite a stir preparing the saloon for service. The midshipmen bring in a number of planks, which are arranged for seats, resting on buckets bottom upwards; they are then covered neatly over with coloured flags, and when everything is in order the bell is tolled for church, the passengers coming from the different parts of the ship as orderly as on land. Mrs. T., though very low, is on the deck wrapped in blankets; I am getting on moderately; sea life is a trying affair; the Lord bring us safely through, and may our future life be spent in grateful remembrance of His past mercies. Lat. 52°, long. 136° 16′.

Tuesday, January 23rd. Yesterday dark and stormy; gale from the north-west; evening—close-reefed, very dark, and afraid of icebergs; none seen as yet. Fearful rolling and shipping of seas. To nervous people it is very trying to hear the officers talk of their encounters, hair-breadth escapes, and shipwrecks.

Wednesday, January 24th. Very fine and cold day; much rolling and discomfort through the night, the wind being direct aft; no sleep for my dear wife. I keep up much better than I expected, for which I am truly thankful. Since yesterday at noon ran 226 miles.

Friday, January 26th. Very strong breeze—royals and top-gallants furled; ran 120 miles last twenty-four hours. South lat. 24° 18′, long. 108° 57′. Thanks to our Heavenly Father, not much shipping of seas, and motion comparatively steady. I have this morning put on my fur cap which has been round the world before. It was lent to me by a friend in the New Mills Circuit, to be returned should I ever come back to England; it is a most comfortable thing, and is quite envied by the other passengers. No appearance of ice; the ladies are chiefly in their cabins; Mrs. T. keeps in bed.

Sunday, 28th. Our fourth Sabbath at sea. Yesterday rather squally. A heavy sea broke through our weather porthole. Mrs. T. was on the deck, in her chair, wrapped in blankets; in running to her assistance my feet slipped from under me and I fell flat on deck; providentially was not hurt. We have passed a good night; light breeze; more people at church this morning; at the request of the captain the service was not spoiled with lame attempts at chanting. Lord help me this evening.

Monday, 29th. Run 200 miles; very fine morning; all comfortable; service last night well attended. To lead the singing and preach is more than I am able to do with comfort. I preached for thirty-five minutes as pointedly as possible: my back and legs ached, and I was glad to creep into my rocking bed. A very good night; and, after my morning ablution, felt much refreshed. So far all goes on well; we are expecting to round the Horn this week, 760 miles distant.

Tuesday, Jan. 30th. The motion to-day is jerking and unpleasant, the wind being south-west, 230 knots, south lat. 55° 47′, west long. 82° 8′; very squally. The sun rises at four and sets at half-past seven; full moon. I am glad we selected this time of the year. We have not seen a particle of ice. How different to be in this latitude in winter, with hardly eight hours daylight; decks covered with snow and ropes covered with ice. The captain and officers say they never rounded the Horn before without seeing ice. The ladies, with one exception, are in their beds.

Wednesday, Jan. 31st. Splendid sailing, 244 knots last twenty-four hours; cold and squally. We are 17 miles off the Island of Diego Ramerez; lat. 56°, long. 75° 3′. To the Horn 276 miles. I am troubled with strong inward pains. Mrs. T. is confined to bed. Strong breeze, with every prospect of rounding the Horn by to-morrow night. Thank God for past and present mercies; I am happy in Jesus.

Thursday, Feb. 1st. Rounding Cape Horn. This morning at five the captain called me up to see the Island of Diego Ramerez: it stands out bold, rocky, and desolate. Progress very rapid; the good ship rolls and groans as if jaded and weary; heavy seas wash her decks. We are delighted with the correctness of our observations, and the sight of the far-famed American promontory. From the forecastle a porpoise has been harpooned, and lies on the deck for all to see. Mrs. Townend is up and able to go on the poop for a few minutes to catch a sight of the Horn. We have now entered the South Atlantic; weather warm; the wind has died away and we have almost a dead calm; snow can be distinctly seen on the hills. A third of our voyage is passed. How grand and solemn and suggestive is old ocean; how frequently and with pensive feelings have I paced the poop, the winds howling, and the billows rolling; how frequently at such times have I repeated the following lines:—

"The surging sea of human life for ever onward rolls—
Bearing to the Eternal shore each day its freight of souls;
But, though our bark sails bravely on, pale Death sits on the prow,
And few shall know we ever lived, a hundred years from now.

. . . .

Earth's empires rise and fall, O Time, like breakers on thy shore,
They rush upon thy rocks of doom—are seen, and seen no more;
The starry wilderness of worlds that gem night's radiant brow,
Will light the skies for other eyes, a hundred years from now.

O Thou before whose sleepless eyes the past and future stand
An open page, like babes we cling to thy protecting hand:
Change, sorrow, death are naught to us, if we may safely bow
Beneath the shadow of thy throne, in a few more years from now."

Friday, February 2nd. Yesterday, calm and light breeze which continues. It is adverse to our course; run last twenty-four hours 116 knots. A ship full rigged on our lee bows, apparently sailing in our direction. This morning close to our bows was floating a huge dead whale in a putrid state, with vast numbers of sea birds gorged with his blubber. Sea unruffled; cold and hazy. A female passenger, a Dane, very ill; she appears to enjoy vital piety, does not expect to recover, and is very anxious to have her will made; has no relative on board. Mrs. T. is much better, we are truly thankful.

Saturday, February 3rd. 196 knots. A heavy head swell, wind nor'-east, pitching very trying, a regular sickening motion. Very, very difficult to shave and dress this morning. It is the price we have to pay for comforts we hope to enjoy in the dear old country. I have much pain to-day, arising from internal derangement. The Lord be merciful to us! South lat. 55° 21′, west long 58° 26′. North the Falkland Isles 158 miles.

Sabbath, 4th. Slow motion, very fine quiet morning. Church well attended, text Joshua 24—15, general remarks on the utility of a religious life; creeds, baptisms, and church ordinances held up; these notions are very distasteful to most of our passengers and officers. Progress 220 knots.

Monday, February 5th. Beautiful sailing in our right course. Since yesterday 186 miles; south lat. 51° 32′ west long 49° 18′. Martin Vas Rocks distant 2075 miles. Last night service very good, numerous attendance, singing excellent. As we can only muster a very few Wesleyan hymn-books, when I have selected my hymns, the doctor, Mrs. Renshaw, and Miss Roberts kindly write out a number of copies to circulate among the congregation; this is better employment than sitting playing at cards, which a number of passengers on the main-deck are engaged at hour after hour. Last night dark and thick with fog, but our good ship, regardless of danger, fearlessly ploughed her onward course.

Tuesday, 6th. Very cold and stormy, leaden skies and murky seas. In the night we passed the "Resignation Rocks," about five miles distant. These sunken rocks are about six feet under water; to strike these rocks and be resigned to one's fate would argue moral safety. Captain Stewart tells a story of two navigators sent out in search of sunken rocks. One said "Yes," and described their exact whereabouts, the other said "No; there are no such rocks." The captain who said there were no such rocks was some time after commanding a ship in the very place where these rocks were said to be. On sitting down to dinner he said, "Now, gentlemen, if there are rocks here, in fifteen minutes we shall be in hell." Presently there was a dreadful crash and few were left to tell the tragic tale. I hardly think our captain believes in these "Resignation Rocks," or he would have kept farther off.

Wednesday, Feb. 7th. Very pleasant; much warmer. Sporting, dancing, and singing of songs; we are thought to be out of danger. Some of the passengers try to convince me there is no harm in these mirthful scenes. Glory be to God, when I am merry I sing psalms, and have my happiness in the service and contemplation of my Maker. No question but the very persons who would be pleased to hear me speak approvingly of these frivolities would be shocked to see me indulge in them. Last night our tars played the farce of "Drowning the Old Horse." They make a figure the form of a horse stuffed with straw, and just at dusk ride the old creature round the main deck, and then hoist him up to the main yard, hanging over the side of the ship. To my mind there is a blending of the ludicrous and the profane, for while all is silent, a clear solemn voice is heard saying, "Ashes to ashes, dust to dust, if the sailors won't have you the devil must," and down drops the bundle of straw and rags into the sea. The third mate then serves out to each of Neptune's sons an allowance of rum. Our run during the last forty-eight hours, 520 miles.

Thursday. Wind variable; very slow, but pleasant; weather warm.

Friday, 9th. Very cold; stormy east wind. Last night at dusk quite a sensation, on reefing the mainsail, wind roaring, vessel pitching, and storm just upon us. It looks fearful to see some twenty men and boys all on the main-yard, the boys at each end, the vessel rolling and almost dipping the yard ends in the sea. We continue to be very agreeable in our department: I see more than ever the necessity of faithful preaching and consistent living. We have plenty of wine and spirits. I am a teetotaller, the captain is very moderate, the officers and doctor have as much as they desire at table, passengers have to purchase what they need, as no beer, wine, or spirits are included in the fare. Cloudy, and no observations can be taken.

Saturday, Feb. 10th. Five weeks since leaving Sandridge Pier and bidding farewell to Australian friends. Since then we have been mercifully preserved; the thing we most dreaded, namely, rounding the Horn, has been done with fine weather, long days, and bright moonlight nights, and without the sight of a particle of ice. The few past severe days are gone, and we are feeling the effects of sickness. To-day, fair light breeze. South lat. 39° 29′, west long. 29° 45′. 235 knots.

Monday, Feb. 12th. Quiet, fine day yesterday. Church and chapel service well attended. The evening service very trying to my strength. The saloon is long, the roof low, and the place crowded: text, John v. 28, 29. May the resolves of last night be permanent! Good wind; warm and soft gentle showers and fleecy clouds. Progress, 230 miles.

Tuesday, Feb. 13th. Towards evening yesterday sultry and sullen. From eleven p.m. to three a.m. a terrible storm of lightning and thunder, and a perfect down-pour of rain. After the first flash, just time to take in sail. What roaring, and shouting, and tramping of feet overhead. The prostration of the passengers shows the effects of the storm. To-day the atmosphere is refreshing, and the sea is forgetting the furious lashings of last night. We are expecting soon to enter the tropics. Run 195 knots.

Wednesday, 14th. A decided calm. It is very hot, and many of the passengers are coming out strong in their summer attire; all looks strange. We are hoping to meet with the south-east trade winds.

Thursday, 15th. Calm and light contrary wind. Only 28 miles progress since yesterday; we are enjoying the fine weather, and hope soon to have a favourable wind. My head is light and giddy; cannot read much.

Friday, Feb. 16th. Still almost wind-bound; all quiet, and still giving the sickly voyager a chance of recruiting strength. Mrs. Townend is much better; yesterday, for the first time since coming on board, she was able to come to the saloon table, and is gaining an appetite. One man is dying of consumption, not expecting to see his wife and daughter in the home country. He left England thirteen years since, hoping to make his fortune in Australia, and is returning poorer than he went. Out of the Geelong Hospital he came on board, professing to be able to work his passage; poor fellow, he has fairly broken down. South lat. 28° 5′, west long. 20° 45′.

Saturday, 17th. Creeping along this great belt of calms, very fine and warm, and if we could forget that we are desirous of a speedy passage we might be content to linger in these calm seas. Our nights are getting longer, and the sunsets are inexpressibly grand; all along the edge of the horizon it is a splendid panorama, having the semblance of a long coast line, with hills and valleys, rocks and trees, and mountains stretching away in the distance. Then shine out the glorious southern lamps: I often sit silently viewing these radiant orbs; I am willing, nevertheless, to exchange these southern for our northern constellations. During last twenty-four hours only gone sixty miles. Captain says it won't pay.

Sabbath, Feb. 18th. Last night we had a serious row. Several of Neptune's sons had been drinking inspiration from King Alcohol given them by the passengers; they kept up singing and noise beyond the time allotted for evening amusements. The captain, from the poop, inquired from whence the singing proceeded, and was roughly answered. He at once went up to the men and asked who had given the insulting reply, "It was me, sir," said one of the men who had formerly been three days and nights in irons; he was in liquor, and cared not what he said. The officers were all called up, and, arming themselves lest there should be an outbreak on the part of the crew, the man was dragged on to the poop loudly vociferating, "Captain, let me go and I will jump overboard and never trouble you again." "Captain, leave off; I'll jump into the sea, I will never submit to lie in irons again!" All the passengers and crew were in commotion, our saloon ladies wildly screaming and running out of their cabins in their night-dresses, and the man shouting "murder! murder!" He was with difficulty prevented jumping overboard, but was at last securely ironed and stowed away. As on land so on the sea, the eve of the blessed Sabbath is robbed of its peace and order by strong drink. This morning a sullen stillness pervades our floating house. Church service on the main deck. A favourable wind for the last six hours has, to our great disappointment, gone back to the north forbidding progress in our right course; run 65 knots.

Monday, 19th. Service last night on the main deck, lighted by the ship lamps, and with the orbs of heaven, the moon in her first quarter, the whole of the passengers, officers, and crew being present or within hearing. The stillness was remarkable, and, with unusual freedom, pathos, and power, I preached for an hour. I think I never in my life had greater liberty, and a more favourable opportunity for ship service could not be given. The captain, chief officer, and many of the passengers gathered round to thank me. Our clergyman was deeply affected, and said, with tears, "O my brother, the word was with power." The captain has promised to liberate the unruly sailor. He is a capital seaman and a general favourite. A set battle early yesterday morning was put a stop to by the chief officer. The quarrel commenced on Saturday night, but on account of the midnight fray the encounter was reserved for Sabbath morning. We are still becalmed; progress, 35 knots.

Tuesday, 20th. Since seven last night a fair wind, and up to twelve at noon made 152 knots. Captain Stewart is in good spirits, believing that we are entering the south east trades. We entered the tropics just as we sat at lunch. South lat. 23° 32', west long 20° 22'. An intelligent, educated woman with her little daughter, from Collingwood, are third cabin passengers returning to England; drunkenness is the cause of her being separated from her husband.

Since coming on board she has evidently been indulging in drink—for so long as passengers have money to pay, an unlimited supply is sold; then the wretched accommodation as a third class passenger and the society she is compelled to be with have no doubt had an effect on her mind. Last night she was quite insane, screaming and threatening to take away her own life and that of her child; the doctor had to confine her in her berth and remove everything by which she could injure herself. Her little girl, a beautiful child four years of age, has been taken into the saloon, one of the ladies kindly volunteering to take care of her during the remainder of the voyage. A subscription is being made to pay a person to attend to the mother. It has been ascertained that neither mother nor child has scarcely a garment except what they have on; the wretched woman must have thrown everything overboard as she used it. The ladies in the saloon are all busy making up a variety of garments for the poor little thing. Oh, cursed drink, how its dire effects meet one at every turn! I incidentally met with this female and her husband a few days after they landed in Melbourne, some four years previous to this; they were evidently then in good circumstances, and had not long been married before leaving England; I never met her again until she made herself known to me on board ship; her husband brought her on board almost at the last moment of sailing to send her back to her friends.

Wednesday, 21st. Sailing quietly on our course. Warm, but not painfully hot. Skirmishes and misunderstandings between decks; some bear the marks of violence. Mrs. Townend's ship chair, being left on deck all night, has disappeared; as it folded together, it can easily have been stowed away in some of the berths below. I never before forgot to bring it every night into our own cabin. As the ship provides no movable seats, it was particularly useful. Ship-life requires great prudence, urbanity, and forbearance.

Monday, February 26th. Last night's service on the main deck passed off well. With considerable energy I preached near an hour. Calm sea, and the queen of night nearly full-horned; the ship as quiet as a chapel on land. Again I received the thanks of the captain and many others. The breeze began to freshen just as we concluded service. Thanks to our heavenly Father for all his goodness. Since eight this morning a dead calm; very little progress the last few days. We are much enervated under the vertical sun. South lat. 11° 48′, west long. 23° 41′.

Tuesday, 27th. At noon no shadow, the sun being vertical, although 9 degrees from the line, it being summer south the equator. It is very hot, but the breeze renders it tolerable. Yesterday our solitary voyage was relieved by the sight of a ship to leeward; only names were signalled though very near. Our captain thought them discourteous. Flying fish in great numbers, also those pretty little fish, called by sailors Spanish men-of-war, which float along with their sails spread. One of the female passengers 'tween decks has been getting intoxicated, and singing songs to the sailors; she has remained on deck all night.

Sabbath, March 4th. Extremely hot; slight thunder and lightning; the passengers between decks suffer much from heat and bad air arising from packs of wool. At eight o'clock last night sent up two rockets and a blue light, an outward vessel being about a mile on our windward side; it was very dark; she answered with a blue light. No service to-day, weather not permitting. We are ten miles north the equinoctial line. During these heavy tropical rains it is amusing to see the turn-out with bare legs and feet, in sou'-westers, catching the fresh water from the clouds. A photograph of the scene to landsmen would look very ludicrous.

Monday, 12th. Strong north-east wind for several days past. Edmond Simmons, the man who was ill in consumption, is dead, and his body committed to the great deep. Yesterday morning a sensible discourse from our clergyman; evening service in the saloon; it was extremely hot and I was very poorly; I improved the death of Simmons. This morning, from five to seven, a perfect gale, upsetting everything, and sending them rolling about the cabins. Two vessels are in sight. We are all very sick. May the Lord deal mercifully with us and bring us to our desired haven in safety! We are glad to see our old friend, the North Star, in the distant horizon.

Tuesday, 13th. A gale from the north-east bearing us on like a strong steed galloping up a hill. We have comparatively a steady-sailing ship, being very broad; on this account we selected her. Some of the clipper-built ships are so long and narrow they are continually shipping seas and scarcely have dry decks the whole voyage to England, but they obtain a good name for quick passages. Our ship was originally a merchantman in the East India trade, but has been altered so as to make her into a passenger vessel for the Australian service. Our captain tells us the reason why she is called the 'Result'* is this. Her present owners made a bet with another company relative to the comparative speed of certain vessels, and, having won, laid the money out in the purchase of this ship, naming it the 'Result,' as being the result of the bet. North lat. 22° 13'; west long. 36° 51'; run 220 knots.

Wednesday, 14th. During the night shipped a very heavy sea, and this morning the mizen top-gallant yard snapped asunder. One of the sailors who was up in the yards let his knife drop, which struck the sail-maker who was sitting at work on deck, the blade cutting through his wrist to the bone; he is in great pain; the doctor fears he will never be able to follow his trade as before. No one will own to the knife, as the sailors are not allowed to carry them loose, but have them fastened by a belt to the waist. We are through the tropics; lat 25° 11', long 37° 23'.

Thursday, 15th. Sailing in the Gulf Stream, with light breeze. Passengers amusing themselves by fishing up seaweed, which plentifully floats in these waters. Others are availing themselves of the present calm, packing up and getting in readiness to land at Plymouth. I do not feel so comfortable as I could wish, being disposed to grumble at the sitting-places on deck being taken up by pet dogs and fancy birds in cages. There are manifestations of selfishness which in this region of Doldrums is somewhat trying to one's patience. Mrs. Townend's chair has never been found.

Friday, 16th. We have been ten weeks on board. Our course is very unsatisfactory, slow, and out of our proper way. We are hoping for a favourable change, that by Easter Sunday we may be on *terra firma*.

Saturday, 17th. Still becalmed, having made *one mile* in our right course during twenty-four hours. The ship is being cleaned and put in order. The sea is like a sheet of glass—not a ripple to be seen. A party of passengers have been out some hours in the ship's boat, and the dogs have afforded no little amusement by swimming after pieces of wood. Scores of empty bottles are being thrown into the sea as targets for the captain and officers to shoot at with a rifle. St. Patrick's day is being merrily kept up, and the second-class

---

* The final fate of the 'Result' was, that she was burnt in Hobson's Bay the very next voyage she made after our return in her; a considerable amount of cargo was on board, but no lives were lost.

passengers having had their weekly allowance of wine, several are staggering or lying about the ship drunk. Sun burning hot, but we have an awning over the poop, which is some protection.

Monday, 19th. Yesterday quiet and calm; service on the main-deck morning and evening. The evening service brought all parties together. The man at the helm, and the man on the look-out could distinctly hear. I had great liberty in opening out the nature and design of the Gospel, with the terrible consequence of final disobedience thereof. A smart shower disconcerted the audience for a few minutes, when our clergyman called out, "It is over, brother; please proceed." In very deed the power of God was felt.

Wednesday, 21st. To-day the sun crosses the line. Warm and sultry, with gentle showers. We are much disappointed with these long calms, fondly hoping for the springing up of a favourable breeze. Solomon says, "Hope deferred maketh the heart sick." We are yet 1800 miles from England, with all the uncertainties of calm and storm before us. Since yesterday this time only made 48 miles. How blessed it is to trust, and be free from disquietude. Lord, help us to be thankful, and do Thou in Thy own good time bring us to our native land.

Thursday, 22nd. A very warm, clear day; blue sky and unruffled sea. Were it not that we are still becalmed, and almost in mind tempest-tossed, we should be led to exult in the view around. Still we have much to be thankful for, and hope soon to be relieved from this Gulf Stream in which for the last seven days we have been bound. Two ships in sight for several days in the same Doldrums.

Friday, 23rd. This morning about three o'clock a favourable breeze sprang up from the south-west, which bids fair to befriend us. The scene is quite changed; the soft balmy air, the sparkling ocean, and our noble vessel, with all her canvas spread, walks along as if pleased at being unchained once more. As plain as she can speak she says, "Give me fair play and a good breeze, and I will soon bear you to your desired haven." Everyone looks pleased and hopeful. Lat. 33° 5', long. 39° 46'.

Saturday, 24th. Last night was very trying. After the moon had retired from view, thick darkness ensued, enlightened only with bright flashes of the electric fluid. Rain fell like water-spouts. The wind being aft, the vessel rolled fearfully, producing great fear among the timid passengers. I feel half ashamed to confess that at such times I am the subject of tremulousness, and promise myself that if once more safe on land, I will no more place myself in circumstances of such discomfort. Our good ship has travelled 218 miles in the last twenty-four hours.

Monday, 26th. Yesterday very stormy and noisy, the ship rolling and groaning, whilst everything not properly fastened rolled and tumbled about. Such spilling of soup and smashing of earthen vessels. For the moment we feel disposed to laugh as each one round the saloon table snatches up their plate in one hand, and knife and fork in the other, to prevent them running to the opposite end; but to the owners and those in command it is no mirthful matter. Mr. Mackie was ill, and the captain read the Church Service in the morning. He is a much better reader than the clergyman. Though sick, I preached in the saloon in the evening; good singing and full attendance. The night was very rough; difficult to keep from being thrown out of bed. Run in the last twenty-four hours, 250 knots.

Tuesday, 27th. Murky atmosphere, with a moderate breeze, carrying us eleven knots per hour. The ship is being well cleaned all round her internal bulwarks. We are very cheerful, like so many children on the eve of holidays. Somehow my joy is tempered with a tinge of fear lest some disaster should come to us, as has often been the case in the very hour of landing. We have a good ship, well manned, and the queen of night full orbed to light us up the stormy channel. If there is a fair opportunity, a number of us will leave the ship at Plymouth.

Wednesday, 28th. Still hazy, and drizzling rain. 265 knots during the last twenty-four hours. About eleven last night the rope holding the boom of the driver broke; we were all aroused from our beds with the noise overhead. Captain Stewart was on the spot in a minute, and, excepting a blow on his head, all was made safe. The man at the helm, who was in the most danger, was running from his post, until the captain compelled him to stay. We are all well, rejoicing in the prospect of a speedy landing. Lat. 48° 16′, long. 20°.

Thursday, 29th. Very thick and foggy; obliged to keep a good look-out, and sound the horn for fear of collision, as many ships must be in the neighbourhood. Our anchors and sounding lines are ready, lest the fog should prevent our seeing the signals.

We cannot take correct observations, but suppose we are about 300 miles from the Lizard, and if the wind continues, hope to be there by to-morrow night.

Good Friday, March 30th. Hot-cross buns to breakfast. The fog still continues, making our progress very dangerous. Captain Stewart and the officers keep a good look-out, especially in the night. The full moon is of great service, giving us nearly half-a-mile of hazy observations, though at times the fog is so dense we cannot see more than the length of the ship. The horn is being blown and the fog-bell rang nearly every minute. Our floating community have just been all on deck to see a French fishing-smack pass close to us to windward. Our progress will be still more dangerous as we get nearer the Channel. Light breeze, south-west; seven knots per hour.

Saturday, March 31st. Last night at supper the captain expressed his serious apprehension of danger, and thought it would be prudent for the ladies not to undress, as the fog continued very dense, and many vessels must be near. I lay down half undressed. At half-past one o'clock the captain came to my cabin and asked if I would not like, after so many years' absence, to see the light off my native land. I said, much excited, "Captain, can you show it me." "Come on deck," said he. In a minute, in my fur cap, overcoat, and slippers, I went on the poop. Sure enough the fog was clearing away, and the light off the Scilly Islands could be seen. I was ready to shout for joy. In an hour the captain called me again; I rose, and witnessed the eclipse of the moon. At eight in the morning we were off the Eddystone Lighthouse. As the pilot-boat neared our vessel, Captain Stewart called out, "What news, pilot?" The answer was clear and alarming, "The loss of the 'London,' sir!" Through the ship the cry was carried from stem to stern, "The loss of the 'London!' the loss of the 'London!'" How often on our homeward voyage had we talked about this splendid steamer, as we knew that she would leave England about the same time we sailed from Australia, and now her living freight had found a watery grave, and we had been mercifully preserved. * * * We had determined to land at Plymouth, if possible; so without any breakfast we entered the pilot-boat, with five or six other passengers, when, 'mid the adieus of friends, the waving of caps and handkerchiefs, we left the good ship to proceed up the Channel, while we scudded along with a fair wind, and reached Plymouth about one p.m. After staying a few hours for rest and refreshment, we went on to Exeter and surprised our good friend the Rev. T. Newton, with whom we spent the Sabbath. Had the privilege of worshipping with our friends in the sanctuary, and heard two eloquent discourses from the Rev. R. Bushell. Collections were made on behalf of the Chapel Fund. In the afternoon I gave an address to the teachers, scholars, and friends; and, in company with Mr. Bushell, we arrived safe in London on Easter-Monday.

What a city is London!—a world in itself. What a perpetual surging scene of busy life! What majestic edifices and wretched hovels! what amazing social distinctions and moral disparities of good, bad, and indifferent; here a Temple for God, and there a Palace for Satan, with all its glare and show to entrap and destroy the unwary. As we drove through the streets we felt how great the change from our solitary voyage on the "lone blue sea." How many anxious thoughts crowd upon the mind of a returned voyager as he reflects on the changes and events which may have happened in the circle of his relatives and friends since last he received any tidings of them. Our last letters received in Australia informed Mrs. Townend of the illness of her only brother, who had been in delicate health for some years, and was slowly sinking by consumption; and we did not expect to find him still an inhabitant of earth; but on reaching Sloane Street, where he resided, we found him still lingering on the shores of time; his anxious prayer and desire had been to live until his sister arrived, that he might see her once more—and her husband whom he had never yet seen. We had the melancholy pleasure of being with him about ten days—when his spirit escaped from the frail tabernacle to join the company of the redeemed in Heaven.

I preached three times in London, but to our churches there I was a stranger, and receiving many pressing invitations to visit Lancashire to preach special sermons for Chapels and Sabbath Schools where I was better known, I gladly responded to the call, and was fully occupied up to the time of the Assembly held in Sheffield, which I attended as a representative for Australia.

The Foreign Missionary committee were holding their sittings in London the week after my arrival, which gave me the opportunity of seeing some of my old friends and brethren in the ministry. I also had the privilege of attending the Missionary meeting in Exeter Hall; but as I was not called on to speak until ten minutes to ten o'clock, when the audience were getting weary, I felt it would be unwise to keep them much longer, as the speech of a returned missionary should be details of labour, which cannot be crowded into the space of a few minutes.

I left London April 28th, to preach on behalf of the Sabbath School at Derby, in the place of the President (Rev. W. R. Brown), who was prevented going by the serious illness of his brother. It was suggested to me that I need not tell the congregation until after evening service, that I was not the President, as we were both strangers in Derby. But it is always best to be honest, for just as I had concluded morning service, a lady came and tapped me on the shoulder, saying, "You are not the President, you are Mr. Townend; I knew you more than twenty years ago when you travelled in Manchester. I wish you had told the congregation, as they would have been pleased to know that a returned missionary was going to preach to-night."

Mrs. Townend and myself were hospitably entertained at the house of the Rev. W. Griffith, whose amiable wife (since gone to join the Church above) shewed us much kindness.

The following Sabbath I spent at Northwich, where my nephew, Rev. T. W. Townend, was stationed; the week following I was engaged to visit my old friends at Bury, to open their Bazaar in the Athenæum. This was my last circuit before going to Australia, and as I had to leave at the end of eighteen months, they still consider I am eighteen months in their debt. I also preached one Sabbath at the opening of our beautiful chapel at Littleborough in the Rochdale circuit, to crowded congregations, and visited and preached at Salford, Heywood, Manchester, Mellor in Derbyshire, and several other places. These services were trying to my strength, but very gratifying to my feelings.

At the Sheffield Assembly I received several invitations to circuits, but not feeling sure that my health and strength would be equal to a large circuit, I consented to be stationed at Blackpool in the Preston circuit. At this fashionable watering-place we have a very large chapel, and the congregations during the summer months are very large. I soon found the internal arrangements of the circuit not congenial to either the members or preacher at Blackpool; and my health being greatly improved I cheerfully accepted in the following December a unanimous invitation to become the superintendent of the Rochdale circuit.

The murky skies, smoking factory chimneys, and clatter of clogs was at first confusing and unpleasant, but I soon felt at home, and schools, chapels, and friends made me, with a gushing, grateful heart, exclaim,

"England, my native land, I love thee still."

O God, our heavenly Father, for all Thy mercies to us help us to be thankful, and when the voyage of life is o'er, may we land safe on the shores of eternal blessedness. AMEN.

www.ingramcontent.com/pod-product-compliance
Lightning Source LLC
Chambersburg PA
CBHW080513090426
42734CB00015B/3038

* 9 7 8 1 5 3 5 8 0 1 0 1 0 *